Emotion Online

Emotion Online

Theorizing Affect on the Internet

Joanne Garde-Hansen
Centre for Cultural Policy Studies, University of Warwick, UK

and

Kristyn Gorton
Department of Theatre, Film and Television, University of York, UK

First published 2013 by
PALGRAVE MACMILLAN

Palgrave Macmillan in the UK is an imprint of Macmillan Publishers Limited, registered in England, company number 785998, of Houndmills, Basingstoke, Hampshire RG21 6XS.

Palgrave Macmillan in the US is a division of St Martin's Press LLC, 175 Fifth Avenue, New York, NY 10010.

Palgrave Macmillan is the global academic imprint of the above companies and has companies and representatives throughout the world.

Palgrave® and Macmillan® are registered trademarks in the United States, the United Kingdom, Europe and other countries

ISBN 978-1-349-32906-9   ISBN 978-1-137-31287-7 (eBook)
DOI 10.1057/9781137312877

This book is printed on paper suitable for recycling and made from fully managed and sustained forest sources. Logging, pulping and manufacturing processes are expected to conform to the environmental regulations of the country of origin.

A catalogue record for this book is available from the British Library.

A catalog record for this book is available from the Library of Congress.

Contents

List of Illustrations

Figures

Table

Acknowledgements

This book emerged out of discussions during the launch of the *Memory Studies* journal in 2008 and out of work in *Media Audiences: Television, Meaning and Emotion* (2009). It became clear to the authors at that time that while memory and digital media were receiving academic scrutiny, digital media and emotion/affect were being overlooked. The successful collaboration of the authors on a number of research projects (especially through the Arts and Humanities Research Council (AHRC)-funded Women, Ageing and Media Network) inspired us to join our research on emotion (Gorton, 2009) and on digital media/memory (Garde-Hansen, 2011). The authors wish to thank many who have inspired our thinking and writing. We are especially in debt to Justin Crouch, Anna Reading, William Merrin, Paul Blackledge, Andrew Hoskins, Ros Jennings, Abigail Gardner, Matthew Allen, Heather McClendon, Owain Jones, and Lindsey McEwen. For the helpful remarks and the support they have offered, we wish to convey thanks to the Palgrave Macmillan staff, especially Catherine Mitchell, Chris Penfold, and Felicity Plester.

Finally, we would like to dedicate this book to those who manage to make us happy, sad, anxious, proud, jealous, angry, scared, and ashamed 24/7 without us ever having to go online: our children, Sam, Josh, Kate, Jack, Johnny, and Matthew.

Parts of Chapter 2 were originally published by Kristyn Gorton (2012) in 'Affect', in *Gender: The Key Concepts,* edited by Mary Evans and Carolyn Williams (London), pp. 3–7, and are reprinted with permission from Taylor & Francis Books.

Introduction

Emotional noise: paying attention and spreading emotion

At the time of writing this book, the online campaign video *Kony 2012* emerged and was watched over 90 million times and received more than 400,000 comments (now disabled) on YouTube alone (see Heather McIntosh's 2012 blog, *'KONY 2012*: Analyzing the Viral Documentary Video'). The opening lines of the filmmaker, Jason Russell, conjoined social media and emotion:

> Right now there are more people on Facebook than there were on the planet 200 years ago. Humanity's greatest desire is to belong and connect and now we see each other, we hear each other.
> 'Grandpa, I love you.'
> 'I love you.'
> 'Why, why won't it take a picture?'
> We share what we love and it reminds us what we all have in common...
> And this connection is changing the way the world works. Governments are trying to keep up and older generations are concerned. The game has new rules. The next 27 minutes are an experiment but in order for it to work you have to pay attention. (*Kony 2012*)

It seemed to fall into our laps (or laptops) as a perfect example of 'emotion online' and it created *emotional noise* both horizontally (across e-mail, blogs, social networks and online video sites) and vertically (through journalism, television programmes, print media, and radio). Not only was *Kony 2012* an emotive online resource; it also generated networked activity – people *liked* Invisible Children (the activist organization that produced the video) on Facebook; celebrities blogged and tweeted about the campaign, millions ordered a Kony 2012 pack and wore the bracelets. With a slicker soundtrack than the amateurism of the video *I Will Survive Auschwitz* (2010) and more serious than Cebu prison inmates' version of *Thriller* (2007), it appeared to have broken the 1% rule.[1]

However, the emotions being performed were not complex, multi-modal and highly individuated ones belonging to local communities, but were presented as universal, fundamentalist precepts *beyond* or even preceding racial and cultural differences.[2] The emotional noise created horizontally and vertically around *Kony 2012* was mobilized by interlinked factors: the agent of emotion (in this case Jason Russell) was asking us in the audience to 'pay attention' because the spreadability (see Jenkins et al. 2013) of online mixed-media compels us to. This spreadability suggests that affect is what ought to/should/could bind individuals to each other and to their mediated environment. However, Bernard Stiegler has argued that

> the capture of attention by technological means is a global phenomenon (affecting all continents), a massive one (affecting all generations and all social strata) and totally new [...]. Humanity has never experienced such a phenomenon of synchronised and hyper-realist collective hallucination, and the consequences of these facts on psychical and collective individuation are as yet hardly theorized. (Stiegler 2008)

When Stiegler says this is 'totally new', he does not mean the newness that Russell advocates above. That is, we only need to see each other *online* in order to feel: online media spread affect so that viewers feel the same emotion as the activists. For Stiegler (2008), the capture of 'hyper-attention' begins with 'the psychotechnologies' of media from the birth of radio to the digital: historical, worldwide, networked, and industrialized. *Kony 2012* is just one example of the online mixed-media call to *pay attention* (in both senses of the phrase) by adding together media and human agency by what we would term emotion agents.[3] They ensured that no single medium contained the affect, that the need to care about the crimes of Joseph Kony was felt both on the ground (gatherings, artefacts, interviews, T-shirts) and in the clouds (the intangibility of the network of media forms).

In this book, we begin to theorize and critique the various ways in which the Internet has become a part of everyday life through the offline/online mediation of emotion and affect and how mixed media perform their affective connections online. This has been a particularly challenging task, considering the abstract nature of both the concepts we apply and the media technologies we are working within. The online media we are paying attention to (text, video, music, photographs) have challenged us to rethink the dynamics of mediation; that is, old media versus new media, the notion of a single medium, and the separation of individuals from their mediated environment.[4] While we accept that there are different performances (national, regional, local and personal) of emotion, both on the ground and in our digital media era, we have become more interested in the ways that emotion is being mobilized and industrialized through online cultures as transmittable, spreadable, networked, and without self-containment.[5] Although we do not subscribe to Stiegler's philosophy in any great detail, we are mindful of the academic attention he is giving to what he terms 'an industrialized libidinal economy' and 'the question of the care of the self' (2008).

It is inevitable that this book will range thinly over many fields (as we do in Part I: Theoretical Approaches) yet drill down in the areas that only we have prospected as worth exploring in depth (as in Part II: Close Readings). We do not pretend that the study of emotion online is both definitive and exhaustive herein. Those seeking exact coordinates to plot emotion online locally, nationally, and globally will be disappointed that we do not have the space within this book to map out how emotion plays out in different parts of the world, to very specific audiences, with and through a variety of distinct media technologies. Rather, we offer this book as an initial making of the case that media and communication theorists of film, television, journalism, radio, print media, and online media need to *pay attention to* (watch out for and to care about) the mediation of emotion in a digital era. To do so, requires a drawing together of a range of knowledge bases, a wider understanding of transmediality and acceptance that the researcher (theorist or practitioner) is affectively implicated in the research design, the methodologies, and the objects of study. While we are not as negative as Stiegler (2008) that this *hyper-attention* (mass, collective watching out for) is ultimately *destructive of attention* (the personal taking care of), we are very aware of the growing *philia* with(in) *attentional technologies*. Objectivist media research has become *very friendly* with its object of study, and this tells us something important about how affect is transmitted in the critique itself.

We are keenly aware of the digital enthusiasts and participatory culture advocates who promote an interactive, grass-roots version of online media. We are equally cognizant of what Geert Lovink in *Networks without a Cause: A Critique of Social Media* has defined as the culture of 'detached engagement' of proliferating discourses, within 'echo chambers' of online discussion 'where groups of like-minded individuals, consciously or not, avoid debate with their cultural or political adversaries' (2011, 2). Our book explores some of those echo chambers, critically reads the discourses we find there, and theoretically reflects upon selected examples. In our making of the case, we have elected to approach emotion online as a *discursive* manifestation. Thus, this book *reads* emotion online as it appears to us as thinking and feeling media theorists. Two key features inform these readings. First, emotion and affect have become fundamental to how online participation and the Internet is theorized and practiced. The danger is that online participants may, as Slavoj Zizek has warned of the Occupy Wall Street activists, 'fall in love with themselves' (2012). Second, and this follows on from the first point, we do not join those who *feel* that our 'new media' are wholly transformed and transforming. Much critical scholarship suggests that long histories of media discourses, forms, and practices shape our contemporary moment. To insist upon a break between old and new or to create boundaries of theory and practice around a media form would be to privilege the cognitive over the affective and the extraordinary over the ordinary. Media are affective tools, and online media present a number of networked tools that can be used by emotion agents to transmit affect.

With this in mind, *Kony 2012* (as youth media, activist media, and remix) seemed an excellent example to begin to interrogate the divisions being suggested between old media and new media that would securitize compassion as newly articulated. Of a similar global activist group, Climate Justice Fast (which involved an Internet-organized hunger strike), Knudsen and Stage have claimed, 'Here we see a new type of mediatized and affectively charged environmental activism (Hjarvard 2008), which uses the internet to construct a new type of protest based on affective processes motivated by geographically dispersed hunger striking' (Knudsen and Stage 2011, 2). The activist group Invisible Children was also gaining recognition through an online platform, yet equally had organized a very old media campaign to 'Cover the night' that involved three approaches: 'Engage your leaders,' 'Serve your local community,' and 'Hit the streets'. These actions were very much of a grass-roots type and were at odds with critiques of 'slacktivism' often aimed at online political campaigns. Interestingly, our first response to *Kony 2012* was scepticism and critical suspicion. We could not decide if *we* were the intended audience and we did not *like* how *Kony 2012* both affected and disaffected us. How were we *meant to feel?* We shed a tear or two, right where we were meant to. Yet, as academics we 'read' the video in negotiated and oppositional ways – we looked at the gendered framing of the father-son legacy and the contrived narration, and wondered where the funding for the production had come from.

We were not alone, and journalists and comedians jumped on the content, and suggested that the success of the video was due to a naive, liberal American misreading of international politics. On the UK television show *10 O'Clock Live*, media critic Charlie Brooker ruthlessly described it as a 'shallow T-mobile advert shot by the Pepsi-Max pricks' and viewed Jason Russell (the filmmaker) as appearing to be 'a clean-cut, Abercrombie & Fitch version of Jesus Christ' (aired 16 March 2012). Some days later, and following the public mental breakdown of Russell, the excitement surrounding *Kony 2012* changed and, perhaps for this reason, the planned 'Cover the Night' was not as successful as it might have been. The press also made a great deal of the lack of viewers to *Kony 2012 Part 2* (which had been produced to address the unanticipated criticism). Articles announcing a 98 per cent drop in viewers were headlined to paint *Kony 2012* as a viral disaster story rather than a success. Yet, if we consider that 2 million did watch *Part 2*, we realize that that is still far more than most online political/charitable videos ever receive.

Whether a success or a failure, *Kony 2012* illustrated the power of the Internet to emotionally engage an audience and to quickly establish a significant following through global hyper-attention. This is happening more often in so-called 'trials by Twitter' or the daily 'Twitch hunts', wherein, even a director general of the BBC resigns while his mainstream news organization falls prey to emotionalized Internet chatter.[6] While global attention is evidenced by a single emotive image as an act of citizen journalism in locked-down regimes,[7] this will resonate in different ways in different parts of the world. The point is that, in spite of the varied technological mediations of emotion online and offline, we may have moved, as Stanley Cohen noted in his introduction to the third edition of *Folk Devils and Moral Panics*, from a period of 'discrete and volatile moral panics' to 'a generalized moral stance, a permanent moral panic resting on a seamless web of social anxieties' (Cohen 2002, xxix). If the computer screen has become the globally networked platform for constructing and mediating affect and if that affect is highly mediated by digitally literate elites, how is hegemonic control maintained if, as Lovink (2011, 3) argues, 'netspaces are noncommittal, and users unrepentantly move on as if their addiction never happened'? We do already know they *unrepentantly move on* through old media addictions, despite the fact that fan theory and participatory media studies would emphasize long-term commitment. Film and television screens have served the function of producing detached engagement for quite some time, and *Kony 2012*, while offering a powerful example of how emotion online can be transmedially produced, also reveals the differing intensities of different emotions and shows that these are nothing new.

On the one hand, the *Kony 2012* allowed mainstream viewers a simplified version of a liberal politics that positions universalized concepts of care, responsibility, empathy, and passion at the forefront of a solution to complex conflict, crisis, and inhumanity.[8] On the other hand, it demonstrated the convergence (see Henry Jenkins's *Convergence Culture: Where Old and New Media Collide*, 2006a) between the Internet, social media networks, grass-roots campaigns, and political action that merits further attention from scholars (see Henry Jenkins, Sam Ford, and Joshua Green's latest publication *Spreadable Media: Creating Value and Meaning in a Networked Society*, 2013). While *Kony 2012* was widely criticized by many (including the government of Uganda), we have to concede that a crucial ingredient of this networked politics was ignored: the intensity of its fandom.

In *Textual Poachers: Television Fans and Participatory Culture* (1992), Jenkins sees fandom in our media ecology in terms of loving an object, and recounts the story of *The Velveteen Rabbit* to describe how fans make culture meaningful through their attentive bodies and emotions:

> Seen from the perspective of the toymaker, who has an interest in preserving the stuffed animal as it was made, the Velveteen Rabbit's loose joints and missing eyes represent vandalism [...] yet for the boy, they are the traces of fondly remembered experiences, evidence of his having held the toy too close and pet it too often, in short, marks of its loving use. (Jenkins 1992, 51)

Jason Russell had been developing a fan base for his films for many years, and these dedicated followers had become fan activists. Not a charity, not a film company, not a sect, and not an evangelical Christian group, Invisible Children was largely misunderstood transmedially[9] because the film was a personal communication from Russell to his fans and this got vertically mobilized. Thus, the unanticipated affective response of dislike toward the maker of this highly emotive activist film was because the majority audience (the millions of non-fans who paid attention) did not understand the cultural production and the culture of viewing this film belonged to. While the intention may have been to let the film travel, it had also moved outside of where it emotionally belonged (its fan base of mainly young, educated Americans) to millions of non-fans (around the world) who did not care about Invisible Children and Jason Russell but were being asked to care about Kony's crimes. Thus, the intended affect became *unspreadable*, and a *disaffected* audience was produced.

The film's inability to spread the intended activist emotion inside the mediation was perhaps because the spreadability of media online is structured by social 'homophily' as danah boyd (2005) defines it. That users of the Internet assume that everyone is like they are is largely because they 'friend' and network with known people along known pathways and rarely venture into the unknown; they have 'created secluded online environments' of 'literally tens of millions of users' (Lovink 2011, 3).[10] Thus, while over 90 million views (not necessarily the same number of viewers) of *Kony 2012* may seem a great deal, compared to the world population, it is not. As boyd states:

> Birds of a feather flock together because there is value in doing so. It is through this commonality that one can find security in one's views, feel validated and supported, and have the kind of environment that fosters motivation and joy. When communities reference the value of 'safe space,' they are referring to the homophilous environments in which people do not have to defend their minority status. (boyd 2005, 198)

These environments (fan sites, activist platforms, political blogs, interest groups, and citizen journalism, blogs for example) may, as boyd argues, 'overstate the success of a movement' and find it 'hard to rally diverse groups' (2005, 198). Hence, although the discursive use of emotion may well become the key factor to address these two pitfalls, it cannot be assumed that its transmedial intensity remains constant and readable.

The discourses in Russell's opening lines to *Kony 2012* were designed to make viewers pay attention and, like millions of others, we did so for 27 minutes (a long time for an online video). We watched the remix of history (images of the Holocaust with African militarism) and listened to Mumford & Sons' 'Roll Away Your Stone', we cared about African children, and were shocked by the victim/aggressor status; yet we were equally charmed by Russell's cute son. The mixture of white, perfect domesticity jarred with the fear-mongering black otherness and an American desire to 'fight war' rather than make it. It held our attention because it contained all the ingredients of a personal communication to create an emotional response. We also paid attention in the same way the Western imaginary has been taught to pay attention by the gurus of inspirational television such as Oprah Winfrey. We felt for the children in the same way we have been taught to feel for children during Band Aid's 'Do They Know It's Christmas' (1984) or USA for Africa's 'We Are The World' (1985). Yet, crucially, we were not attentive in the way Invisible Children hoped we would be. The authors had paid attention for 27 minutes, but we did not care enough to act. In fact, as critical theorists of media, we became so concerned about the unspreadability of the compassion intended by the mediated emotion that we sought to understand in more depth the networked discourses of emotive content online.

First, we began with the notion that all media are presented and practiced as emotional media. There is not media (object) then and me (subject), but media inside me and me inside media. As Teresa Brennan states in *The Transmission of Affect* (2004, 19), 'the transmission of affect does not sit well with an emphasis on individualism, on sight, and cognition' that is 'based on the notion that the objective is in some way free from affect'. Second, we understood this campaign as an example of emotion, media, and audience, discursively imbricated. Therefore, the layering of emotion, media, and technology is discursively built into the activist framework, with the aim of producing online fans. As we know from the extensive work on fans by Lewis (1992), Jenkins (1992, 2006b), Hills (2002), Brooker (2002), Sandvoss (2005), and Abbott (2010), emotional attachment, resonance, involvement and payoff are critical to the social and cultural capital of the fan/audience. This is seen as a grass-roots, bottom-up, and consumer-driven process by Jenkins in *Convergence Culture* (2006a, 18). *Kony 2012*'s Russell reinforced this *right to communicate* in the film:

> It's always been that the decisions made by the few with the money and the power dictated the priorities of their government and the stories in the media. They determine the lives and the opportunities of their citizens. But now there is something bigger than that. The people of the world see each other and can protect each other. It's turning the system upside down and changes everything. (Jason Russell, *Kony 2012*)

Although Invisible Children may have anticipated 500,000 views from the fandom of the early years, it had achieved over 70 million views from non-fans within a few days, thus seemingly proving the point that 'people of the world see each other' and that such global transparency allows stories to be shared within friendship- and interest-driven networks. These networks are built upon intimacy and affectual relationships, not on the business plans of top-down media corporations, Russell would argue. Yet they are also used 'to accelerate the flow of media content across delivery channels to expand revenue opportunities, broaden markets, and reinforce viewer commitments' (Jenkins 2006a, 18). Although we know that social media 'as a buzzword of the outgoing Web 2.0 era' is also a 'product of business management strategies' (Lovink 2011, 6), it remains to be proven just how committed viewers really are and how much they really care in the longer term.

The modus operandi of new technologies is simplicity: simple tools, simple design, simple messages, and simple communications. In that simplicity lies a powerful rhetoric that uses the concept of 'affect' as a theory, discourse, form, and practice toward securitizing emotion within media economies. In our book, theories of emotion and affect contribute toward our critique of social and online media, which is a collaborative effort to take stock and create sustainable concepts. As Lovink states:

> By using concepts as individual building blocks, assembled through endless dialogues and debates, such collaborative efforts will ultimately culminate in a comprehensive materialist (read: hardware- and software-focused) and affect-related theory. This has not happened so far on a large scale, but maybe we should slow down, relax, and be patient. (2011, 22)

With this in mind, we offer *Emotion Online: Theorizing Affect on the Internet* as one such building block in our taking stock of where we are emotionally with regard to the Internet in social and cultural terms.

Clearly, the demystification of techno-cultural power to reveal an affective core is problematic if it gets layered into a technology that is unevenly distributed across the world yet is continually represented as an agent of simplicity and everydayness. Our book seeks to understand this problematic imbrication of emotion and online culture, for we understand that 'people not only conduct their lives with affects and emotions but also in the absence of capacities for evaluating full and transparent information' (Isin 2004, 220). Information is not always evenly spread in our online ecology (despite the spreadability of media content), and mass caring does not necessarily lead to action if mass online witnessing can be said to produce a bystander effect.[11] Unable to establish the veracity of the content of *Kony 2012*, aware of a century of cinematic manipulations of the viewer's gaze, socialized into a discourse of benign neglect of developing countries with their complex postcolonial conflicts, millions of viewers did nothing but share a link.

So what did make us pay attention to *Kony 2012* for those 27 minutes? The assumption of course was that there was something new and old to see in this film and something new and old to feel (while others were feeling it too). As in mass broadcasting of an event, it was moving and it moved viewers *en masse* enough for them to spread it around their networked intimacy, taking on the role of emotion agents. We wanted to be moved perhaps in the ways that those young American fans of Invisible Children were being moved. Maybe it was the focus upon the son, the paternalistic narrative, the inheritance of the earth, and the desire for a new world order from an ordinary man that moved us. Or was it that we saw a white American man *care*: care for his son, care for African children, care about the world, about history and feel responsibility toward the Other? We watched one young white male make his life emotionally meaningful through entrepreneurial media activism. Although he made the solution look as simple as online active engagement, we found that the simplicity of feeling something about Kony's crimes was supposed to be enough for us to be active and engaged.

Yet, clearly it was not all that new. Women were largely absent from *Kony 2012*; the wife and daughter not in the film and the girls sold into sex slavery had a brief mention. From the perspective of emotion and affect, the lack of attention to women is telling.[12] We have watched wealthy white men care about global poverty and political struggle since the 1980s (Midge Ure, Bono, Sting, Brad Pitt, George Clooney, and Sean Penn, for example). What was new was the method of technologically communicating that care toward the production of a caring community of ordinary people, for the 'Internet is a perfect instrument for a world in which community is understood as a network' (Barney 2004, 164).

We wanted to understand in more depth what was new and old about emotion online, and where better to start than to explain what early explorations of the Internet and communications technologies anticipated would be new, and what in fact has remained old?

New media, old emotions

In the year 2000, *The Cybercultures Reader* presented 48 chapters that were the culmination of academic research filled with the promise, possibility, and cautionary tales of a deregulated, free, open cultural space where humans and technology interacted. Key terms from many of the chapter titles such as *becomings, first steps, community, welcome, the world, warriors, alternative, new age, technophilic, prosthetic, radical, hacking, counter-culture, unbounded, subcultures, manifesto, envisioning, commonality* and *globalization* denote the ideologies underpinning the anthology. These editors compiled cyberculture thinking as broad, inclusive, and nonspecific (covering online communities, games, digital art, biomedical technologies, e-mail, websites, and any form of techno-logically enabled communication). The 'decentralized, non-linear, *rhizo-matic* textures of cyberspace' provided the landscape, and it was the job of the reader to select, connect, and construct (Bell and Kennedy 2000, 1). This was a liquid reader in nonliquid form and it resonated with Web 2.0, which was just emerging out of the dot-com era. Its through lines were centred on the imaginary, the prophetic, the experimental and, at times, the esoteric. It was no ordinary explication of cyberculture, and it did not present cyberculture as ordinary.

Since then, our theoretical literature (in response to Web 2.0) has moved away from the relationship between technology and culture as a 'technocultural construction', a 'biotechno matrix', or a 'posthuman' trajectory of 'cyborgization' (Bell and Kennedy 2000, 1, 3, 5). The term 'cyberculture' itself has much less resonance than it did in those early theorizations. It is the ordinary experiences of being online that have emotional impact within everyday life that concern us now, and media convergence has accelerated this ordinariness. There have been significant shifts toward interrogating the everyday and the ordinary in cultural studies (see Stewart 2007; Hartley 2009; Highmore 2010b; and Turner 2010), and this has begun to permeate Internet studies and mobile media research (see Goggin and Hjorth 2008 and Lásen 2010a/b). Cultural studies of affect, public feelings, and the politics of emotion on the one hand, and scholarship on digital culture, new media, and information-communication technologies on the other have also begun to converge (see Vincent and Fortunati's [2009] *Electronic Emotion: The Mediation of Emotion via Information and Communication Technologies*). We will engage with many of these new ideas throughout this book, because we are taking for granted that in our encountering of emotion online we seek to understand its ordinary and everyday discursive articulation through technologies that are imcreasingly ubiquitous.

In the last decade, there have been significant shifts in our academic understanding of the ways in which humans use, engage with, and interact with ubiquitous computing (see Dourish and Bell's [2011] *Divining the Digital Future: Mess and Mythology in Ubiquitous Computing*).

Moreover, the most recent theoretical intervention casts the net wide in uncovering the everyday and ordinary emotions that are articulated and consumed through technologically enabled networks. 'What are the structures of feeling that operate in our everyday digital life, and what kind of virtual public spheres do they create?' asks Adi Kuntsman in her introduction to the collection *Digital Cultures and the Politics of Emotion: Feelings, Affect and Technological Change* (2012, 4). She continues: 'How do digital media shape our everyday experiences and political horizons of love, boredom, fear, anxiety, compassion, hate, hope?' (Kuntsman 2012, 4). This attention to the ordinary and the everyday can recede from view when much research on emotion and feeling in digital cultures may be produced through the lens of intense, sublime, or traumatic human experiences – for example, war (Hoskins and O'Loughlin 2010; Kuntsman 2010; Clough 2012), terrorism (Weimann 2006; Chen 2012), racism (Kuntsman 2009), death (Ferreday 2010; Walter et al. 2011/12), and conflict/global politics (Karatzogianni 2009). Here, we offer a coordinated approach to theorizations of emotion so as to attend to the questions that Kuntsman poses by focusing upon ordinary experiences and by regarding ourselves as ordinarily and affectively implicated in what we are theorizing about.

At first, it may seem that the increased access to media and communications in online culture means that the most dominant and dominating narratives are those from hidden lives, untold histories, or oppressed peoples. As Patricia T. Clough has recently argued:

> These stories of children-soldiers [see *Kony 2012*], prisoners, sex workers, orphans left by parents dead of AIDS, those abandoned, depressed, near suicidal confronted by the hatred of neighbours of different ethnicities, if not the same ethnicities, communities and families, these stories really are not unheard of or overlooked stories. (2012, 22)

These untold stories seem to form the very basis of how the affective economy of online emotional culture operates in the twenty-first century. Emotion is here securitized as appropriately belonging to those who deserve to express it, not to those who seek out emotionalization in order to explore their own self-expression.[13] However, many online users do routinely seek out such raw emotion, from the last mobile phone calls of those who died in the Twin Towers to the final tweets of a person about to die. Perhaps they have become desensitized by highly stylized televisual and cinematic content and want to 'keep it real'. Maybe mainstream media and communications have globally, commercially, and institutionally packaged reality along well-trodden and known pathways. Yet, what we learned from *Kony 2012* is that we were not all moved by stories and images in the same way, in spite of their spreadability.

In this book, we argue that emotion online is encountered when the culture we live is performed on the intersection of the personal and the global through mixed media, one that makes it hard to think compartmentally about specific technologies, audiences, and parts of the world. We are on that 'slippery nexus between the Internet's reinforcement of existing power structures, and parallel – and increasingly penetrating – worlds where control is diffused' (Lovink 2011, 3). Above all, we want to feel that we belong in the many worlds we (could) inhabit. Furthermore, we desire to belong, argues Debra Ferreday (2009) in *Online Belongings: Fantasy, Virtuality, Community*, just as much in 'the highly visual and commercialized culture of the web' we use daily as in the 'sense of community' from 'more obscure sites of virtual belonging such as chat rooms and UseNet groups'. She continues: 'this sense of community [in commercialized culture] is perhaps less likely to require the erasure of specificity and difference. Instead, it is based on a sense of shared experience and, importantly, shared emotion' (2009, 98).

Thus, any continued theorization of a technologically informed culture as cyber, separate, alternative, radical, counter, or sub becomes null, void, and potentially dangerous in an online culture where fascist mash-ups on YouTube are ignored as fabricated. Worryingly, online emotions of 'testimonies of violence' may also 'operate within a regime of suspicion, where digitalized evidence is always already suspected of being photoshopped, made-up, fabricated – and as such, these testimonies fail to move, cause annoyance or mockery instead of compassion' (Kuntsman 2012, 3). Extreme violence expressed through amateur constructions of copies of texts, images, and videos produce an 'affective regime of disbelief' (Kuntsman 2012, 3).[14] It would be better to see emotions online as operating in a regime of performativity, reiteration, citation or 'reverberation', as Kuntsman defines it (2012, 1–3).

Although we have defined emotion, media, and technology above as imbricated and layered, Kuntsman notes that such intertwinedness is more an 'affective fabric of digital cultures'. These are 'the lived and deeply felt everyday sociality of connections, ruptures, emotions, worlds, politics and sensory energies, some of which can be pinned down to words and structures; others are intense yet ephemeral' (2012, 3). Drawing on Sara Ahmed's ideas in *The Cultural Politics of Emotion* (2004) around the emotionality of texts as performative, Kuntsman states that 'online performative acts of naming an emotion can create *communities* of feelings (Ferreday 2003, 2009; Kuntsman 2009), as well as *objects and subjects* of feeling: love, hate, mourning or nostalgia' (Kuntsman 2012, 6). We would also add that many have strong feelings about what we waste in the fabric of the material world in terms of online culture: time (with family); energy (slothful inactivity); resources (electricity); human creativity (digital sweatshops); and, as Jennifer Gabrys (2011) brilliantly shows in *Digital Rubbish: A Natural History of Electronics*, electronic detritus and hazardous waste from the seemingly immaterial virtual media technologies we so love and desire.

With all this in mind, we seek to contribute to an emerging and growing attention to the mainstreaming of ordinary emotions articulated and performed online that have then become practiced in everyday life. Although Karatzogianni and Kuntsman's volume *Digital Cultures and the Politics of Emotion* (2012) understandably intervenes from the perspective of theoretical literature on emotion and affect, as an opening gesture their edited collection houses an eclectic mix of approaches. We do not reattempt the breadth and variety of theoretical and analytical positions that are successfully produced in that volume. Rather, our intention is to offer the growing interest in emotions and online media a more comprehensive theoretical framework to illuminate our critical readings. In the *Cultural Politics of Emotion*, Ahmed successfully produced close readings of printed material of charity campaigns (like *Kony 2012*) that sought to move the reader to appropriate others' feelings: of feeling sad *about* them rather than *with* them (2004, 21). In our book, we approach emotion online in a transmediated readerly way, but draw out the multiply-mediated ways in which the Internet is now also used to empower the reader and distance the Other.

Therefore, this book draws upon an equal amount of literature from television and film studies, as well as cultural studies of technology, globalization, online media, and the Internet, to pursue a sustainable conceptual framework for approaching some key moments in the history of online mediated emotion. This book is also informed by feminist theories of emotion, because women can get absented from the techno-masculinization of care and global responsibility, as *Kony 2012* made apparent. We do not promote online life as a new, radical alternative to offline life or as postbroadcast in its mediation of the world. Neither are we invested in the more traumatic archives of feeling that have come to define key theories of emotion, memory, mourning, grieving, and terror (such as genocide, the Holocaust, wars, and acts of terror). These emotions have increasingly become securitized by emotion agents of film, television, radio, journalism, and online media. In fact, we approach online emotion from the perspective of media studies and popular culture, taking the position that online media *is* popular culture so that we can track the continuities among media forms. As Tara Brabazon has argued of popular culture: 'films, music, television, food and magazines – preserves something of a life lived, pleasures shared, joyous laughter or empathic tears. It is not accurate or verifiable, but it is affective' (Brabazon 2005, 67).

Old media, new emotions

Although it acknowledges that some key forms of online media have had a potentially liberating and democratic impact for users (for example, the fan activism that forms the basis of Jenkins et al.'s [2013] *Spreadable Media*), our book remains critical throughout of notions of decentralization, openness, transparency, authenticity, and 'rhizomes'. These notions informed those foundational ideas of cyberculture in the early 2000s and they continue to positively present online media and culture as creativity- and community-driven, even in the face of the exploitation of these two factors by Internet businesses. The numerous publications of Robert McChesney have emphasized the illusion of a deregulated media landscape, a landscape that cyberculture theorists of the 1990s imagined as potentially offered by human–computer interaction (HCI). In McChesney and Nichols's (2002) *Our Media, Not Theirs: The Democratic Struggle against Corporate Media*, the authors launched a scathing polemic against US media (very generally) and argued that what should have been a media system for the people and of the people 'fails to provide basic support for citizenship'. The media system is owned by a 'handful of enormous conglomerates that have secured monopoly control of vast stretches of the media landscape' (2000, 24).

In the last decade, some critics argue that this ownership has changed little, considering the astonishing rise in social networking sites. Matthew Hindman argues in *The Myth of Digital Democracy* (2009), for instance, that the opportunity for citizens to post their views online offers largely 'trivial' content because of the 'powerful hierarchies shaping a medium that continues to be celebrated for its openness' (2009, 18–19). Hindman is certain that the 'hierarchy is structural, woven into the hyperlinks that make up the Web; it is economic, in the dominance of companies like Google, Yahoo! and Microsoft; and it is social, in the small group of white, mainly educated, male, professionals who are vastly overrepresented in online opinion' (2009, 19). This may be challenged with the rise of social networking and participatory media, but is such online culture providing an alternative discourse? Certainly, digital enthusiasts emotionalize it as such[15] and certainly academic research has found a good deal of evidence that evokes a culture of connectivity (see Gauntlett 2011; boyd 2012a/b; van Dijck 2013).

Initially, Google, Inc., emerging in the late 1990s out of Larry Page and Sergey Brin's radical and innovative ideas and working practices, offered the possibility of open connectivity. Yet, it became a multinational, bureaucratic conglomerate, employing over 30,000 workers and trying to sustain that early counter-corporate-culture vision. The Google motto of 'don't be evil' (an emotional plea) has to be set against CEO Eric Schmidt's suggestion to the *Wall Street Journal* that the future of Google may not be in search-offering at all. 'I actually think most people don't want Google to answer their questions', he stated. 'They want Google to tell them what they should be doing next' (Jenkins Jr. 2010). Perhaps they do not, because Eric Schmidt stepped down and Larry Page stepped back up as CEO in April 2011, and the overriding issue he faced revolves around trust and privacy. How we *feel* about the size, scope, and power of such an online giant of the Internet is vital to Google's representation of itself to users,[16] and this feeling cannot be separated from the disempowerment experienced by consumers of offline media either.

What percentage of Internet users, in even the most advanced information societies, have blogs, are civically engaged, upload videos, or are fan activists? What percentage feels powerless to hold any media giant to account? If we follow the digital enthusiasm of advocates such as Clay Shirky (2010a, 2009a/b), Charles Leadbeater (2010), and James Surowiecki (2005), we are led to believe that online social media will make us (feel) more empowered as consumers. The mediation (micro) and mediatization (macro) of emotion, to borrow Sonia Livingstone's (2009) phrasing, and the concomitant use of online media to both represent and vent everyday emotions, can have real impact across old and new media alike, stitching them together as vital to civic life and to care of the self.

For example, 'public anger' (or at least the perception of it) in the United Kingdom at phone hacking closed a UK newspaper (*The News of the World*) that had been in print for 168 years – a newspaper well known as an emotion agent with a long history of being 'liked' by readers. Family companies such as Ford pulled their advertising in corporate fear of being associated with the newspaper and in corporate pride in their brand. The betrayal of a grieving family (whose murdered daughter's phone was hacked for newspaper stories) led to the newspaper's owner (Rupert Murdoch) to put his head in his hands, seeking the parents' forgiveness. Moreover, there was the human cost of 200 journalists that were left suddenly jobless. The mediated emotion of those workers joined the public expressions of pride, hurt, and betrayal to produce a mediatized offline final celebratory edition of the paper and the website www.newsoftheworld.com as an 1843 to 2011 online memorial. This mixed the journalism of guilty pleasures with the compassion of its final act of charitable giving. Media and emotion became transmedially produced as the public, journalists, and industries responded horizontally (across online discussions boards) and vertically (through print, television, radio) on both mediated (micro) and mediatized (macro) levels. A year later, former deputy editor Neil Wallis (2012) lamented its loss to a tabloid industry 'terrified' by The Leveson Inquiry of running 'astonishing stories' and to a 'great British public' that knew what it liked and it liked emotionalized print media.

Therefore, while we are principally researching and offering insights about emotion online, we do not lose sight of offline and everyday emotional practices and of the traditional media forms that have hitherto defined how we should feel in and about society and culture. In line with this, newspapers, magazines, television, and film form continual referents in our mixed-media approach to reading everyday online culture. This is largely because we view the separation between media forms into discrete or single mediums as unhelpful, but mostly it is because we read powerful continua between old and new mediations in the consumption practices of audiences, as well as in the production practices of powerful emotion agents. We do not, though, imagine we can cover everything; readers specializing in one media form will no doubt find that their area may only be touched upon in our theoretical syntheses of emotion and online media culture.

We are very aware that we are using the word *audience* and not *users, produsers, prosumers,* or *fans*. The latter four categories may appear to have the most significant presence in online media culture research, but all these categories are likewise cultural, academic, political, or market constructions (see van Dijck 2009). We are not denying that there are ordinary Internet users who produce creative content in a *writerly* way as a contribution to 'transmedia storytelling', who engage with the 'transmedia story' as it 'unfolds across multiple media platforms, with each new text making a distinctive and valuable contribution to the whole' (Jenkins 2006a, 95–96). Yet, considering the relatively nascent status of transmedia storytelling and the competitiveness of media industries, it is more likely that the vast majority of content produced for online consumption is there to be *read*. Those active online are busy literally *writing themselves into being* so as to be read. In fact, online and social-media entrepreneurs of media content production may be newly and emotionally engaged, but they have not yet left behind old media practices of mass broadcasting. They may be the new emotion agents, but they too view their content through a 'commodity logic', view their audiences as 'present on a multitude of channels' and they know how much we all 'love the commodity fetish', as Lovink defines the 'Googlization of our lives' (2011, 147).

Globality/Emotion

Google also knows that a closed systematization of readerly content is vitally important for fast mass global engagement and consumption transported down the tubes of the Internet. For Larry Page of Google, affective responses are immaterial if they cannot be systematized and monetized very quickly. Testing 41 shades of blue for links is not about discovering how to make icons on pages more aesthetically pleasing, personally relevant, or democratically representative. It is simply about data producing profitable patterns from billions of human actions. Systematizing and informationalizing serendipity becomes a driver for Internet giants. Therefore, for this book, mainstream, networked, professional, commercial, or public-financed media are seen as global and competitive, because our 'media ecology' is 'composed of competing organizations, mediums, genres, formats and forms, and their distribution by traditional and new media technologies' (Cottle 2006, 8). Furthermore, media archives are also being globally repurposed. David Hesmondhalgh thanks 1970s/80s punk for expanding 'the emotional range' of his 'small record collection', and finds that 'music could be shocking or coolly detached; intelligent or belligerent; hilarious or deadly serious' (2007, 25). He uses this as self-evident proof that the cultural industries do not support a 'monstrous system for the maintenance of conformity' (2007, 25). Yet punk now competes on the global media stage for a much wider share of the music market than British subcultural youth. Thus, the mediation (micro) and mediatization (macro) of everything (Livingstone 2009) forms a conceptual framework for understanding our intimate connections with discourses of globality and emotion as they permeate our past and present media.

Media theorists have known for some time that the cultural imperialism of the global flow of media images, ideas, and discourses exports

Western concepts of 'globality', which have emotional resonance for media audiences.

> Globality is a blockbuster new script – action, drama, suspense, and road picture all packed into one – with a sprawling cast of characters and locations in every corner of the earth. We have met, worked with, and had extensive conversations with many of the key figures in this unfolding scenario. (Sirkin et al. 2008, 2)

Thus, Sirkin, Hemerling, and Bhattacharya, three management consultants, partners in the Boston Consulting Group (BCG), define a new global economy and imagine it as a US mediation of the world. They could have easily been describing ABC's six-season television series *Lost* (2004–2010), which was averaging 15+ million US viewers per episode during the writing of their pre-financial-crisis book *Globality: Competing with Everyone from Everywhere for Everything* (Sirkin et al. 2008). *Lost* was a TV series that knew how to dig deep into audiences and extract loyalty through presenting weekly doses of jeopardy. With the new global relationship after the trauma of 9/11, *Lost* rediscovered a rich and fertile island. ABC marketed the new show in 2004 by extending its reach out into everyday life, through putting messages in bottles left on beaches where vacationers relaxed *away* from television. Viewers sought it out online. It survived because its narrative offered universalized emotions of fear, hatred, love, grief, jealousy, pride, anger, and desire in the face of difference (national, racial, ethnic, gender, age, physical ability, and class). The finale, after 114 episodes, simultaneously broadcast in the United States and the United Kingdom on 24 May 2010, was a trans-Atlantic, emotionally charged denouement.

This globetrotting TV drama, with a multicultural, international ensemble cast, produced just the effect of globality that Sirkin et al. (2008) imagine above: panoramic, inclusive, heterogeneous, and engaging with Others. In the context of global recession, this concept of globality has been challenged, but still emerges within discourses of social networking, microblogging, online citizen journalism, and online gaming. This does not mean that national, regional, local, and hyperlocal emotionally charged narratives do not compete with globality.[17] Globality in terms of *Lost* was the appearance of international, cross-cultural difference, although the corporate production power was firmly rooted in the long histories of US television networks. Even if *Lost* drew upon audience engagement and interactive script production from fans' creative ideas, this did not undermine the hierarchies of power in television as they opened up to online networks.

Thus, if research about global media structures show that the long histories of power continue to shape the contemporary moment (see Curran 2002; Curran and Seaton 2009), then how is emotion being used as a universalizing factor that moves audiences and users across geopolitical boundaries? What makes the affect of *Kony 2012* so spreadable but the intended emotional response unspreadable? Underlying any exploration of the literature that has converged upon the conceptualization of emotion online is the critical tension between the global and the local conditions upon which emotions are represented, produced, or consumed. For example, Adi Kuntsman's research explores the 'passionate politics of militarism' that pervades 'on- and off-line military violence, the mediation of wars and conflicts, and the affective regimes that emerge in cyberspace at the time of imperial invasions, "wars on terror", and globalised mediascapes' (2012, 3). Her examples are historically specific to Russia, Israel, and the United Kingdom.

Alongside this we can place the idea that online culture is fast becoming an emotion culture of public intimacy (see Berlant 1997), the expression of feelings (see Cvetkovich 2003), of ugly feelings (see Ngai 2005), of queer emotions (see Sedgwick 2003), and of ordinary affects (see Stewart 2007). The fact that these can be shared globally but mean so many different things locally shows that affective value has both economic value and cross-cultural value. While our book, because of the constraints of time and space, will not be covering the many local variations and the cross-cultural articulations of emotion online, we are mindful that a more comprehensive treatment of the very many national and regional emotion cultures found on the Internet would be welcomed by scholars (see Danet and Herring 2007).

Our approach to emotion online

Our turn to the affective domain within media studies is born out of a 'feeling' as researchers that (even as non-fans) we are not quite separate from the objects of study we have been analysing for decades. We have also not been able to sever our affective ties to those well-established media forms that have moved us. As happens with many Internet users, our emotions (and, because of the archiving power of technololgy, our memories) are being mobilized horizontally (with e-mail, blogs, messaging, YouTube, Facebook, iTunes, commercial/public/third sector websites) and vertically (with radio, music, television, film, newspapers, and magazines). There are too many things to remember and there are too many things to feel and we do not have the time to interpret the significance of all the mediations that affect us. So, we have avoided both the 'bias toward the cognitive individual' and 'the prominence of ideas of unilateral self-containment' in our readings of emotion online (Brennan 2004, 62). By approaching the Internet as researchers with feelings and approaching media as lacking self-containment, we unpack the most useful literature on emotion, affect, and globalized media in Part I and offer three close readings of online emotionality in Part II. The aim is to provide future researchers (empirical or not) with some useful thinking and analysis, so that they might then interrogate the differences, distinction, and specifics that we have been unable to cover more closely. Although we read closely, this is not toward a fixed interpretation, and so we invite readers to reinterpret the material in other directions, mindful of Kathleen Stewart's reflection upon 'ordinary affects':

> Their significance lies in the intensities they build and what thoughts and feelings they make possible. The question they beg is not what they might mean in an order of representation, or whether they are good or bad in an overarching scheme of things, but where they might go and what potential modes of knowing, relating, and attending to things are already somehow present in them in a state of potentiality and resonance. (Stewart 2007, 3)

In spite of the renewed interest in the concepts of emotion and affect (for example Gregg and Seigworth's [2010] *The Affect Theory Reader*; Shaviro's [2010] *Post Cinematic Affect*; or Karatzogianni and Kuntsman's [2012] *Digital Cultures and the Politics of Emotion*), there is still a significant gap in work that explores the ordinary ways that ordinary people engage with emotional online media content. Such content is always, already available and mobile, from offices to homes, due to what Melissa Gregg (2011) has called the 'presence bleed' of our technological intimacy.

It is noteworthy that we use the word 'explores', for this book is an exploration, an enquiry, and a scoping exercise of the terrain that should and could be covered. Kuntsman notes that many of the works on emotion and affect have yet to make it into research on digital media and technology and observes that 'the work on emotions and feelings, in turn, has yet to address the challenges posed by digital cultures to affective politics' (2012, 5). Karatzogianni and Kuntsman rightly highlight the parallel nature of the two fields (cultural studies of affect/feelings/emotion and scholarship on digital/new media/ICTs [information communication technologies]) and say that 'it would be naïve to attempt to grasp them both in all their complexity' (2012, 5). Likewise, we are not attempting here to simplify and although we have deliberately not approached the study of emotion online empirically on either a micro or macro level, our aim is not to overgeneralize either. Rather, inspired by Kuntsman's notion that a book on emotion and online media might 'think creatively through their possible intersections', we have sought to bring 'distinct bodies of theory into a conversation' (2012, 5) with some key examples that pertain to ordinary affects as prospected by us, as researchers with feelings.

It is worth noting to the reader who is expecting an ethnographic/ netnographic study, a survey of opinions, a focus group of online users and bloggers, or a participant observation of the domestic uses of mobile phones, laptops, digital TVs, and e-readers, that this book is not focused upon active and interactive engagement with the Internet through tool-user-based analyses. We have researched many of these approaches for this book and find them illuminating. For our theorization, they would be in danger of cordoning off sections of the online audience/ user/fan group to their single use of one medium/genre. As Janice Radway argued quite some time ago regarding the problems of 'dispersed audiences', ethnographic approaches can remain 'locked within the particular topical field defined by our prior segmentation of the audience' and 'have often reified or ignored totally other cultural determinants beside the one specifically highlighted' (1988, 367). As authors, we have been determined not to ignore these other cultural determinants and have recognized that we belong to the vast majority of fairly passive online readers, viewers, and listeners that approach online media with *masterly inactivity* and *detached engagement*.

This is not to say that we do not actively construct meanings, just as film and television audiences have done for some time (at least we do in terms of what is emotionally relevant to our lives). A wealth of reception theory and audience studies in the late 1980s and 1990s showed, through a variety of methods, the cultural competencies of audiences, the work they do on/with media texts, and their uses of media in the domestic and public spheres (see Gauntlett and Hill 1999; Turner 1999; Hartley 1999, 1992a/b; Gray 1992; Morley 1992 and Fiske 1989a/b). As in the early work of Fiske and Morley, our book continues the focus upon 'those social forces that produce audiences, effectively leading us away from the examination of texts and audiences and toward a more wide-ranging study of the practices and discourses of everyday life' (Turner 2003, 123). We approach the Internet in much the same way as we would other media forms and from the established discipline of media studies, by taking a reader-oriented position, but without a narrowly circumscribed ethnographic-style method of interviewing, surveying, and observing in detail preselected research data. We do not wish to separate a single phenomenon from any other and we do not, as Virginia Nightingale warns, wish to fall into the trap of co-opting audiences' and users' descriptions of their experience as authentic and/or substantiating our own (1989, 55).

Thus, this book does not even attempt to offer empirical research in our cultural study of emotion online. Rather, we approach emotion online as most Internet users do: as emotionally dis/engaged *readers*, rather than producers. This may fly in the face of the 'strong current of digital optimism' in 'the industry, in the academy, among policy makers, and even among the general public' which predicts 'a dramatic shift in all kinds of potentialities as a result of what is understood as the consumer securing increased control over the production and distribution of media content' (Turner 2010, 127). Yet, we agree with Turner's summation that 'much of the importance of the claims made for the "produser" lies in projections made about what kind of role they will play in the future, rather than in the evidence of what they are doing now' (2010, 127).

It is not surprising, therefore, that considering a reorientation of media studies toward postbroadcast, Web 2.0, or social media, we find many projects emerging on very specific online forms and practices, many of which begin to address emotion, attachment, and engagement. For example, there are studies of participatory culture (Jenkins 2006b; Delwiche and Henderson 2012), citizen journalism (Nip 2009), online video (Lovink and Niederer 2008; Raun 2012), social networking (Hjorth 2008a; Gregg 2012), fan cultures (Hellekson and Busse 2006; Bury 2008), mobile phone culture (Vincent and Fortunati 2009; Sirisena 2012), and transmedia storytelling (Evans 2011). While these may well dovetail with our theorization of affect on the Internet, so too will our approach synergize with studies of traditional media and emotion, such as work on video games (see Shinkle 2008, 2012), news and journalism (see Uribe and Gunter 2007; Kitch 2008; Peters 2011), television (see Kavka 2008; Gorton 2009; Skeggs and Wood 2012), film (Plantinga and Smith 1999; Smith 2003; Tan 2011), and popular music (Brabazon 2005; Vernallis 2004).

In *Emotion Online: Theorizing Affect on the Internet* we are observing the usage, the dialogue, the interactions and the shared content in a *readerly* as much as in a *writerly* way. We do this because of a nagging feeling that in daily life what we are encountering online is very much easily readable, relatively closed, and does not often challenge the reader's position. In fact, the reader may even be positioned as a passive receiver of a fixed message, because there is recognition among content producers (emotion agents) that the vast majority of Internet users only read. These may even include journalists and television producers, who neglect to critically question what they read online prior to broadcasting it, with disastrous results (see the previous reference to the resignation of the director general of the BBC in 2012). This does not foreclose the *writerly* texts that are open, need to be decoded, and challenge the reader through the violation of codes. Here the reader is active and produces meaning, but we certainly do not presume that all users behave like fans, actively using the Internet to participate and interact. It may be controversial not to include a focus upon a specific pattern of media consumption among a specific community, but we do so knowingly and in the light of much 'current practice that eschews the attempt to understand large-scale processes' (Turner 2003, 132). For all the theorization that the Internet is an active space of interactive participation, we do not desire to reinvent/reify categories of participation that Lev Manovich has also seen privileged in academic discussions. While we did begin this introduction with *Kony 2012*, we did so because of its mass recognisability and realize that a 'disproportional attention is given to certain genres such as "youth media", "activist media", "political mashups" which are indeed important but do not represent the more typical usage of hundreds of millions of people' (Manovich 2008, 35).

In what follows, we introduce the reader to the broader theories of emotion and affect that underpin our engagement with online media and what Manovich defines as 'the practice of everyday (media) life' (2008, 33). We start from the position that this media life is always already a mixed-media life and that no single media tool or practice is in ascendancy. We also start from the position that all media discourses, forms, and practices function as what we call emotion agents (some more powerful than others perhaps) or carriers of affect. They connect individuals to their environments and to one another, and they cannot be separated from the individual subject into discrete or isolated objects of study (to rethink Teresa Brennan's *The Transmission of Affect* [2004] in terms of media). There is a subtheme in here concerning the death of the idea of a single medium, but that will not be our main issue. Rather, through a focus upon emotion and affect we aim to unstress the cognitive/objectivist approach to researching media cultures and to pay more attention to the mediation of emotion. This may take us some distance away from the increasingly popular neuroscientific accounts of emotion and affect, but we recognize that even these accounts are likely to socially construct their versions of the brain as machine, archive, calculator, network, transmitter or tubal.

In Part I: Theoretical Approaches, we cover theories of affect, emotion, feeling, intimacy, and touch, as they pertain to media and screen studies in the context of theories of globalization. Thus, in 'Chapter 1, Theorizing Emotion and Affect,' we consider the ways in which these terms have been defined and discussed within critical and cultural theory. Beginning with 'emotion,' the chapter travels through the theoretical background and context to consider how one might 'theorise emotion and affect' online. It also considers recent work on the divide between the public and private sphere and the rise in therapeutic culture. 'Chapter 2, Screening Emotion', moves from the position of defining the concepts of emotion and affect to thinking more specifically about how they have been theorized within screen studies. This chapter begins by focusing on emotion and affect in screen media, cinema and television, and then expands to think about fan culture, convergence, participatory culture, desire, pleasure, and face-to-face communication. It considers how the screen mediates emotion and affect, so that we may establish a background for thinking through how the computer screen functions in a theorization of emotion. 'Chapter 3, Global Emotion', covers theoretical ground in the focus on media, emotion, and globalization. In so doing, it critiques the position that online media offer more authentic, emotionally real, and unfettered communication that provides deep insight into our connections with others. Drawing on concepts of globality and the 'globital' (Reading 2011) for thinking about global emotion, we trace the theorization of affect as transmedial and technologized.

The articulation of these theoretical themes as they pertain to ordinary online experiences is best expressed in the emotion and affect that have become a more visible part of daily life, as the intimate sphere is made more public and consumable: 'What was before ephemeral, transient, unmappable, and invisible become permanent, mappable and viewable' (Manovich 2008, 38). In Part II, Close Readings, we use the key theoretical themes of our book to invite the reader to delve deeper into understanding how emotion and affect are mobilized as permanent, mappable, and viewable in order to critically analyse what emotion agents are saying and doing with those emotions horizontally (across online social networks of text and video) and vertically (through connections with traditional media forms).

Love, happiness, and joy are key mobilizers of and consequences of media fandom. In Chapter 4, 'Social Media, Happiness, and Virtual Communities', we build upon well-established theorizations of audience pleasure to understand happiness online. There is a danger in studies of emotions online to think of them only as social and meaningful or anti-social and meaningless, because the bodies socially interacting cannot be seen by each other, at least not in the text-based online world, and appear without place or location. Our focus upon happiness bridges this divide by focusing upon flashmobs on and offline. In Chapter 5, 'Emo-techno-ecology: Fear and Anger about Climate Change', we address this issue of place and geography in our attention to the personal/local rootedness of discursive representations of climate change as personal–global. On the whole, ordinary people read the mixed mediation of climate change through a weather-war dyad in the same way they think about clouds in cloud computing: large-scale, intangible, irruptive, and a potentially erasive threat. However, the exchange of data, locations, environments, and profiles to produce intimate place relationships will mean little if the domestication of technology continues to position women and their bodies as inferior. In Chapter 6, 'The Hate and Shame of Women's Bodies Online', we explore the cultural and economic exchange of data that shores up misogynistic ideas around the image of the female body. Here emotion is embodied with women digitally remediated as reposi-tories of negative affects.

Part I
Theoretical Approaches

1
Theorizing Emotion and Affect

Towards an understanding of emotion and affect

Scholars attempting to cover the history of research on emotion often chart a course through work by Aristotle, Baruch Spinoza, Sigmund Freud, and William James. These names become anchoring points in a chronological overview of emotion as a concept. Of course, like all broad-brush attempts to survey such a vast and complicated area, they leave out several other important scholars, such as Adam Smith, David Hume, Silvan S. Tomkins, and Raymond Williams. This chapter is not intended as a history of the concept of emotion. Several books have been written already that successfully move through the theoretical development of the term. Robert C. Solomon's (2003) *What Is an Emotion? Classic and Contemporary Readings* ([1984] 2003), for instance, provides an excellent historical overview alongside written work from Aristotle to Martha Nussbaum. *The Secret History of Emotion: From Aristotle's Rhetoric to Modern Brain Science* (2006) by Daniel M. Gross is a radical reading of similar writers. Jennifer Harding and E. Deidre Pribram's *Emotions: A Cultural Studies Reader* (2009) offers recent work within the fields of cultural and critical studies, and Jerome Kagan's *What Is Emotion?: History, Measures and Meanings* (2007) charts a sophisticated course through the history of emotion in fields as diverse as anthropology, psychology, and neurobiology. Instead, this chapter will draw out some of the key definitions and ideas, particularly as they will later concern the issue of emotion and affect in online media culture.

William James posed the question 'What is an emotion?' over a hundred years ago. Robert C. Solomon begins his excellent collection on classic and contemporary readings of emotion with James's question; he remarks that ever since James uttered this in the British journal *Mind*, people have been debating and revising their answers ([1984] 2003, 1). Most scholars begin their study of emotion with Aristotle and Spinoza. For example, Harding and Pribram commence their reader with 'disciplinary developments', which also include work from Williams ('on structure of feeling', 1961), from Alison Jaggar's 'Love and knowledge' (1989), and Grossberg's 'Postmodernity and affect' (1988. Contributions from anthropology, geology, and sociology, such as those of Lila Abu-Lughod (2002) and Catherine Lutz (1986), also figure as pivotal in the study of emotion. *Emotions in Social Life: Critical Themes and Contemporary Issues* (1998), edited by Gillian Bendelow and Simon J. Williams, maps the sociological landscape of research on emotion to consider issues of 'the mediation of emotional experience', 'emotion as a way of seeing', 'emotions and health', 'ageing and emotions', and 'sexuality, intimacy and personal relations'.

A renewed focus on emotions, particularly within critical and cultural theory, has led to books and collections that examine particular feelings and states of being, such as David L. Eng's and David Kazanjian's *Loss* (2003), which considers the remains of the body, space, and ideas. Sianne Ngai's *Ugly Feelings* (2005) examines negative emotions such as envy, anxiety, and paranoia to reflect on the 'ugly' side of the way we feel. In so doing, she exposes the political and cultural underpinnings of such emotions and their gendered and racial overtones.

There has also been a regeneration of interest in the emotions in neuroscience and philosophy. Dylan Evans and Pierre Cruse's *Emotion, Evolution and Rationality* (2004), for example, highlights pivotal work in neuroscience from scholars such as Antonio Damasio, Andrew D. Lawrence, and Andrew J. Calder, as well as philosophical work from Finn Spicer and Peter Goldie. The reader interested in exploring the history and application of the concept in greater depth would do well to consult the texts cited above. For our purposes, it is only necessary to interrogate the main theorizations of emotion and affect that fall within the purview of media and cultural studies.

So where do we begin in terms of defining emotion?

In basic terms, emotion is seen as something that people express about the feelings they have, whether the feelings refer to a state of being or to a physical condition. Emotions can be individual or can be expressed by the masses, and people often refer to the emotional climate/atmosphere of events such as funerals, weddings, or riots. These public gatherings capture an emotional mood and can have positive or adverse affects on individuals. Emotion is defined in various ways, but is generally seen as a sociological expression of feelings. It is not as often associated with the body, although it might describe a particular response to feelings such as a blush or clammy hands. Therefore, for this book, emotion should be understood as something that can be distributed and exchanged through psychic and physical contact, but also by social and technological means. Sara Ahmed argues, in *The Cultural Politics of Emotion* (2004), for instance, that emotions are simultaneously psychic and social, individual and collective: 'The emotions are not "in" either individual or social, but produce the very surfaces and boundaries that allow the individual and the social to be delineated as if they are objects' (Ahmed 2004, 10). Such a definition will be important for our close readings in Part II, because here Ahmed is articulating the tension that could inform an idea of networked individuality. For now though, it is enough to acknowledge the way in which emotion is being theorized as a joining or jointing of the individual and the social.

In his work on art and emotion, Derek Matravers argues that 'an emotion is a complex state; it has both cognitive and affective components' (1998, 4). In so doing, he reminds us that there is often an intellectual response and a physiological response to emotion – or, in some cases, just one or the other. Jerome Neu expands on this notion of an embodied and mindful approach to emotion and applies it to the act of crying. In *A Tear Is an Intellectual Thing* (2000), he muses on the question 'Why do we cry?' and answers, 'because we think' (2000, 14). However, he then goes on to reflect upon the times we might hurt ourselves by accident (he uses the example of stubbing a toe) and cry, and yet we may not have an intellectual thought in correspondence to those tears. This moment of question to something so outwardly simple as crying leads him to pursue and unpack the complexity of emotions and the role of emotions in our lives.

Sociologists have long been interested in the concept of emotion. Arlie Russell Hochschild's *The Managed Heart* (2003 [1983]) and *The Second Shift* (1990) are considered as landmark texts, along with David D. Franks and E. Doyle McCarthy's collection entitled *The Sociology of Emotions* (1989). More recently, Simon Williams's *Emotion and Social Theory* (2001) expertly maps the terrain to consider 'Why emotions, why now?' He considers the debates between emotion and reason, biology versus society, the 'lived' body, and 'transformations of intimacy' that have dominated discussions regarding the concept of emotion within sociology. Usefully for our close readings in Part II, he also considers digital/virtual emotions and argues that 'Events are reported in such as (sic) way that clear appeals are made to news-consumers as to the "appropriate" emotional response regarding these tragedies, from school minibus crashes and the murder of innocent children to the carnage of Northern Ireland' (2001, 122).

In the light of Williams's insight on the mediation of emotion, it is noteworthy that sociologists of memory have become equally involved in the study of emotions and, in particular, of emotional responses to trauma, terrorism, torture, and war during the last century (see Radstone & Hodgkin's *Memory Cultures: Memory, Subjectivity and Recognition*, 2005). Not surprisingly, within the emergent field of memory studies (driven by research into commemoration, mourning, remembrance, and reconciliation), emotion is seen as a collective response dominated by the thinking of Maurice Halbwachs's *The Collective Memory* ([1950] 1992) or Paul Ricoeur's *Memory, History and Forgetting* (2004). Less attention is paid to personal memory such that it is the deterministic nature of 'collective memory' that 'confines and binds our most intimate remembrances' (Halbwachs 1992 [1950], 53). Thus, suggesting memory makes a social container for emotions. Grief, shame, anger, and jealousy become private emotions in the face of collective responses to genocide, the Holocaust, political repression, or physical and psychological abuse.

Therefore, emotion, as a concept, has been pivotal in trauma and memory studies, where debates may rage regarding the harnessing of emotions such as suffering or grief for political or ideological purposes. Adrian Kear and Deborah Lynn Steinberg's *Mourning Diana: Nation, Culture and the Performance of Grief* (1999) pinpoint 'emotion' (the lack of it in the case of the Royal Family and the abundance of it in the case of Diana's mourners) as the pivotal tipping point for breaking down the private/public class divisions in the short period directly after Princess Diana's death. We shall turn our attention to the theorizations of the role of media in harnessing, projecting, and collectivizing emotions in the following chapter. Although it is important to underscore that memory studies has become more interested in the power of media to shape, control, and affect audiences' emotions around memorable and newsworthy events (see Garde-Hansen 2011), our book will be more concerned with ordinary emotions in people's everyday encounters within online media culture.

The affective turn

Like the concept of emotion, *affect* has been defined in various ways, though affect seems to attract more confusion in the way it is used. In its basic definition, the noun *affect* means the conscious, subjective aspect of an emotion; and generally this refers to a physical response from the body, a blush or tear, for instance. Some argue that *emotion* refers to a sociological expression of feelings whereas *affect* is more firmly rooted in biology and in our physical response to feelings; others attempt to differentiate on the basis that emotion requires a subject while affect does not; and some ignore these distinctions altogether. Elspeth Probyn suggests: 'A basic distinction is that emotion refers to cultural and social expression, whereas affects are of a biological and physiological nature' (2005, 11).

In her excellent collection, *The Affective Turn: Theorizing the Social*, Patricia T. Clough (2007) reminds us that the 'affective turn' refers to a shift in thought and to a synthesis of understanding. Affect asks us to think of both the body and the mind and of rationality and irrationality or of the passions (ix). '[Affects] illuminate [...] both our power to affect the world around us and our power to be affected by it, along with the relationship between these two powers' (2007, ix). Staiger, Cvetkovich and Reynolds point out that the 'affective turn's sources and lineages are many, and its hybrid formation is part of its strength' (2010, 5). Together, these ideas show what is at stake for audiences, users, and consumers of media, who have long been in positions of oscillating between empowerment and disempowerment in relation to the messages, ideas, and communications they give and receive. What is important to note in terms of 'affect' rather than 'emotion' in relation to media, is that both Clough (2007) and Cvetkovich's (2003) ideas resonate with a notion of liminality or hybridity. That is, there is a sense of being on the interface in some kind of technosomatic way, which we shall explore in more detail in Part II.

In her work on the 'cultural politics of emotion', Sara Ahmed argues: 'Affect is what sticks, or what sustains or preserves the connection between ideas, values, and objects' (Ahmed 2010, 30). Here affect is a sort of glue that binds and connects those ideas, values, and objects, and as such we might come to view media objects that transmit ideas and values as affective in their very nature. Some media objects (a pop song, a children's TV programme, a video game, a photograph, or a news report) just *stick to and with* us throughout our lives. Moreover, and this will be crucial in the following chapter, where we focus more upon audience, affect also functions as a collective energy that initiates and sustains gatherings of people or ideas. Ben Highmore offers a more physiological interpretation, writing, 'Affect gives you away: the telltale heart; my clammy hands; the note of anger in your voice; the sparkle of glee in their eyes' (Highmore 2010a, 118). Here affect is more of a bodily response that is visible and palpable and as such could be measured.

In her work on 'ordinary affects', Kathleen Stewart (2007) puts forward another way of thinking about affects, and argues, 'Affects are not so much forms of signification, or units of knowledge, as they are expressions of ideas or problems performed as a kind of involuntary and powerful learning and participation' (40). Here affect is conceived more abstractly and complexly as 'varied, surging capacities', 'that give everyday life the quality of a continual motion of relations, scenes, contingencies and emergences' (2). Affect is, then, more about becoming than being, a form of expressive learning and participation, just as finding something online to cry about may say less about us and more about what we could be. For our purposes, this formulation offers a practical application of how media audiences and online users cannot help but be affected, because online there are things that happen 'in impulses, sensations, expectations, daydreams, encounters and habits of relating, in strategies and their failures, in forms or persuasion, contagion, and compulsion, in modes of attention, attachment and agency, and in publics that catch people up in something that feels like *some*thing' (Stewart 2007, 2).

Interpretations such as Stewart's have had a great influence on the social sciences in their attempt to understand the materiality of space, time, and place in a lived way, because she describes a process by which ordinary affects 'pick up density and texture as they move through bodies, dreams, dramas and social worldings of all kinds' (2007, 3). For example, Elizabeth Wissinger suggests, 'The concept of affect resolves some of the difficulties of treating forces that may only be observable in the interstices between bodies, between bodies and technologies, or between bodily forces and conscious knowledge' (2007, 232). Again the notion of in-between-ness and liminality is structured into the definition of affect and makes coming to full interpretations of emotion online increasingly impossible. Wissinger sees affect as the bridging of gaps that are otherwise unseen and the traversing of spaces that we live in but do not always observe closely.

These definitions illustrate the various ways in which affect is used within cultural and critical theory and demonstrate the slipperiness of the term and its usage within academic study. In their introduction to *The Affect Theory Reader*, Melissa Gregg and Gregory J. Seigworth also make reference to affect's messy in-between-ness, arguing that 'There is no single unwavering line that might unfurl toward or around affect and its singularities, let alone its theories' (2010, 5). It is this messy in-between-ness that emerges and reemerges throughout our research of online cultures in the close readings in Part II, not only in the way in which such cultures are inhabited by users, but also in the ways such cultures are produced in their relation to offline and traditional media cultures. Thus, to borrow from Gregg and Seigworth, there is no single and unwavering line that might unfurl toward or around online life and culture and their singularities either.

The affective turn can be traced to a return to the body or 'a demand for the concrete' (Highmore 2010a, 119). The two dominant locations for this return are in feminist theory and in philosophical renderings of the body via Spinoza (1993 [1677]) and Deleuze (1988). Silvan Tomkins (see Sedgwick 1995; Demos 1995), a radical American psychologist, is often seen as one of the primary originators of the concept of affect within the humanities. The affective turn has been pivotal to the production of nonrepresentational theoretical approaches in the social sciences. Nigel Thrift's (2008) work in cultural geography grew out of a dissatisfaction with representational approaches because the latter drove too deep a wedge between the object of study and the process of study, and because they missed not only the bulk of everyday life in practice, but also its richness. Other key expressions of nonrepresentational geographies (Anderson & Harrison 2010; Harrison 2007, 2008; McCormack 2007) have explored *affect, emotion, body,* and *self* as key themes. Although this book will not be explicitly applying nonrepresentational theories from cultural geography, we will be drawing upon some of these ideas within Part II, largely because Thrift's approach to affect takes into consideration the rich performative accounts of being-in-landscape and opening up embodied practices with nonhuman objects, artefacts, and technologies (see Jones & Garde-Hansen 2012).

For the most part, we will be drawing upon the humanities (arts, cultural studies, and sociology) for our understanding. Tomkins argues that 'Reason without affect would be impotent, affect without reason would be blind. The combination of affect and reason guarantees man's high degree of freedom' (1995, 37). Here affect works in combination with reason, instead of straddling reason and passion. Tomkins theorises affect in relation to Freud's theories of drives and offers an alternative way of understanding human motivations and passions. He designates affects as a primary motivational system and considers shame, interest, surprise, joy, anger, fear, distress, and disgust as the basic set of affects (Sedgwick 1995, 5). His work has had a significant influence on feminist theorists such as Eve Kosofsky Sedgwick and Adam Frank (*Touching Feeling: Affect, Pedagogy, Performativity* 2003). The idea of drives couched in Freud has been significant to the psychoanalytic approaches of feminist theory, and emotional drives that cross between humans and animals have also been picked up by Thrift (2008) in his Darwinian approach to affect across cultures. We shall return to Thrift's ideas in more detail in Chapter 5's reading of geographies of feeling around climate change.

In her work on affect in cultural theory, Clare Hemmings argues that 'In contrast to Tomkins, who breaks down affect into a topography of myriad distinct parts, Deleuze understands affect as describing the passage from one state to another, as an *intensity* characterized by an increase or decrease in power' (2005, 552). Deleuzian interpretations of affect, which stem from his reading of Spinoza, also dominate work on the concept of affect. Spinoza uses the terms *affectio* and *affectus* to differentiate between the way in which 'affects can be either active or passive [...]. The more the mind has inadequate ideas, the more it is liable to the passions; the more it has adequate ideas, the more it is active' (quoted in Lloyd 1996, 73). Deleuze draws upon Spinoza's theorization of affect in *Spinoza: Practical Philosophy* (1988). Deleuze understands affections as modes, 'corporeal traces', images, and ideas that involve 'both the nature of the affected body and that of the affecting external body' (48). He argues that 'these image affections or ideas form a certain state (*constitutio*) of the affected body and mind, which implies more or less perfection than the preceding state. Therefore, from one state to another, from one image or idea to another, there are transitions, passages that are experienced, durations through which we pass to a greater or a lesser perfection [...]. These continual durations or variations of perfection are called "affects" or feelings (*affectus*)' (48–49).

The way in which Deleuze emphasises both the corporeality and the indeterminacy involved in affect has appealed to writers such as Brian Massumi and, by extension, cultural theorists interested in media, art, literature, and performance. In his *Parables of the Virtual: Movement, Affect, Sensation,* Massumi argues that 'the problem with the dominant models in cultural and literary theory is not that they are too abstract to grasp the concreteness of the real. The problem is that they are not *abstract enough* to grasp the real incorporeality of the concrete' (2002, 5). Thus, as Thrift (2008) has argued, they are too representational and miss the richness that nonrepresentational theoretical approaches can offer. Massumi's reconceptualization of the body, along with that of others, has therefore led to interest in 'new media' and 'biomedia' and sensory approaches to research (see, for instance, Parisi 2004; Zylinska 2009; Pink 2009).

Although Tomkins and Spinoza (or Deleuze on Spinoza) are perhaps the most referenced in terms of studying affect, some theorists draw on Freud, William James's work on emotion, J. L. Austin's interpretation of speech acts, Aristotle's *Rhetoric,* and eighteenth-century notions of sensibility (for instance, David Hume & Adam Smith) in their understanding of affect. The concept of affect has also been linked to work by Raymond Williams by numerous theorists. Stewart (2007), for instance, defines 'ordinary affects', as 'public feelings that begin and end in broad circulation, but they're also stuff that seemingly intimate lives are made of' (2). Her use of *affect* in this context shares similarities with Williams's *structures of feeling*. Williams's interest in the 'ordinary' and the everyday has led to work such as that by Lawrence Grossberg, that rethinks the significance of peoples' affective relationships. Indeed, Grossberg identifies Williams's structure of feeling and Hoggart's *what it feels like* as the moment he 'met' affect (2010, 310). These approaches to affect as public sentiment will be particularly important in our close readings of online media culture in Part II. For now though, it is vital to track the feminist engagement with emotion and affect, which bears upon media studies and cultural studies.

Feminist theory's engagement with emotion and affect

Culturally, emotion and affect have been long associated with femininity in the Western world. Indeed, historically women have been cautioned for getting 'too emotional'; emotion and affect have been understood to work against rational thought. As Alison Jaggar writes: 'Not only has reason been contrasted with emotion, but it has also been associated with the mental, the cultural, the universal, the public and the male, whereas emotion has been associated with the irrational, the physical, the natural, the particular, the private, and, of course, the female' (1989, 145). However, recent work, particularly within neuroscience, has challenged this assumption and argues instead that emotion and affect are fundamental to rational decision-making. In *Descartes' Error: Emotion, Reason and the Human Brain* (1994), for instance, Antonio Damasio challenges Descartes's proclamation 'I think; therefore I am' through modern neuroscience. His trilogy of research into emotions and affect has attracted a great deal of attention within neuroscience and the humanities. In *The Feeling of What Happens*, Damasio writes: 'We DO NOT need to be conscious of the inducer of an emotion and often are not, and we cannot control emotions wilfully' (2000, 47). Rather, for Damasio the causes of an emotion can range from an 'image of an event' (conscious or not); it may be 'no image at all but rather a transient change in the chemical profile of your internal milieu' (47, 48) due to hormones, diet, the weather or exercise, making collective accounts of emotion very difficult to prove.

Still, our research within media and cultural studies has shown that emotional or affective expressions are often described as collectively feminine. A father might tell his son to stop 'acting like a girl', for instance, if his son is getting upset too easily; a woman might be dismissed as 'being a woman' if she passionately objects to something. Given these culturally constructed understandings of emotion and affect, it is not surprising that feminist theorists have long been interested in this work and that it continues to raise essential questions for gender studies. In the context of care, attention, and responsibility, this is very important for thinking about how online culture is being ethically critiqued and rationalized, which we will cover in more depth in Part II.

In feminist theory, a focus upon the body and on the emotions and women has led to a vast corpus of work on emotion and affect (see Gorton 2007). In the 1980s, feminist theorists such as Lila Abu-Lughod (1986), Arlie Russell Hochschild (2003 [1983]), and Alison Jaggar (1989) took interest in women's emotional lives and labours. In fact, Elspeth Probyn suggests that Alison Jaggar's chapter, 'Love and knowledge: emotion in feminist epistemology' (1989), was one of the first to consider what emotion might mean for feminism (Probyn 2005, 8).

Although these earlier influences are still resonant, it is only over the last decade that we have witnessed what Woodward (1996), Berlant (1997), and Nicholson (1999) have referred to as an 'affective turn'. The body still plays a central role in these examinations. However, they extend into an interest in language, shame, public sentiment, and the proximity we have towards others, which then extends into discussions on race (see Ahmed 2004; Probyn 2005). Ahmed's work in *The Cultural Politics of Emotion*, mentioned above, focuses on how 'emotions work to shape the "surfaces" of individual and collective bodies' (2004, 1). In contrast, in *The Transmission of Affect*, Teresa Brennan takes a more physiological approach, beginning her exploration of affect with the following question: 'Is there anyone who has not, at least once, walked into a room and "felt the atmosphere?"' (2004, 1). She argues that an increase in the perceived 'catchiness' of emotions 'makes the Western individual especially more concerned with securing a private fortress, personal boundaries, against the unsolicited emotional intrusions of the other' (15). It might reasonably be argued that one aspect of this process of retreat, privacy, and fortification is the rise of DIY (do-it-yourself) and lifestyle television programmes and websites, which help foster a tendency for creating your own sense of home. She argues that:

> The transmission of affect, whether it is grief, anxiety, or anger, is social or psychological in origin. But the transmission is also responsible for bodily changes; some are brief changes, as in a whiff of the

room's atmosphere, some longer lasting. In other words, the transmission of affect, if only for an instant, alters the biochemistry and
neurology of the subject. The 'atmosphere' or the environment literally gets into the individual. (Brennan 2004, 1)

One of the emotions Sara Ahmed pays particular attention to in terms
of contagion is disgust. Drawing on Darwin's description of a 'native's'
disgust at foreign food and of his own disgust at the closeness of the
'naked savage's' body to his food, Ahmed considers how this emotion
circulates and racially configures bodies. She draws attention to the
ambivalent structure of disgust, which involves both attraction to and
repulsion for its objects. For this reason, proximity and distance become
crucial in thinking through the affect of disgust –the closer one is to
the disgusting object, the more one's body will pull back in abjection.
Ahmed also considers the way in which disgust 'sticks' to some objects
more than others and how disgust works performatively 'not only as
the intensification of contact between bodies and objects, but also as a
speech act' (2004, 92).[1] Considering Damasio's ideas that an image and
even the thought of an image may be enough, it seems that proximity
to a screened object would disgust.

One of the issues that these models of affective contagion raise is that
of proximity and distance – how do spatial relationships affect the way
we *feel?* How do these models of contagion respond to issues such as
(representations of) the object of disgust? Ahmed refers to an '"inside
out" model of emotions' (2004, 9), which underlines the way 'we
respond to objects and others, that surfaces and boundaries are made:
the "I" and "we" are shaped by, and even take the shape of, contact with
others' (2004, 10). Ahmed draws on emotional responses to fear, specifically those that are incited by racial difference. In the context of our
case studies that draw upon the online representation of fearful peoples,
events, or ideas, it is important to recognize the tension between proximity and distance to such representations within online users. They
are close to the screen representing the object of disgust, yet they may
be very distant (geographically, socially, racially) from the reality being
represented.

Therefore, use of the term *affect* has generated a significant amount
of momentum and has been considered a 'trendy' concept, despite the
fact that work on affect has been going on since (at least) the seven-
teenth century. Academic research on the concept of affect has led to
a greater understanding of the role of emotions within sociological
and cultural studies, and this in turn has helped to identify the close

emotional engagements viewers have with the screen – whether film, television or computer, as we shall show in the next chapter. Research has also helped to counter cultural assumptions regarding the gendered nature of affect, and it highlights the importance of emotion and affect in rational decision-making. This decision-making, in turn, leads to the notion that there is an economy of choices to be responded to in terms of our emotional engagement.

The affective economy

As we noted in the introduction, theoretical encounters with affect online have started to be addressed, most recently in *Digital Cultures and the Politics of Emotion: Feelings, Affect and Technological Change* (2012), edited by Athina Karatzogianni and Adi Kuntsman. Their book offers a broader approach to the digital than Jane Vincent and Leopoldina Fortunati's edited collection, *Electronic Emotion: The Mediation of Emotion via Information and Communication Technologies* (2009), which took as its premise that emotions and information and communication technologies (ICTs) function as a kind of social glue. The reader would do well to read Vincent and Fortunati's introduction to get a sense of how emotion and ICTs are synergised through communication theories. They only touch upon mediations of emotion through television and film. However, we remain more sceptical of the social-glue approach and find in Karatzogianni and Kuntsman's (2012) collection a critical questioning of any overarching theory that would bind emotion to technology.

In their collection, the editors draw together a diverse and international range of scholarship that theorises and analyses affect, fantasy, intimacy, seduction, touch, and corporeality in a range of digital cultures such as gaming, YouTube videos, mobile phones, e-mail, wikis, and digital art. Affect is the through line that draws together quite disconnected activities and experiences that occur in very different places and spaces. The concept of *affective fabrics* is provided as a way of thinking about the material landscapes that emotional experiences reside in, and the concept of *reverberation* is offered as a way of bridging the online/offline divide that appears to break down as emotions are communicated and intensified (Karatzogianni & Kunstman 2012, 1–3). This is emotion functioning not so much as glue, but as the textiles themselves. We shall attend to these issues in more detail in Chapter 3, but what is important to note here is the way that affect has come to reverberate within a range of discursive fields, from media to technology to economics.

In *The Cultural Politics of Emotion* (2004), Ahmed posits 'affective economies' as a way of drawing together psychoanalysis and Marxism into a
discussion about emotional capital. She argues that 'affect does not reside
positively in the sign or commodity, but is produced as an effect of its
circulation' (Ahmed 2004, 45–46). We agree, and yet commodities are
produced with both an intended use value and a preemptive symbolic
(hereafter, *affective*) value. It is the affective value that can be seen as the
most sustainable aspect of a commodity, product, or sign. Contra Marx,
this value already resides in signs and commodities, waiting to be activated,
developed, and sustained by the consumer; it is not born out of human
labour (advertising and marketing aside) and it has no carbon footprint.
Its value (often seen as inferior to the morally virtuous use value created
from men's and women's productive labour) is in fact the very backbone
of an affective economy. It may be the pet name we give to our car, the
proud polishing of screens, tablets, and laptops we do habitually, or the
nostalgic memories of cassette mix-tapes and vinyl records. While affect
does indeed circulate in an economy, it is also built in to the commodity
or sign from its inception, and is inseparable from its use-value.[2] Media
content is just such a commodity, and in this book we are keenly aware of
the media fan cultures that trade in an affective economy.

Clough (2012) has argued: 'Affect is a vector of unqualified intensity
seeking future actualization; it is a vehicle from one dimension of time
to another' (2012, 23). Similarly, in a different context, *affective branding*,
argue Parisi and Goodman (2012), is control of future memory/emotion.
We are persuaded to consume signs and commodities that always already
have a preemptive affective value built into them, which will be activated in the future. For many commodities designated as vintage, their
future emotional value will be their lost use-value, which itself functions as a memory or nostalgia. For other commodities, the affective
value is, as Brian Massumi (1993) has argued, preemptive in its control
of the anticipated memories and feelings we *will have but are yet to have*
about the commodity. It is our desire to see the emotional value grow,
to sustain the emotions built in, that advertisers encourage. This shows
the affective economy to be highly valuable and future-proofing (eBay's
and Preloved's success is testament to this), not just in financial terms,
but also in sustainability terms.

However, while commodity culture ensures that human labour does
not have to continue ad infinitum as if this labour were indefatigable, it
also realizes that careful online management of the commodity sign once
it enters online culture (if affect is a vector) may no longer be possible.
We understand affect as designed into a commodity (constructed and

nurtured by the first purchaser), and then transmitted to, and enhanced and protected by subsequent consumers. Yet, at the same time we understand that such affect is vehicular (as Clough points out above), it is mobile and goes unprotected from one dimension to another. We shall return to these ideas in Chapter 6, when we focus upon the precariousness of the private intimate images exchanged between lovers over e-mail or mobile phone that then enter an affective online economy. For now though, it is important to note that ICTs and media technologies are more than ever touched, felt, held, worn, caressed, pressed, thumbed, dropped, scratched, protected, stolen, remembered, and forgotten within the affective economy of pervasive and ubiquitous computing.

(Keeping in) Touch: intimacy, feelings and haptics

It is important to mention intimacy, feelings, and touch, which have also attracted a great deal of attention in critical and cultural theory following the 'affective turn', as these terms all carry different meanings from emotion and affect, though also share many similarities. Touch, for example, is a very sensual, tactile, and often loving expression of intimacy and emotion. If we see a couple holding hands, we often think they must be in a loving relationship with each other. A mother might gently rest her hand on her child's head or shoulder as an expression of love and protection. If a child utters innocently 'he touched me' of an adult male who is not a trusted intimate, fear and anxiety prevail. Trusted forms of touch signal a deeply felt emotion and an intimacy. But how does touch function online? Surakka and Vanhala remind us that the 'mouse-driven user interface' is still the 'most visible milestone for an ordinary user' in human-computer interaction (2011, 213). As they argue: 'The most important consequences are that the user receives feedback about his or her actions when operating a desktop computer or another kind of information technology, such as handheld devices, televisions, and mobile telephones' (2011, 213–214).

In *Thumb Culture: The Meaning of Mobile Phones for Society* (2005), edited by Glotz, Bertschi, and Locke, the editors note that *keeping in touch* is cited as the primary function of the mobile phone and that this is manifested through the sensory capacities and movement capabilities of thumbs. In her chapter for the collection titled 'Emotional Attachment and Mobile Phones', Jane Vincent shows how 'the mobile phone engenders intimacy and a feeling of being permanently tethered to loved ones' (2005, 117), even though, as we shall explore in Chapter 6, those loved ones have the power to exploit that intimacy online. Following this, we might also think of the touch necessary for using touch screens, whether iPad, iPod, or e-readers. In Facebook parlance, a user can 'poke' one of their friends, which means to send her a message, and gestures towards a physical touching. If a user's Facebook profile is stolen and despoiled through the posting of malicious content, it is said to have been *fraped*, thus referring back to corporeality and shame. The body is central in the turn towards emotion and affect online, and yet the body cannot enter into the virtual world in real terms. There are devices that can make one feel connected or able to experience a kind of touch, but these are stimulated by electronic means, not through a physical interaction. Yet, recent research has suggested that the physical is not always necessary for an emotional response. Surakka and Vanhala note that 'social signals, such as simulated emotional touch (i.e., haptics, non-verbal touch-based communication, and emotions), simulated proximity, and virtual facial expressions of an embodied agent character may affect our subjective feelings and physiological arousal' (2011, 214).

Despite new ways of theorizing the body virtually, touch seems to remain something firmly rooted in the flesh. As Simon Williams suggests: 'The cuddle for a crying child, the supportive arm around a friend in need, the gentle caress of a passionate lover, these and many other similarly embodied gestures touch us deeply, communicating a shared sense of trust, intimacy and vulnerability, grounded in the fleshy predicaments of our mortal human bodies' (2001, 126–127). Yet the demand for online representations of such ordinary intimacy accords with Massumi's argument in 'The Thinking-Feeling of What Happens' (2008) that haptics is not simply touch but also about the perception of it: 'touch as it appears virtually in vision – touch as it can only be *seen*' (2008). Thus, it is the perception of somebody there on the other end of the mobile phone, on the other side of the world at a computer (just as we are) that is felt and translated into a contagion, into something that sticks, and into something we involuntarily participate in.

It is in this act of translation that the liminality, the messy in-between-ness of affect can be said to reside. Drawing on Spinoza and Simondon, Massumi explains:

> What I'm trying to say is that formations communicate only imma-
> nently, at the points where they live themselves in, or at their
> self-embracing fringes. They only virtually relate. All relation is virtual.
> [...] It is only because relation is virtual that there is any freedom or
> creativity in the world. If formations were in actual causal connection,
> how they effectively connect would be completely determined. They

might interact, but they would not creatively relate. There would be no gap in the chain of connection for anything new to emerge from and pass contagiously across. There'd be no margin of creative indeterminacy. No wriggle room. (Massumi 2008)

The perception of others' feelings is important here. In defining feeling, emotion, and affect, Eric Shouse argues that 'feelings are *personal* and *biographical*, emotions are *social*, and affects are *prepersonal*' (2005). Drawing largely on Massumi's work, Shouse helpfully unpacks the differences between the terms. Feelings are understood as 'personal and biographical', because when we feel something we check it against our past experiences; what makes one person sad will not affect another. Emotions are 'social' because they are exhibited, whether authentic or contrived. A person might express sadness in a social setting because s/he feels that doing so is socially appropriate. Facebook offers an interesting way to consider Shouse's definitions of emotion and feelings. Status updates are filled with emotional displays, and many users are conscious that when someone posts something it is not necessarily an expression of their 'real' feelings. A post about a new baby, for example, can affect people very differently, depending on their personal experiences. So, someone who already has children might feel happy that this person does too, or someone wanting children might feel sad as she does not have one, and others will feel completely uninterested. But most will reply 'Congratulations, I'm so happy for you', or something of this nature.

Lisa Blackman and John Cromby (2007) offer similar definitions and suggest that 'Where *feeling* is often used to refer to phenomenological or subjective experiences, *affect* is often taken to refer to a force or intensity that can belie the movement of the subject who is always in a process of becoming' (5–6). In *An Archive of Feelings: Trauma, Sexuality, and Lesbian Public Cultures* (2003), Ann Cvetkovich defines 'archives of feelings' as 'repositories of feelings and emotions, which are encoded not only in the content of the texts themselves but in the practices that surround their production and reception' (7). Again, perception of feelings and the creative connections those perceptions can bring forth are important here. Cvetkovich's conceptualization of 'archives of feelings' works particularly well when we think of the 'timeline' feature introduced by Facebook. The format suggests the importance of archiving one's personal thoughts, pictures, moments and 'feelings' from 'birth' (when the person first opened a Facebook profile) to the present day.

Feelings are the focus of A. R. Hochschild's influential *The Managed Heart: Commercialization of Human Feeling* (2003 [1983]). She introduces the term *emotional labor* and defines it as 'the management of feeling to create a publicly observable facial and bodily display; emotional labour is sold for a wage and therefore has *exchange value*' (1983, 7). Hochschild carefully considers the 'costs and benefits of managing emotion in private life and work', and in so doing generates crucial questions and issues regarding emotion in public spheres that continue in discussions of emotion today (9). In thinking about feelings as 'senses' and as something not necessarily 'inside us', Hochschild persuades us to consider how we 'manage' our feelings in our everyday lives and 'contribute to the creation' of those feelings (2003 [1983], 17–18). Her understanding of feelings is pertinent to a neoliberal economy that is constantly putting pressure on individuals to manage their own bodies, deal with their own emotional problems, and to keep their feelings in check *on the job* (over e-mail, in online evaluations, on Skype, in meetings). It applies equally to the ways in which people are expected to control their feelings in the face of disappointment or in moments of frustration, while at the same time media culture demands to see those moments of jeopardy, particularly on reality television shows. Clear messages are posted on trains, airplanes, buses, and other forms of transportation that remind passengers that they must control their feelings and not let their frustrations out on staff. Again, it is the perception of feelings and that one *has* feelings (appropriate or not) that is being communicated here and that we shall focus upon in our close readings, particularly in relation to the calls for managing bad feelings online or the production of hurt by abuse of online material.[3]

Intimacy is often thought about in relation to sexual relationships, but what happens when this is mixed in with economic concerns? Viviana A. Zelizer's intriguing book *The Purchase of Intimacy* (2005) draws attention to the difficulties in understanding intimacy in relation to legal and economic situations where 'you imagine that the world splits sharply into separate spheres of rationality and sentiment' (2). In fact, Zelizer seeks to understand the 'purchase in the sense of grasp – how the powerful grip of intimacy affects the ways we organize economic life' (2). For example, she draws attention to the 9/11 compensation funds established for the deaths in the United States and questions how Americans as a society negotiate the bonds of intimacy in such a tragedy. When relationships are not clearly defined, then who becomes the rightful heir: the lover, the children, or the siblings? Likewise, who has the right to create an online memorial to a deceased person: the family, a lover, or an enemy? Who has the right to profit from a website that exchanges intimate images of ex-girlfriends? Intimacy extends into relationships between siblings, between parents and children, and friendships. Indeed, one of the hallmarks of a good friendship is the ability to be intimate with the other person. Intimacy involves a kind of knowing about the person that means that you have access to that person's 'inner' life. In other words, if you are in an intimate relationship with someone, you probably know more about his feelings or his emotional state of being than most people do. You are also in a position of power to exploit that knowledge, as we shall show in Chapter 6, when we encounter the misuse of nude images of ordinary young women. As Zelizer maintains, intimacy 'ranges from damaging to sustaining, from threatening to satisfying' (2005, 18).

Intimacy often carries a sexual connotation, and its lack is cited as one of the reasons for the failure of marriages. 'It lacked intimacy' is often read as 'It lacked passion, sex, intercourse', and yet the two are not always the same. One can have sex without intimacy; this is often seen as the downside to casual dating. In terms of online media, intimacy has been a very difficult area to understand and study (see Ellison, Steinfeld, & Lampe 2007 on Facebook 'friends'). There is a discrepancy between how people imagine themselves and how they present themselves online: perceptions, semblances, and presentational immediacies are creatively produced between appearance and reality. Online dating sites such as match.com, eHarmony, and meetmymatch strive to bring people together, but they also bring together appearances so that they 'affectively, effectively overlap' (Massumi 2008). These social networking sites (SNSs) are examples of moving from online to offline communication; often the online persona may seem very different from the offline one and yet they are the same (see Ellison, Heino, & Gibbs 2006).

We can widen our discussion of the affective economy to consider the ways in which people compete through forms of intimacy in what we might call 'competitive intimacy'. For example, on Valentine's Day, posts either photographing or explaining ways in which loved ones have recognized the day are designed to say something about the superiority of one's own intimate relationship. One photo showed 'Happy Valentine's Love You Lots xxx' written in the snow and visible from the poster's apartment window. Replies ranged from advice that the boyfriend (who wrote the message) was a 'keeper' to suggestions that he was a 'show-off'. In another post, a picture of oatmeal with a heart made from strawberries accompanied the message 'Breakfast from my Sweetheart'. The posters of these messages clearly want to share their intimacy with their 'friends' in a performative way, reiterating powerfully and visually the bonds they have created. Yet, there is also an element of competition here. This form of tacit competitiveness can be seen as destructive, yet it can also be reassuring. On the one hand, it can cause people to feel that their own lives are lacking as they witness mediatized intimacy that celebrifies love. On the other hand, it can make them feel more content with what they have because they do not feel the need to showcase their emotional attachments to a network.

In *Intimacy* (2000) Lauren Berlant argues that 'the inwardness of the intimate is met by a corresponding publicness [...]. At present, in the U.S., therapy saturates the scene of intimacy, from psychoanalysis and twelve-step groups to girl talk, talk shows, and other witnessing genres' (1). The essays in this collection address the 'contradictory desires' that 'mark the intimacy of daily life' (5). Berlant's work is useful insofar as it explains ways in which the intimate meets the public, and she articulates the relationship between emotion and the public sphere:

> But intimacy also involves an aspiration for a narrative about something shared, a story about both oneself and others that will turn out a particular way. Usually, this story is set within zones of familiarity and comfort: friendship, the couple, and the family form, animated by expressive and emancipating kinds of love. Yet the inwardness of the intimate is met by a corresponding publicness. (Berlant 2000, 1)

Berlant's observation is particularly germane to online examples of this kind of intimacy. People's blogs or individual web pages will tell a story, an intimate one about their family, their travels, their parenting experiences. In comparison, the *sidebar of shame* (so to speak) of the UK's *Daily Mail* website is widely recognized as a totally absorbing and clickable image-list of intimate titbits from the world of celebrity. The address is often intimate and private, as if the emotion agent (be it blogger or newspaper) is talking to a friend or family member, and yet the information is accessible to an invisible audience, open for anyone to read and (involuntarily) participate in their intimate revelations. The creative possibilities that the invisible audience are producing online will be focused upon in Chapters 4 and 6.

Public sentiment, the 'intimate public sphere', and therapeutic discourse

How do we negotiate the boundaries of the public and private in terms of emotion and affect? This question has dominated a good deal of the emergent work on emotion and affect, with a burgeoning attention to media and communications.[4] In their chapter on emotions in culture, for instance, Jennifer Harding and E. Deidre Pribram (2002), consider 'how emotions as a category of experience might be implicated in negotiations of the (hierarchically arranged) public/private divide in contemporary popular discourse' (408). In their consideration of the public/private divide, they raise the case of Princess Diana's death as an example of a moment when the private enters the public domain. It is also worth mentioning Marita Sturken's notion of *emotional reassurance* and her formulation of 'comfort culture and the consumerism of kitsch objects' in *Tourists of History* (2007), as well as Matthew J. Allen and Steven D. Brown's work on the 'affective labour of remembering' in reference to the memorials for the 2005 London bombings (2011). As we noted earlier, memory studies have played a pivotal role in examining the way the private meets the public in affective ways. Garde-Hansen's *Media and Memory* (2011), Neiger, Meyers, and Zandberg's *On Media Memory* (2011), and Garde-Hansen, Hoskins, and Reading's (2009) *Save As...Digital Memories*, have covered this terrain with reference to the public domain of media very well.

Indeed, one of the directions in which the interest in the divide between the personal and political takes us is towards a contemplation of public displays of sentimentalism. In her book *Impersonal Passion: Language as Affect* (2005), Denise Riley refers to the handwritten cards, flowers, and teddy bears that grace scenes of public mourning. The cards contain the question *Why?* and, as Riley argues, 'Such cards have become part of today's panoply of public mourning'. These public expressions of mourning lead Riley to consider how 'this WHY [a prostrated inert thing, is also a provocation. To whom is it put? The writers of such cards will realize perfectly well that the only answer to their implied "Why was this innocent life destroyed?" is swift and brutal-sounding: that here there is no *why* to be answered other than by a terse "Because"' (2005, 59).

Her analysis of these public displays also leads Riley to consider why these metaphysical interrogatives have replaced questions of moral responsibility. For example, 'I must be involved in this somewhere' vies with 'I am not responsible for this' (Riley 2005, 69). 'Why?' and 'Why me?' allow its speaker to replace moral responsibility with accusation, destiny, and bad fortune, but also involve the audience in answering the question. One might also think of the way in which people refer to an event as 'tragic', instead of attending to the political or social structures that allow these 'tragic' events to happen in the first place.

Lauren Berlant, in *The Queen of America Goes to Washington City* (1997) intelligently addresses what she sees as an increase of the private in the public sphere, what she terms 'the intimate public sphere'. Her work has been influential to feminist theorists writing about emotion and affect, but it is also crucial to those working on mediated public spheres such as online media. In the next chapter, we argue that these are spheres that form continua with television and film and certainly run parallel to them. Berlant differentiates what she calls 'the intimate public sphere' from a Habermasian 'intimate sphere' of modernity and goes so far as to argue that 'there is no public sphere in the contemporary United States' (2002, 3–4). Instead, a 'kind of vicious yet sentimental cultural politics' dominates (2002, 4). She explores this claim through what she refers to as a 'counterpolitics of the silly object', and interrogates the 'waste materials of everyday communication' (1997,12) to observe the ways in which intimacy configures national culture. Her book provides a fundamental critique of the right-wing agenda in the United States as well as a decisive insight into the use of intimacy in the public sphere.

In *Cold Intimacies: The Making of Emotional Capitalism* (2007), Eva Illouz charts the rise of capitalism alongside a narrative of emotion in fascinating ways. She argues that advice literature is largely responsible for the rise in therapeutic cultures, which now dominate Western culture. She points out that at the beginning of the twentieth century, two influential thinkers, Samuel Smiles and Sigmund Freud, stood at opposite ends to each other on the notion of recovery. Smiles held up an aspirational model in which every individual was morally responsible to 'better' his or her situation through hard work and determination. Freud, in contrast, saw therapy as class-bound and believed that even if working-class people could work through their neuroses, they might be worse off 'because the hard life that awaits them if they recover offers them no attraction, and illness gives them one more claim to social help' (Freud 2001 [1958], 167). Illouz argues that by the end of the twentieth century, the two opposing narratives become 'so intertwined as to be virtually indistinguishable' and notes the way in which 'recovery has strangely become an enormously lucrative business and a flourishing industry' (2007, 42). Part of the democratization of such therapeutic discourses, as Illouz points out, was the result of the 'paperback revolution' that made self-help books more affordable and available to the middle and lower-middle classes (2007, 43). With the invention of the Internet, this is even more possible, and yet most of the therapeutic services are still really about making money. Chapter 4 will consider this dimension in more detail. Suffice to say here that this is important for how online culture is characterized as both a therapeutic DIY toolbox and a folk devil – the cause and cure for all social ills in one indistinguishable stroke.

Among the reasons why the therapeutic narrative has had such a wide cultural resonance, Illouz suggests, is that 'The internet is the latest development in this process, as it presupposes a psychological self which can apprehend itself through texts, classify and quantify itself, and present and perform itself publicly, its problem being precisely how to convert that public psychological performance back into a private emotional relationship' (2007, 108). It is the ability to be 'emotionally competent', however detached and alienated this is, that remains a sign of one's ability to thrive in a capitalist economy. One has to be competent in emotions in new and digitally literate ways.[5] The Internet is problematic because it divorces the mind from the body in ways that highlight our self-selecting. Illouz uses the example of dating sites and, interestingly, suggests the ways in which the Romantic notion of love has changed due to 'love on the Internet'. While previously love was defined as a 'thunderbolt' (see Illouz 2007, 89), now that is unlikely to happen, because a user would first be attracted, almost as a consumer, to a person, and then would have to meet the person, at which point judgment is often made on very superficial grounds; Illouz uses the example of someone not liking the person's weak handshake. Illouz's most recent work, *Why Love Hurts: A Sociological Explanation* (2012), continues this interrogation of the expansion and development of choice within our affective economy and the *institutional forces shaping how we love*.

Therapy culture has meant that feelings have been given more importance than ever in the Western world. Although Illouz's (2012) book takes the attention off individuals as the cause of their own misery and places the spotlight on forces, structures, and organizations, there has also been the focus upon personal and private emotions as offering the key to managing emotions. Dana L. Cloud has argued that 'the therapeutic, as a situated, strategic discourse (or rhetoric), dislocates social and political conflicts onto individuals or families, privatizes both the experience of oppression and possible modes of resistance to it, and translates political questions into psychological issues to be resolved through personal, psychological change' (1998, xviii–xix). As Cloud suggests, responsibility is increasingly given to individuals to 'manage' their feelings, emotions, and affective lives, especially in the public sphere. The Internet becomes a space to do so, but it is also a very public domain for blowing the whistle on oneself, which problematizes notions of intimacy and constructions of the self as private. As we shall show in Chapter 6, the forces, structures, and organizations that exist online make managing feelings difficult. Although, as we will go on to explore, online media have been celebrated for their liberating potential, they are also sites of intense observation, power, and archiving. Users might feel free to disclose their feelings and get in touch with their emotions, but they must also recognize the way in which their expressions of intimacy are logged, tagged, and shared. Which is to say that feelings presented online are, like Massumi's 'perceptual artefacts', lending themselves 'to regimes of power' or enveloping 'in themselves power potentials as well as powers of resistance' (2008).

There is a wealth of work within critical and cultural theory on the concepts of emotion and affect. Over the last decade, in particular, theorists have articulated the various ways in which the concepts of emotion and affect play an integral role in our everyday lives. Pertinent to the second half of this book is work that has been undertaken regarding the concepts of emotion and affect in television, film studies, and face-to-face and interfaced communication – in other words, on work that has been produced within what is sometimes called 'screen studies'. Although we will not be applying the dramaturgical frameworks of sociologist Erving Goffman (1961) for understanding the self, symbolic interaction, and society in terms of online culture, it is worth highlighting that in Turner and Stets's (2005) *The Sociology of Emotions*, Goffman's notion of the *focused encounter* is useful for connecting emotion theory to screen studies. Goffman emphasised cultural context as vital for understanding individual emotional responses in gatherings of people. For 'encounters are lodged within larger structural and cultural units. Each encounter is embedded in a gathering, which assembles individuals in space', who are 'embedded within a more inclusive social occasion composed of fixed equipment, distinctive cultural ethos, program, and agenda, rules of proper and improper conduct, and pre-established sequences of activities' (Turner & Stets 2005, 27–28). From face-to-face encounters to encounters on and with screens, our present book is interested in the gatherings of screen audiences and online crowds and the preexisting cultural scripts that are shaping these focused encounters. Therefore, in the next chapter we take a close look at the research that offers the reader an overview of screening emotion.

2
Screening Emotion

Time to lean forward

A common distinction made between televisions and computer screens is that for the television you lean back and for the computer you lean forward. Indeed msnbc's tagline is: 'It's time to lean forward': 'to lean forward is to think bigger, listen closer, fight smarter and act faster' (www. msnbc.msn.com/id/39310817/ – United States). Leaning back implies a lack of interaction and participation, while leaning forward suggests engagement and agency.[1] Scholarship in television audiences and media theory has upset both assumptions, and most theorists seem to agree that there is both activity and inactivity in contemporary television audiences and computer screen audiences. In this chapter, we explore that scholarship that disallows the positing of simple binary oppositions about how we position our selves, bodies, minds, and emotions in relation to different screens.

These screens can be found on multiple platforms (broadcaster websites, video on demand, news sites, online games, blogs, discussion boards, and social networking sites, for example) in multiple places (in the home, on the street, and in the workplace), and in different parts of the world (some parts with regulated Internet). It is clear that how we feel about a mobile phone image of happiness uploaded to Renren (Chinese social networking site) will play out differently to the same image uploaded to Facebook. It is also clear that particular kinds of technologies and platforms such as Facebook, YouTube, mobile phones, on-demand television, online games, and discussions forums are distinct phenomena. Viewing footage on a mobile phone of environmental disaster recorded by a survivor and uploaded to YouTube is quite a different emotional experience to viewing the same footage framed as breaking news and streamed through the BBC news website.

We cannot and do not attempt in this book to cover all the emotion landscapes, structures, and logics of how emotion is played out online, played out in different parts of the world, and for very specific audiences, but we do attend to the layering of screen media and emotion in the Western imaginary as it appears to us. As individuals, we find ourselves traversing many online landscapes that may well be distinct structurally, logically, and rationally, but we creatively connect our emotional attention across them. It is in this chapter that we attend to the emotional saturation of online media culture as it pertains to continua of theories from television and film studies. These theoretical explorations of emotional engagement with the screen began (rightly or wrongly) by conceiving of the audience (personally, locally, and globally) in terms of how they engage and how they work things through, with less attention to the distinct differences in delivery systems, types of distribution, and contexts of consumption. Likewise, in laying the foundations for future research into the exact coordinates of emotion online in our media-saturated world (for different parts of the world, for specific audiences, with distinct technologies, on individual platforms), we need to weave together a framework of theoretical ideas about screening emotion.

The last chapter considered the theoretical history of the concepts of emotion and affect, how these have been used in a range of disciplines, and how their articulation has drawn upon differing disciplinary areas. Crucially, for this book, it is their relationship to terms such as intimacy, touch, and feeling that resonate with new and old articulations of emotion and experiences of affect encountered online. This chapter develops from that basis and considers how concepts of emotion and affect have been theorized in media studies, with a particular focus upon screen studies. While the last chapter aimed to provide a working understanding of the concepts of emotion and affect and how they have been used within critical and cultural studies, this chapter considers how emotion has been theorized 'on screen' and in relation to screens – primarily through work in film and television studies.

Media, emotion, and affect

There has been a range of work already undertaken more generally on the relationship between media, emotion, and affect. Largely this is because, as Ahmed has pointed out in *The Cultural Politics of Emotion* (2004), texts have emotionality. Likewise, Katrin Döveling, Christian von Scheve, and

Elly A. Konijn suggest in the introduction to their book, *The Routledge Handbook of Emotions and Mass Media* (2010), 'how we feel in and about our society, or indeed about the world in which we live, is affected by our experiencing this world through the mass media' (2). On the one hand, in *Regarding the Pain of Others*, Susan Sontag (2004) has explored the cultural mediation of suffering in photography. On the other hand, as stated in the introduction to this book, Tara Brabazon has noted that

> Popular culture – like films, music, television, food, and magazines – preserves something of a life lived, pleasures shared, joyous laughter or empathic tears. It is not accurate or verifiable, but it is affective' (2005, 67).

In understanding the representation and transmission of empathy in the media, Carolyn Calloway-Thomas (2010) has been able to pinpoint the moments when celebrities function as global conduits for imagining the feelings of others, thus drawing upon media and emotion in the context of sympathetic communication that is shared textually between media and audiences. Maria Angel and Anna Gibbs's (2006) research has understood the transmission of affect through media images as a process of biomediation of politics, of danger, and of friendship. Gibbs's chapter 'Disaffected' (2002) offered a new approach to media studies in terms of a biological interpretation of affect, a focus on the 'biological' that has largely been rejected by feminist-inspired media and film studies. She states:

> I would want to argue – as I have elsewhere in relation to a particular instance (Gibbs 2001) –that what is co-opted by the media is primarily affect, and that the media function as amplifiers and modulators of affect which is transmitted by the human face and voice, and also by music and other forms of sound, and also by the image. Moreover, the media inaugurate and orchestrate affective sequences. (2002, 338)

With this in mind, in what follows, we cover terrain that is connected with these previous studies, but with the aim of steering the reader toward emotion, affect, feeling, intimacy, and touch at the interface of the screen.

Cinema, emotion, and affect

Emotion as a concept does not appear as a central interest within film theory until cognitive theorists, in particular, see it as something crucial to understanding the film audience. As Torben Grodal asks in *Moving Pictures: A New Theory of Film Genres, Feelings, and Cognition* (1997, 1), 'Is it possible to "comprehend" the narrative in *Casablanca* or *Psycho* without any idea of the types of emotions cued in the film and their relative response?' Plantinga and Smith's collection entitled *Passionate Views: Film, Cognition, and Emotion* (1999) is an incredibly important text that helps to lay out some of the ways we, as theorists and scholars, might think about the use and the transmission of emotion on screen. This transmission is not entirely visual either; Plantinga's collection includes the important work of Jeff Smith (1999) who, in 'Movie Music as Moving Music: Emotion, Cognition, and the Film Score', begins with a self-analysis of the 'lump in the throat' brought about by Samuel Barber's *Adagio for Strings* that plays in the final death scene of David Lynch's *Elephant Man* (1980). Film theory takes an affective turn and theorists become unafraid to ask questions about what moves them as viewers. Plantinga's emphasis on close-up shots, Jeff Smith's work on music, Noël Carroll's attention to affective dimensions of the text, and Greg M. Smith's mood-cues (all in Plantinga's 1999 collection) help us to consider how we might think about emotion and film/television.

For instance, in 'Local Emotions, Global Moods: The Emotion System and Film Structure', Greg M. Smith argues that 'The orienting function of emotion encourages us to seek out environmental cues that confirm our internal state' (1999, 113). In other words, our mood or emotional state may determine what programme or film we decide to watch: if we feel sad, we might choose a melodrama or if we are feeling happy we might be drawn to a comedy. Smith also suggests that there are *emotion markers*: 'configurations of highly visible textual cues for the primary purpose of eliciting brief moments of emotion' (1999, 118). These 'emotion markers' support and emphasize the mood of the viewer; these are moments of intense emotion in the text that serve to continue the mood of the film and that are interpreted from the bottom up by audiences rather than applied from the top down by producers: *emotion from below,* so to speak.

In *Film Structure and the Emotion System* (2003), Greg M. Smith argues that 'Films offer invitations to feel. Film audiences can accept the invitation and experience some of the range of feelings proffered by the text, or they can reject the film's invitation' (2003, 12). In other words, films and television do not *make* viewers feel, rather, we, as viewers, are *invited* to feel and must acquire some level of understanding of emotion cues and markers (from our previous film 'reading') in order to make sense of what we watch. As Smith explains: 'To accept the invitation [to feel], one must be an "educated viewer" who has the prerequisite skills required to read the emotion cues' (2003, 12). This ability to 'read' the emotional cues can present some problems when we transport these ideas to online media in terms of text-based communication. However, considering the proliferation of audiovisual media in online culture and the notion that we will gravitate towards or away from particular sites based on emotional 'moods' seems very apt.

In *Moving Viewers: American Film and the Spectator's Experience* (2009), Plantinga develops and expands on ideas from his earlier work in *Passionate Views* and advances the importance of the concept of emotion within film studies. He considers why there has been relatively little study of emotion and affect and comes up with some very interesting answers, including the notion that emotion is 'antithetical to reason and an obstacle to logical and/or critical thinking' (2009, 4). As we explored in Chapter 1, this presumption has come under attack in both the humanities and in fields such as neuroscience, where recent work has not only challenged the notion that emotion is an obstacle to logical thinking, but has suggested that it is a necessary component to rational decision-making and critical thought. Anna Gibbs (2002), cited above, believes that emotion and affect have largely been ignored in media studies due to their inclusion of biology and therefore an essentialism that flies in the face of decades of cultural constructionist accounts of the audience. Plantinga also suggests that the emphasis on psychoanalysis in earlier film studies (often referred to as 'screen studies') meant that there was a move away from emotions and towards drives and unconscious pleasures. Because emotions are thought to be subjective and private, they were not seen as proper objects of academic focus (2009, 4). In response to this neglect, Plantinga argues that emotion and affect play a key role in a film's narrative, the physical pleasure of the cinematic experience, the ways in which viewers make meaning from what they watch, and even the reason viewers go to the cinema. In other words, Plantinga makes emotion and affect central to the cinematic viewing experience.

Plantinga's work is crucial in terms of revaluing the role that the concepts of emotion and affect should play in cinema studies, and, by extension, he gestures towards the importance that emotion and affect should have in a study of online media. Many viewers are now watching films on their computer screens and engaging with paratexts on the Internet. Indeed, viewers may consult their tablets whilst watching movies on the television screen in order to find out more about the film's subject matter, the actors, or other background information.

Plantinga's work explores what cognitive film theory tell us about the ways in which emotion is elicited and figured into the experience of the viewer (2009, 5). One of the primary ways, as Plantinga notes, is that emotion is a central motivation for watching movies (2009, 5). Not only do viewers enjoy the film emotionally, perhaps signalled affectively by tears or laughter: they often share their enjoyment with friends and family, encouraging others to watch it, who do so because of the emotional connection it has had on the first viewer. This chain of affective experience of one viewer to another is then contagious and extends to others and leads to conversation, often over the Internet, whether on e-mail, blogs, or web forums. In fact, Gibbs argues that consumer economies 'actually rely on contagion for everyday functioning, connecting people, money, goods, resources, ideas, and beliefs in global flows of communication and exchange' (2010, 186).

This is often true of television, which will be explored in further detail in the next section. Emotion is also crucial in terms of the way viewers interpret, understand, and share a film's narrative. Good storytelling involves getting viewers (or readers) emotionally attached to either the characters or to the narrative's trajectory, or to both. It is very difficult to sustain interest in any text if there is no emotional involvement. This emotional involvement usually leads to memorable experiences that become connected. So, for instance, most of us can remember a time of being emotionally moved by something we watched, whether this is an individual experience or a cultural one. Some of us may have been moved by exactly the same cinematic experience at the same time (Barber's *Adagio for Strings* in *The Elephant Man,* for example). These moments shape our memories of the cinematic experience and also link us to collective cultural moments.

How does this extend to our thinking about online media? The sharing and sending of a flashmob clip, for example, elicits an emotional response from many of its viewers, which is then shared amongst friends and family over e-mail, blogs, and on social networking sites. The short films of a collective 'happening' (such as pillow-fight flashmobs[2] across the world in major cities) often move people emotionally and garner feelings of community, collectivity, and humanity in similar ways to a good film. Chapter 4 will explore the affective nature of flashmobs and their emotional importance in more detail. It is worth noting here that flashmobs have now spread back into traditional screen production with the viral success of *The Big Bang Theory Flash Mob!* which reached 13 million views and 9000 comments in three days, performing mutual affection of all involved in the show.[3]

In his work on fans of spaghetti Westerns and users of the Spaghetti Western Web Board, Lee Broughton (2011) refers to the social practices and the virtual community that is established through mutual affection for these films. The emotional attachment that fans have for spaghetti Westerns not only results in their posting and sharing online, but also in real-life interactions where they cross national boundaries and meet in Spain to see film location sites before redevelopment and time destroy them (305). Broughton sees this 'real-life' meeting as an example of the online/offline interaction of fans with their beloved objects and an example of the ways in which this fandom creates virtual communities; he comments, 'Most Internet users' on-line activities reflect their off-line interests too' (2011, 306). Broughton's research highlights how emotional attachments to films inspires online interaction and offline socialization in ways that speak to nonrepresentational geographies, as noted in the previous chapter. This completes the circle that film tourism has been exploring from a heritage industry perspective. At the end of her book *Film-Induced Tourism*, for example, Sue Beeton notes that future research needs to focus on how 'we put ourselves into the story, sights, sounds and emotions of the movie through our personal experience, knowledge and analogy' to create a sense of place out of the film (2005, 229). Online film fandom is one mechanism for laying down such roots.

Television, emotion, and affect

Following the 'affective turn,' discussed in Chapter 1, Theorists such as Misha Kavka (2008), Kristyn Gorton (2009), Beverley Skeggs and Helen Wood (2012) have considered how emotion and affect function in television programmes and its audiences. Their work has helped to fill a gap in research on the use of emotion and affect within television, in terms of how it is valued, how writers construct 'emotional' moments and ways in which audiences affectively engage with programmes. More recently, theorists have used emotion and affect in their analyses of film and television to examine particular genres, such as E. Deidre Pribram's *Emotions, Genres, Justice in Film and Television: Detecting Feeling* (2011) or to examine specific concepts, such as Rebecca Coleman's *Transforming Images: Screens, Affects, Futures* (2012).

Kristyn Gorton's work in *Media Audiences: Television, Meaning, and Emotion* (2009) was one of the first to explore the concepts of emotion and affect solely in terms of television. Although primarily a theoretical and textual exploration, it also included ethnographic work in the UK soap industry to consider the extent to which television writers and directors placed value on emotion. The book takes the question of the viewers' emotional engagement seriously, thereby placing the question of emotion and affect centre stage. The first half of the book focuses on the literature surrounding the concepts of emotion and affect and the medium of television; the second half draws on textual readings in contemporary television as a means of exploring how emotion is valued, fashioned, and manipulated within television. One of the more interesting findings is the way in which emotion has been fashioned in reality television. Gorton argues that emotion is sometimes used as a social tool in a way that obscures differences of class, gender, and race. It is worth quoting her analysis at length:

> Thus, while superficially operating as light entertainment, many reality or lifestyle programmes such as *Wife Swap* (Channel 4, 2003–2009) seek legitimacy through a suggestion that they play a deeper pedagogic role: they invite us, the audience, to reflect on our intimate feelings and relationships through an empathetic engagement with the participants. Using devices such as the video diary and the staging of final meetings between the participants, these programmes use emotion as a tool to suggest that differences of class, race, sexuality, and gender can easily be overcome through the emotional medium of a 'good cry'. Indeed, *Wife Swap* fashions emotional responses as a way of overcoming differences between the participants and between viewers and participants (Gorton 2009, 100–101).

Through a discussion both of how emotions are mediated by the television screen and of the mechanisms by which these emotions of self-becoming become contagious, Gorton's work questions the implication that these programmes teach their participants lessons about themselves or about their parenting skills (2009, 101). This is important for thinking about the social learning and participation encountered online, whereby emotion, particularly shame (around parenting, for example), is constructed in a similar way and resonates with users from their experience of reality television.

In *Blush: Faces of Shame* (2005), Elspeth Probyn notes that 'Television in particular exploits the individual viewer's response to what resembles an intimate shared shameful moment, which is aired for all to see' (85–86). Television becomes, as Probyn suggests, a particular exploiter of these catchy emotions, and we can see that such public shaming is certainly central to the online outing or Twitch hunts of racist tweeters, for example. Yet, as Ahmed (2004) has commented, it is necessary to think about how emotions circulate – they do not necessarily move from one person to another in a straightforward manner. As Ahmed explains, 'Even when we feel we have the same feeling, we don't necessarily have the same relationship to the feeling' (2004, 10). In other words, while television may create intimate moments, as Probyn describes, viewers will not experience emotions or 'catch' the emotions in the same ways. In Chapter 6 we will explore this differentiated contagion of emotion in relation to how online users exchange images of women and women's bodies as a form of visually mediated gossip. With respect to such repurposing of online self-portraiture, we find that emotion is mobilized in the ways that Ahmed suggests.

In *The Cultural Politics of Emotion* (2004), Ahmed observes that 'emotions are not simply something "I" or "we" have. Rather, it is through emotions, or how we respond to objects and others, that surfaces or boundaries are made: the "I" and the "we" are shaped by, and even take the shape of, contact with others' (10). This notion of emotional contagion is crucial in terms of understanding emotion online. Social media, for example, are full of intimate moments shared for all to see: scans of unborn babies, admissions of love and hate for partners, secrets about jobs, and whistle-blowing blogs, for example. These statements often become objects or affective contents, which are then passed around and circulated, taking on different meanings as they meet with others who may comment in supportive or ironic ways.

The therapeutic discourse, as discussed in Chapter 1, saturates television schedules. Indeed, as Mimi White suggests, 'As an integral apparatus of post-World War II American consumer culture, television is centrally implicated in confessional and therapeutic strategies (2002, 313). Television talk programmes such as *Loose Women* (ITV, 1999–) or *The Ellen DeGeneres Show* (NBC, 2003–), for instance, are designed around the ideas that it is good to 'talk through' our feelings and to voice our thoughts on matters from abortion to holiday dresses. Presenters on talk shows often address the audience in an intimate fashion, relating personal anecdotes as if we are all just friends having a coffee. The intimacy, however manipulated, in the address also extends to the way the programmes are presented.

As Helen Wood points out in *Talking with Television: Women, Talk Shows and Modern Self-Reflexivity*, even the organization of the studio set on programmes such as UK ITV1's *Good Morning* 'replay the arena of the domestic': 'Their living room is extended into our living room' (2009, 44). This illusion of intimacy emphasizes the importance of feelings and works to draw the audiences in: thus the set leans forward, in toward the viewer, disallowing passive consumption. In her work on 'affect contagion', Anna Gibbs refers to the intimate nature of television in that it 'aims to create the illusion of intimacy, as if the viewer were the only person watching and were being addressed directly by the medium' (2005, para. 3). This idea of intimacy is even more apt for the computer screen. As users, we often feel as though we are having a private conversation with whatever happens to be on screen. This illusion of intimacy is extended when we think of handheld computers (tablets) or laptops, which can be transported easily into bedrooms and other places we consider private in the home.

Kavka sees the following as defining elements of television: 'as mechanism of social integration, as apparatus in the domestic environment, as technology of presence' (2008, 4). While we completely agree with these attributes of television, we think her definition also extends into our thinking about the home computer, especially laptops and netbooks, which are often used to watch television in bed or on the couch. It is also possible to extend this into thinking about immersive 3D TV and about how a multidimensional view can affect a viewers' experience of a text. We must keep in mind television's changing nature and its continual convergence as a multiplatform product. In an interview with television scholar Elizabeth Jane Evans, the head of Multiplatform Commissioning for Drama, Comedy and Entertainment at the BBC, Victoria Jaye mentions *Doctor Who* (1963–1989, 2005–) and *EastEnders* (1985–) as 'premier brands' and programmes that have 'storyworlds where television just cannot contain the world; it flows over' (2011a, 110). Despite being very different kinds of stories (one soap, one science fiction) and attracting different kinds of audiences, they each tell stories that 'flow over' into another world, whether into a spin-off television series (such as *E20*), into television-induced tourism worlds, or on the Internet as fan sites.

We must also think of the ways in which people watch television and how this affects notions of the public and private (for instance, see Anna McCarthy's *Ambient Television: Visual Culture and Public Space*, 2001). Elizabeth Evans notes that 'If you are watching television on your mobile phone you are watching it alone but, being a portable device, the mobile phone is primarily used in public spaces. It has the potential to combine public space with private viewing and as such raises questions about the importance of private space to the specific act of engaging with television drama' (2011b, 133). As discussed already, television's intimacy is partly the allure for viewers: the sense that what is being seen is private and even confessional, especially with regard to reality television. As viewers, we feel drawn into private worlds. Yet, as

Evans points out, how does watching these private worlds in a public space affect the emotional engagement that viewers have with the text itself? In her work on television and emotion, Gorton considers the phenomenological relationship we have with television and the way in which viewers often get themselves 'prepared' for a favourite television programme or film: viewers might dim the lights, get a blanket, a glass of wine in hand, and so on (2009, ix). Questions regarding the nature of our engagement with drama, the relationship between private and public space, and our physical relationship to the screen extend to our thinking about emotion online. Do users of laptops or iPads in airport terminals, for instance, have a less emotional engagement with a chosen website, a Facebook chat, or an e-mail exchange with a friend than they would at home?

Kavka's work takes the genre of reality television as the sole focus for her study of emotion and affect in television. In so doing, she comes up with some very interesting ideas regarding the use of emotion and affect in television and in the public sphere. She notes, for instance, that 'The affective power of the mediated image, its ability to bring out feelings where the real world may leave us cold, is one of the defining paradoxes of our technological era' (2008, 1). Kavka takes issue with Berlant's compartmentalization of private worlds, discussed in the last chapter, and suggests we 'recognize the ability of (reality) television to make the private sphere public by paying attention to its "capacious-ness"' (2008, 75). Kavka notes that 'Instead of bringing private persons into realms of public discourse, as Jurgen Habermas characterizes the eighteenth-century liberal press, the TV relation goes the other way: reality television brings the public sphere into private spaces, binding public discourse to the interested, invested *Intimisphere* (for Habermas, the intimate sphere of the conjugal family)' (2008, 49–50).

Drawing upon work by Wendy Brown, Kavka sees the potential in reality television to expand our notion of the public sphere. Unlike Brown, who sees a limitation to the 'capacity to experience privacy and intimacy', Kavka argues that 'capaciousness names the feeling of being on the cusp between public and private, experiencing one's own posi-tion in a box nested within many, as part of the peopled neighbourhood we come to know and belong to via the screen' (2008, 76). She goes on to suggest that 'in this way, the private extends the public, giving it capa-ciousness through our mediated intimacy with people we have never met, but who are "out there"' (2008, 77). As with Massumi's notion of the *virtual seen,* noted in the previous chapter, Kavka's conceptualiza-tion of capaciousness of reality television is easily transported to the mediated intimacy of online media, in particular, social network sites or blogs. Here we feel and perceive the other's presence, like the infamous viral cartoon of a stick man seated hunched over his computer, banging away at his keyboard while a voice (presumably a wife) shouts, 'Are you coming to bed?' He: 'I can't. This is important' She: 'Why?' He: 'Someone is *wrong* on the Internet'.

Beverley Skeggs and Helen Wood's *Reacting to Reality Television: Performance, Audience and Value* (2012) does an excellent job of posing the question of affect in terms of the television audience. The culmination of an ESRC Identities and Social Action research grant, their work reflects a deeper engagement with the audience itself. For them, affect is seen as 'a force in the social relations between audiences and television' (5). Drawing upon empirical data from interviews, Skeggs and Wood conclude that 'Affect enables connections to be made to the television participants and their characterizations, situations and position in narrative structures', therefore allowing audiences to 'evoke judgment, replay morality, assuage ambivalence, generate self-criticism, produce affective reach, incite resonances, reproduce cultural in/difference' (184). As with the theories of affect covered in Chapter 1, it is this notion of participation and learning that resonates, as audiences' emotional practices become opportunities to experiment with being and becoming.

We have placed emphasis on reality television and emotion because it is most relevant in terms of studying emotion and affect on the Internet.[4] Largely this is to debunk the notion that somehow new media and what goes on online is so very different from old media such as television. In many ways, it can be argued that the profiles on a site such as Facebook are designed as if in a kind of reality programme, as users attempt to put their best faces forward. Emotion often drives searches on the Internet, with search engines such as Google acting as verbs of assurance: *I Googled it and it said so*. For instance, a pregnant woman might use the search engine on a regular basis as fears and anxieties surface. Or perhaps someone is concerned about their relationship, health, or their children's education. These emotional attachments and relationships often motivate our use of the Internet as a potential site for finding answers and reassurance, in much the same way as television has functioned to work through domestic issues.

Fan cultures

To some extent, studies of fan cultures have always been interested in the emotional involvement of its fans. Matt Hills, for instance, observes that 'Without the emotional attachments and passions of fans, fan cultures would not exist, but fans and academics often take these attachments for granted or do not place them centre-stage in their explorations of fandom' (2002, 90). Perhaps for similar reasons to those cited by Plantinga, fan theorists have not always put the emotional or affective relationship to the text centre-stage. Early fan research, in particular, had to defend fans' engagement as something *more than* just an emotional involvement. Jenkins's work, for instance, focussed on the active participation a fan took in terms of making stories, creating alternative narratives, and attending conferences, for example. He points out the way in which fans are dismissed for being too emotional about their chosen text. So, in many ways, the concept of emotion had to be revalued first, before there could be a successful way of applying it to screen studies. It is not surprising that theorists of fan cultures have gone on to produce interesting and important work on how fans emotionally involve themselves in media.

Jenkins's early work on fandom exposed the way in which fans' emotional, intellectual, and personal choices are attacked by virtue of their choice of television programme. There is a sense that this person is unable to have a healthy relationship to the text and therefore becomes an object of ridicule. Jenkins's work was pivotal in terms of articulating the cultural assumptions made of fans and in terms of unveiling the importance fans had given to the texts they were beholden to. Jenkins returns to the notion of an emotional dimension to fandom in his book *The Wow Climax: Tracing the Emotional Impact of Popular Culture* (2007). He observes that 'Most popular culture is shaped by a logic of emotional intensification' (2007, 3). He also suggests that emotions from popular culture are not personal, but are 'broadly shared feelings' (2007, 4). Indeed, if feelings are to be understood and even identified with by a large group of people, they need to be easily recognizable.

Lawrence Grossberg argues that it 'is in their affective lives that fans constantly struggle to care about something, and to find the energy to survive, to find the passion necessary to imagine and enact their own projects and possibilities' (1992, 59). By way of explaining this affective energy, he uses the term 'mattering maps' (57–58). Fans often have a range of programmes they invest their energy in, but only one or two that they are devoted to; in other words, they might be casual viewers of several programmes but only dedicated to a couple. The concept of affect, and the renewed interest in it, has led to a resurgence within the study of fan cultures whereby affect and emotion have now become central in examinations of fan cultures and of ordinary viewers' relationship with television texts (see Jenkins 2007; Kavka 2008; Gorton 2009). The movement away from thinking of emotion and affect as detrimental and immature towards seeing them as a form of investment and creative production has given the fan new importance. Kompare (2010), for example, notes the way in which the creative industries, particularly the television industry, now courts fans for free labour. This was particularly the case in the BBC series *Sherlock* (2010–), in which Dr Watson's blog and the tie-in website *The Science of Deduction* inside the television show existed online and became a focal points for fans to figure out what would happen next in the series. Scriptwriters were then able to use this fan knowledge to build into scripts and anticipate and cement fans' emotional involvement and investment.

Such involvement and investment was prefigured in Howard Rheingold's *The Virtual Community: Homesteading on the Electronic Frontier* (1993), which helped set the stage for thinking about the ways in which fans interact in computer-mediated communication (CMC). Since then, other important research has helped us to better understand the ways in which fans establish and sustain communities online. Nancy Baym's (2000) work on soaps and fandom, for instance, straddles research on CMC and audience studies to provide an ethnographic account of women in a soap opera's Usenet newsgroup. Likewise, Karen Hellekson's and Kristina Busse's collection, entitled *Fan Fiction and Fan Communities in the Age of the Internet* (2006), usefully explores key ideas regarding fans in CMC, while also offering an excellent bibliography and overview of fan fiction.

Fans account for a great deal of mixed-media activity online. Blogs, web forums, and sites dedicated to particular celebrities, television programmes, and films abound. The fan him/herself has expanded in definition, as people who would not typically think of themselves as fans now find themselves contributing to these sites and enjoying conversation about a favourite programme or character. This does not mean the end of fandom as a theoretical concept distinct from mainstream audience pleasure, but it does mean the boundaries between fans and audiences has become permeable in the light of interactivity. Sarah Lund, for example, a character from the successful Danish television series *Forbrydelsen* (DR1 2007, known in English as *The Killing*), not only has several websites dedicated to her as an actress and character in the series, but also one website dedicated to the jumper she wore (Sarahlundsweater.com). This gives detailed information on the jumper Sofie Gråbol made famous – such as how it was chosen, where it could be bought, and even some ideas on how to knit it yourself. Therefore, the Internet has opened entirely new and creative ways for fans/audiences to communicate and construct alternative stories about characters or programmes they are attached to, ways that share more with practices of gaming than of film. On Twitter, for example, Carri Bugbee posed as the character Peggy Olson (@peggyolson) for the popular US series *Mad Men* (AMC 2007–).[5] Her regular tweets drew a strong fan base and changed the way producers and networks perceived the fan. Thus, on the one hand, fans, television, and the Internet are redefining their relationship with far more accessibility for the fan to the objects they love. On the other hand, as we noted in the introduction to this book, fan producers are the new emotion agents that continue to produce the mediated content within a 'commodity logic', with audiences 'present on a multitude of channels' who 'love the commodity fetish' and its 'Googlization' (Lovink 2011, 147).

Media convergence and participatory culture

Talking about a television character on Twitter is a good example of convergence, as is looking at a website about how to make a jumper (sweater) from your favourite television character's wardrobe. In *Media Convergence: Networked Digital Media in Everyday Life*, Graham Meikle and Sherman Young (2012) use the term 'convergent media' to refer to 'media content, industries, technologies and practices that are both digital and networked' (2), in part to avoid the terms 'new media' and 'digital media', which they feel can be misleading, particularly since 'all media were new once' and some media, such as the Internet, is no longer 'new' at over 40 years old (2–3). Likewise, in rethinking ideas around remediation, Richard Grusin in *Premediation: Affect and Mediality After 9/11* (2010), considers the role of affect not in reactionary terms to something that is or at least once was new (such as the Internet), but as anticipatory, which is not dissimilar to Massumi's ideas on immanence, semblance, and the anticipatory cited in the previous chapter. This is not about media getting the future right 'but about proliferating multiple remediations of the future both to maintain a low level of fear in the present and to prevent a recurrence of [the] tremendous media shock that the United States and much of the networked world experienced on 9/11' (2010, 4).

In this context, convergence functions affectively in that media that are not ours or made by us look like they are ours and made by us because they most resemble how we too participate in media content, and this feeling of closeness because we have seen this before (it is anticipatory) shocks us when its content is graphic: Abu Ghraib photos, 7/7 bombing (the 7 July 2005 London bombing) mobile phone images, YouTube videos from Syria. We are shocked and then we are sad, not we are shocked because we are sad (see William James, 1950 [1890]), claims Grusin (2010, 81). Therefore, while such convergence and mediality might imply uncertainty, Luciana Parisi and Steve Goodman (2012) claim that they lead to 'mnemonic control' or a 'refined mode of preemptive power', designed into the environment of ports, connections, mobile and wireless devices, hubs and hotspots, to become a 'mnemonic ecology' (165–166). It is served by a 'collective intelligence', and its purpose is to have 'power over futurity, which is seen as the power to foreclose an uncertain, indeterminate future by producing it in the present' (167–168). We will return to these ideas around emotion, affect, mnemonics, and mediality in Part II. For now though, it is worth the reader thinking about the use of convergent media for producing premediated emotions in audiences by what we have termed emotion agents.

Henry Jenkins's work on 'convergence culture' continues to be influential in terms of thinking about the ways in which technological developments affect culture and the way we use media in our everyday lives. Jenkins defines convergence as 'the flow of content across multiple media platforms, the cooperation between multiple media industries, and the migratory behaviour of media audiences who will go almost anywhere in search of the kinds of entertainment experiences they want' (Jenkins 2006a, 2). His definition of convergence is not just about the overlapping of media, but encompasses the ways in which people will seek out new forms of connection through various media platforms (3).

Developing from his interpretation of convergence, Jenkins argues that 'according to the logic of "affective economics," the ideal consumer is active, emotionally engaged, and socially networked' (2006a, 20), what Grusin would term popular culture's 'participation in the practices' of circulating content 'across premediated socio-technical networks like the Internet or email' (2010, 70). One example of the kind of convergence and 'affective economics' that Jenkins refers to can be found on the websites of television programmes such as *Lost* and *24*. On these websites, users can download 'mobisodes' at a cost to see some extra scenes not aired on television; see Evans's discussion of *24: Conspiracy* (2011b, 115–144). Here technologies converge: television, the Internet, and mobile phones work together to provide a para-service to their users. But, as Jenkins suggests, this is also about 'affective economics', as the websites rely on the fact that their viewers will be emotionally involved enough in the series to want to pay to find out more about the show or to experience simulated stories related to the programmes they enjoy.

Scholarship within film and television studies has increasingly devoted attention to viewers' extratextual pleasure. Plantinga (1999), for instance, comments on the importance of the external features of the film as well as the intratextual pleasures. Researchers recognize the way in which fans continue their pleasure with the text even after they have left the cinema or turned off the television (see Hills 2010, for example). In other words, there is pleasure beyond the screen. Yet, most of this pleasure now happens on another screen – the computer screen, even if this is simply using a favourite scene for the wallpaper of our desktop. Television, in particular, extends viewers' emotional engagement with the use of para-texts (see Jonathan Gray's *Show Sold Separately: Promos, Spoilers, and Other Media Paratexts* 2010). Fans of a television programme can go to the corresponding website and find out more about the characters through tie-in content and about the actors who play them. They can participate in a game, blog about the latest episode, get cooking advice, or produce their own tie-in content. This kind of engagement with television used to be seen as fan activity, and yet now this is a much more commonplace premediation that anticipates future content production through affect and mediality.

Jason Mittell, for example, makes reference to the 'narrative complexity' (2006) in contemporary American television. Referring to television programming in the United States from the 1990s to the present, Mittell examines the narrative shifts that have enabled more complex narratives and therefore, more complex fan engagement. He notes that: 'The internet's ubiquity has enabled fans to embrace a "collective intelligence" for information, interpretations and discussions of complex narratives that invite participatory engagement – and in instances such as *Babylon 5* or *Veronica Mars*, creators join in the discussions and use these forums as feedback mechanisms to test for comprehension and pleasures' (31–32).

Paul Booth's *Digital Fandom: New Media Studies* (2010) uses the term 'new media studies' to refer to 'a new way of looking at the practice of contemporary media studies that takes into account, and uses, the technologies that audiences are using to engage with media' (3). In response to William Merrin's call for 'ongoing changes in digital media' to be put at the centre of the discipline in his article on Media Studies 2.0 (2009), Booth illustrates a move within media studies towards a more encompassing model of the relationship between new technologies and their audiences/users. Interactive media become something that focus not only on how media influence audiences and produce markets, but also on how audiences influence media and produce the content they take pleasure from (2010, 3). In this way, Booth's work reflects the long history of audience studies that has moved from interpretations of media as dominant via Theodor Adorno (1979) to the audience as influential via John Fiske (1989a/b), to a more integrated approach that sees a holistic synergy between technology and its users.

One of the reasons for this approach, as Booth notes, is that 'new media' is constantly updatable and changing. It is not static text. Wikis, blogs, and social networking sites are constantly evolving and changing, as input from users comes in (2010, 3–4). Fans are prime examples of users who are influencing, producing, and creating text on the web, and as Booth argues, new media and fandom are intimately linked (2010, 4): 'Digital Fandom examines fandom as the work of a collective community, and not fans as individual audience members' (2010, 22). His model of fandom is implicated in media studies as a discipline: 'Fans rewrite not just the extant media object, but also the state of media studies itself' (2010, 39). Booth's understanding of 'digital fandom', through his study of alternate reality games (ARG), leads him to think about the web as a 'web commons', which is a new way of understanding how people collectively make use of the Internet (2010, 23). Instead of seeing the Internet as a static source of information (of links to information), Booth thinks about the web as a 'mind-set', that is something that 'extends beyond the Internet and represents a substantive alteration in how we conceive of the socialization of information' (2010, 23). Booth's model of the Internet chimes well with Broughton's research (2011), cited earlier, on spaghetti Western fans. There, fandom was not limited to the web. Indeed, part of Broughton's research is on 'offline' meetings. The 'web commons' model that Booth proposes is a more fluid and encompassing model of fandom and of human interaction with new technology.

Booth's model is important in terms of emotion and affect in that it gestures towards the more affective relationship people have with online media – one that does not necessarily stop when a person shuts off the computer. One of the examples of a 'web commons' that Booth draws on are the wikis created for contemporary television series by their fans. Heroeswiki.com, for example, is a wiki site dedicated to fans of the television series *Heroes*. On the site, fans can create alternative endings and stories, and can discuss characters and plot lines. This site, like many others dedicated to television programmes, exemplifies the ways in which fans actively participate with a text that they have become emotionally involved with. Booth recognizes these sites as a repository of information and as a shared space for people to swap stories and knowledge. Like Broughton and his work undertaken on the Spaghetti Western Web Board, and like Mittell with his notion of 'collective intelligence', Booth sees these sites as a positive example of digital community and interactive sharing.

Desire/fantasy/pleasure on screens

Plantinga's work has largely omitted psychoanalytic film studies, or screen studies, in favour of cognitive theory to account for emotional engagements in film. However, in his more recent turn to understand American films – or, more precisely, Hollywood films – in *Moving Viewers: American Film and the Spectator's Experience* (2009), he draws on folk psychology, acknowledging the importance screen theory has played in our understanding of terms such as *desire, fantasy,* and *pleasure* (19). Desire, fantasy, and pleasure are certainly important to an understanding of the ways in which viewers and fans become emotionally and affectively moved by what they see/read/hear online. For Plantinga (unlike people with more esoteric theories in film and media studies), 'Our folk psychological knowledge, in many contexts, is remarkably adept at gauging the psychology of others', otherwise 'social life as we know it would cease to exist' because 'the intentions, motivations, thoughts, and desires of others' would be 'utterly baffling and unpredictable' (2009, 19). This will be important for thinking through the adeptness of online users at dealing with the sometimes difficult and antisocial emotions they encounter on the Internet, as we shall show in Part II.

In *Reading the Popular* (1989a) and *Understanding Popular Culture* (1989b), John Fiske persuasively interrogates the pleasures one finds in the popular (see also Nick Stevenson's 2002 comprehensive coverage of Fiske's ideas in *Understanding Media Cultures*). Fiske argues in *Understanding Popular Culture*, for instance, that 'Popular culture is made by the people, not produced by the culture industry. All the culture industries can do is produce a repertoire of texts or cultural resources for the various formations of the people to use or reject in the on-going process of producing their popular culture' (1989b, 24). Writing against Adorno and the Frankfurt School, Fiske sees popular culture as belonging to the people and therefore something capable of giving them immense personal pleasure. Like Fiske's work, studies in media and sociology such as Simon Frith's *Music for Pleasure: Essays in the Sociology of Pop* (1988) have examined the role these concepts play in our consumption of media. One of the most accessible theorists on the psychoanalytic dimensions of desire, fantasy, and pleasure in film and television is Ien Ang (1996).

Ang's work on 'melodramatic identifications' (1996, 85) is especially important in terms of thinking about how viewers engage with fictional characters. She argues that viewers identify with fictional personas *in fantasy*; that is, they do not see the characters as 'role models', rather they serve as 'symbolic' identities through which they can work through various different emotions and affective relationships (1996, 92).

In her influential work on *Dallas*, Ang suggests that viewers, particularly women, are able to escape their lives and can indulge in feelings they do not ordinarily allow themselves. She calls these moments, 'moments of peace, of truth, of redemption, moments in which the complexity of the task of being a woman is fully realized and accepted' (1996, 95). Although not all viewers will desire or need this kind of escape, Ang's framework accounts for the pleasure many take in watching programmes such as soaps, which thus could account for concomitant pleasures that women and other users discover online.

Indeed, Ang associates the *pleasure* viewers get from watching fictionalized programmes such as *Dallas* with the 'ever changing emotions' they find within the text; indeed, she argues that 'it is emotions which count in a structure of feeling' (1985, 45). Ang combines 'tragic' with Raymond Williams's 'structure of feeling' because she feels that any happiness in the text is always complicated or challenged, which constructs the emotional journey viewers enjoy so much: 'In the tragic structure of feeling, emotional ups and downs occupy a central place' (1985, 46). Chapters 4 and 5 will return to the notion of happiness and to Ang's construction of a 'tragic structure of feeling' in more detail, but it is interesting to note here the way in which fans engage in the 'complex narratives' of their favourite texts, which has been discussed above. Similar to Mittell's and Booth's arguments, Ang's theorization of the way emotion works in texts suggests the need for an emotional journey for viewers/users to participate in. Ang's work also gestures towards a form of escapism that allows viewers/readers/users to try out alternative ways of living and experiencing life.

Online worlds, such as *Second Life* and *World of Warcraft*, open doors into new ways of imagining pleasure and living out fantasies online. *Second Life*, for instance, advertises itself as a space where you can 'Have fun, flirt, or simply flaunt your creativity in a world where you can experience and create anything you can imagine' (http://secondlife.com). The suggestion is that all your desires, pleasures, and fantasies can be realized in a space that is not only free, but also free from moral consequences.

In this imagined space you can have affairs, experience pleasure with the opposite sex, and/or have multiple partners as long as your imagination can sustain it. In Chapter 6, we show in the case of 'revenge porn' sites and cyberstalking that desires, pleasures, and fantasies are not free from moral consequences; mainstream media from print journalism to television are creating emotive moral panics from this notion of a free Internet. Here though, Plantinga's positing of the importance of 'folk psychology' within theories of spectatorship is important, for an online user adeptly knows the motivations, intentions, feelings, and desires of other users/ viewers/spectators, which is not to say they cannot be fooled, but rather to say they operate within a contingent consensus of shared feelings.

Online worlds are not so different from television soaps, films, alternative reality games, and fan sites in that they provide people with a way of vicariously experiencing desire or living out fantasies without having to risk physical, moral, or ethical consequences. There is more active participation in some of these worlds, however, and therefore, perhaps more risk of an emotional consequence (for example *World of Warcraft* invites its participant to 'descend into a world of myth, magic and legendary adventure' https://us.battle.net/account/creation/wow/ signup). Although we have not used multiuser domain sites and online games in our close readings, they do seem to set themselves up in similar ways to 'soaps' and 'adventure series', respectively, while also offering interactive and participatory learning. They allow for a form of escapism that is more emotive and personal, and they come with their exceptional examples of everyday fear and terror.

At the same time, we can link the kind of creative play to the interaction that fans have with their preferred film or television texts. In his work on the virtual community, Howard Rheingold (1993) points to the similarities between fans who pretend to be certain television characters and romances that happen online. He argues that the 'phenomenon of fandom is evidence that not everyone can have a life as "having a life" is defined by the mainstream, and some people just go out and try to build an alternative life' (167). Indeed, understanding these alternative lives and creative practices has long been at issue and in debate within audience studies and fan research. In Chapter 6, we draw upon those alternative lives and experiences that undermine the consensus that the Internet is or should be a positive space of friendship, community, social networking, and public good. Just as television (youth/subculture) and film (video nasties) produced ordinary anxieties, so too emotion online continues to be represented in terms of fear of and for the vulnerable: women and children.

Face-to-face communication on screen

Carl Plantinga's work on the 'scene of empathy and the human face on film' draws attention to the importance of the face in eliciting emotion from spectators. He also suggests that emotion in the close-up shot can be contagious to its viewers. He notes that 'emotional contagion is the phenomenon of "catching" others' emotions or affective states. [...] When our friends laugh and smile while telling us a story, we often laugh and smile in response even if we fail to see the humor in the story itself' (1999, 243). Gibbs's research on news media has also drawn attention to the biomediation of the human face for producing affective states within audiences (2005). Research has expanded to consider the way face-to-face communication happens on screen. With the growing popularity of face-to-face communications such as Skype, scholars are questioning the role of the face in terms of our emotional experience online. They are also interested in the heavy usage of sites such as *Second Life* and *World of Warcraft*, which do not involve face-to-face communication, and the ways in which the lack of face-to-face communication can sometimes be preferred.

In their work on emotions in human-computer interaction, Veikko Surakka and Toni Vanhala (2011) note that, 'Generally speaking, people react to virtual cues of emotion and sociality in much the same manner as they do to those expressed by other humans' (214). However, as they point out, computers 'have limited access to the social signals that we give out, and therefore cannot respond properly to their users' (215). So, although users can experience emotion in response to social cues online, computers have limited ways to extend and return this emotion. The same can be said about the television or film screens. Although it is more of a one-way trajectory at first (first watch of a movie, first time seeing a series, for example), the fictional world, as already discussed, can be revisited, reexplored, and renewed by the fan or even casual viewer online.

Thus, as we have shown in the theories outlined so far, the transmission of affect refers not to emotion but to a bodily capacity, a bodily readiness, and a trigger to action, including the action of feeling an emotion (Clough 2012, 23). In terms of our concern with emotion online, if the creative juice designed into online worlds produces affective value, then the conceptualization of being online in terms of functionality, usability, service, and provision may be a misunderstanding of how we are already feeling before we become users. Indeed, how can it be possible to mobilize and share emotionalized content across media and transnationally if the devices and delivery systems are all differently produced, consumed, and used? Further research will be needed to account for all these differences and distinctions in order to understand the multidirectional ways that emotion and affect work in online media generally, in particular kinds of technologies and platforms, and in relation to global media-on-demand television, actively scheduled but passively consumed, smartphones used in a variety of passive/active ways to produce and consume media content, YouTube videos produced by a minority and passively consumed by a majority, or online/mobile games with high or (very) low production values. The powerful discourse of connectedness and openness of online media and the zeitgeist of sharing content of the early twenty-first century have contributed to blurry affective economics across all these media forms. It has led to Stiegler's gnostic conviction about how the web 'radically modifies public and private spaces and times' (2012), as we will highlight in the next chapter. Yet, what is shared is so differently produced and differentially consumed. It will be for future researchers to use our layering of the cultural dynamics of media, technology, and emotional saturation as a basis for exploring the distinct, the different, and the specific.

When we consider the vast literature on film, television, and emotion that has preceded online culture, we discover areas of resistance to a globalizing concept of emotion. Theoretical work in these specific media forms works within and across those media to produce a mixed-media framework, and this reminds us that quite a few parts of online media are not open and shared. While we cannot ignore the many debates about commons, sharing, and a new economy that have been emerging in academic settings and public discourses, we need to explore in more depth the ways in which these debates have dovetailed with theories of globalization and global networked online media. Emotion and affect in this context can be articulated very differently, almost as if there has been a *death of the idea of a single medium.*[6]

3
Global Emotion

From global village to global psyche

In 'How the Internet Gets Inside Us', *New Yorker* critic Adam Gopnik explored the tensions between the technophobes and technophiles, as both groups have something to say about the 'cognitive entanglement' of humans and technology. He commented that if television produced the global village, the Internet produces the global psyche, with 'everyone keyed in like a neuron, so that to the eyes of a watching Martian we are really part of a single planetary brain. Contraptions don't change consciousness; contraptions are part of consciousness' (Gopnik 2011, 2).

At stake here is emotion: the intimacy with screens and machines; empathy at a distance; and the betrayal of spouses, children, and friends in real life or away from keyboard in favour of relationships online. Everything that was once inside us is now put outside (from paranoia, to fetishes, to hatred and fear), says Gopnik, and his response is more affectual than intellectual. No doubt, as we foregrounded in the previous chapter, this may be because online content makes us lean forward and into rather than back and away from, as in those ideas around cinema and television. Yet, Gopnik's low-level anxiety is no different from the criticisms hurled at television in the 1970s, film in the 1950s, and the novel in the 1890s. Here is the internalized next stage of Anthony Giddens's statement concerning 'an intensification of worldwide social relations which link distant localities in such a way that local happenings are shaped by events occurring many miles away and vice versa' (1990, 64). While not dealt with in this book, we have to acknowledge the wider context of corporeality and technology, whereby pervasive computing translates bodies, affects, and emotions into measurable codes, images and maps: from computed tomography (CT) scans, magnetic resonance images (MRIs), three-dimensional (3D) ultrasound, airport security imaging and polygraphs to intelligently tagged clothing. As Kathleen Stewart has suggested, we have no filter on our attention, for the 'affective subject is a collection of trajectories and circuits' (2007, 59).

Therefore, in the previous chapters we have traced the conceptualization of emotion and affect in and between different disciplines and we have drawn out the applications of these concepts within a range of accounts, with Chapter 2 focusing more specifically on screen media and emotion at the interface. It should be clear to the reader that the last decade has seen an 'emotion boom' within academic research, not unlike Andreas Huyssen's 'memory boom' (2003, 17). Part of this research has been more and more directed at our differentiated and mediated cultural landscape. Sociological and psychological approaches to emotion and affect are now being developed to incorporate media as social, physical, and psychic artefacts/spaces (see the emergence of research by Rebecca Coleman 2008, 2009, 2012; Lisa Blackman 2001, 2007, 2010, 2011; Blackman & Harbord 2010). Within neuroscientific research and psychology, the primary focus on the 'cognitive' has opened up to cross-disciplinary exchanges with cultural studies, identities, and media (see the work of Felicity Callard 2006; Callard & Papoulias 2010a/b). Within media studies itself, we have argued in Chapter 2 that affect is emerging as a prime mover for understanding digital cultural phenomena and identities; see the developing research of Debra Ferreday (2005, 2009, 2010); and Ferreday and Coleman (2010).

We are particularly interested in how the concepts of emotion and affect have been and are being put to work in current research of online media and culture within the context of what might be termed an *ethics of (global) connectivity*. Modes of attention, connective possibilities, and contingent interactions become 'moments of legibility and emergence', 'moments of impact' producing a 'surge of affect' (Stewart 2005, 1027); but how far can affects be 'composed through worldly interactions' of bodies, objects, sounds, images, movements, and encounters (Nayak & Jeffrey 2011, 289)? It is little wonder that media (film, television, radio, journalism, music, and photography) are seen to play a key part in the 'transmission of affect' (Brennan 2004; Angel & Gibbs 2006, Gibbs 2008), the production of empathy (Calloway-Thomas 2010) and the technologization of life itself (Zylinska 2009). We have covered the reasons for this increased theorization in the previous chapters. Here, it is around the positing and contestation of global feelings that this chapter offers a review of literature that has sought to understand why and how online media are being presented as global, connected, and shared, while at the same time immersive, tactile, and individuated.

There have been many theorizations of globalization as cultural sharing (see Featherstone 1990; Tomlinson 1999), as a 'triumph of the universal' (Featherstone & Lash 1995, 2), as universalized technologies (Lash & Urry 1987), or as the universalism of the dominant ideology, 'shared by exploiters and exploited alike' (Balibar & Wallerstein 1991, 4). This does not mean, as Franklin, Lury, and Stacey point out in *Global Nature, Global Culture* (2000) that such a concept is entirely closed and determinate. As Chapter 2 suggested, in the light of fan cultures, online culture is constantly changing, incomplete, added to, indeterminate, not straightforward, competitive, and heterogeneous. Yet, Franklin et al. argue that Western views on individualism are influenced by the 'easternized version of life, death, nature and the planet' which 'places the subject firmly within the new universal processes of global culture' (2000, 125). In the light of global flows of media from East to West, such as the Japanese cinema of Studio Ghibli and especially *Princess Mononoke* (1997), it makes sense to ask that if 'the global is implicitly within each of us in this easternized model' then 'how might this affect our changing sense of interiority and embodiment'? (Franklin et al. 2000, 125). In this understanding of globality, the global flows, technological flows, and media flows converge with the body and suggest that the division between internal and external is hard to maintain. Thus we may envision a biomediated version of embodied subjectivity (see Rosi Braidotti's 'informational body' 1994), inspired by feminist criticism.

Having said this, the trend toward giving cyberculture a soul may probably have run its course. Howard Rheingold began with reality as 'virtual' (1992), showed the emerging connections being made in 'virtual communities' (1993), and has now arrived at real, everyday online communities that need lessons in intelligence, humanity, and mindfulness (2012). We are at the point at which emotion goes online, becomes technologized and ubiquitous, and needs rules. These rules could be informed by Plantinga's folk psychological approaches in *Passionate Views* (2009), noted in the previous chapter. However, as in Huyssen's research on the 'memory boom' (2003) and the observation that media – from print to the Internet – are blamed for cultural amnesia, so too are those same media blamed for either feeling too much or having no feeling at all. What if both observations were true (to rewrite Huyssen's same questions about memory and forgetting)? What if the current boom in emotion is inevitably accompanied by a boom in a lack of feeling? What if the relationship between emotion and the lack of it 'were actually being transformed under cultural pressures in which new information technologies, media politics, and fast-paced consumption are beginning to take their toll' (Huyssen 2003, 17)? In this chapter, we seek to understand how key thinkers have understood emotion in relation to globalization and technology, how feeling and thinking about being online have developed, how the feelings encountered there are being theorized, and what issues are at stake.

Before we get there we need to take a step back and think through what the current discourses on mediated emotions and emotionalized media forget as they turn media technologies affective. We ought to remember those theorizations of the technological and the global that have led us to the messianic messages of Facebook founder Mark Zuckerberg, who on 1 February 2012 posted a statement of intent as company shares were offered publicly:

> Facebook was not originally created to be a company. It was built to accomplish a social mission – to make the world more open and connected. [...] We live at a moment when the majority of people in the world have access to the internet or mobile phones – the raw tools necessary to start sharing what they're thinking, feeling and doing with whomever they want.[1]

This discursive revolution around the 'social' as a concept: social by design, social by intent, social through impact, and social in ethics, shows Zuckerberg's world as driven to be connected through a technological infrastructure that is built upon sharing feelings. This bears witness to Licklider and Taylor's much earlier proposal in 1968 that when communicating face to face through a computer the 'communication system should make a positive contribution to the discovery and arousal of interests', illustrated by a doodle of a boy sending an image of a heart through the screen to a girl (26). In fact, Richard Grusin states in *Premediation: Affect and Mediality after 9/11* (2010) that in 'hypermediacy' is 'the proliferation of diverse and interconnected media formats of social networking' that are 'defined in terms of [the] desirability' to be on them (2010, 4). 'Are you on Facebook, MySpace, Twitter?' is asked with the obvious expectation that you would and should be. Grusin notes:

> Leaving multiple traces of yourself on socially networked media sites is seen as a necessary goal – and interacting with such sites is made pleasurable or desirable in part because they work to produce and

maintain positive affective relations with their users, to set up affec-tive feedback loops that make one want to proliferate one's media transactions. (Grusin 2010, 4–5)

It appears that globally mediated communications promote sharing, connectedness, decentralization, and cross-cultural sensitivity (Shirky 2008, 2010a) as a direct alternative to old-media economies of distance, objectivity, privacy, and rationality. Do such discourses imply the possible exchange and transmission of universal feelings across networked communications (especially social networks)? Zuckerberg believes that Facebook's 'collective' power of sharing will transform governments, institutions, and industries. Yet, as Grusin argues, Facebook's seemingly innocuous 'like' or 'unlike', rather than 'dislike' buttons, 'epitomizes its bias towards fostering positive individual and collective affect' (2010, 4). We shall return to this in Chapter 4 on social media and happiness and in Chapter 6, as such a bias is smashed apart by the use of interest networks to upload images of women's bodies in order to shame them.

The discourse being promoted is that online media offer more authentic, emotionally real, and unfettered communication that provides deep insight into our connections with others. Again, Zuckerberg believes that Facebook (which we view as a platform for emotion agents and emotional agency or lack thereof) offers the tools for honest and transparent dialogue. For academic research into the global distribution of an ideology of sharing feelings, collective feelings, and the technological creation of affective domains, the concern is that big players like Facebook with their 'hacker way' may move too fast, too iteratively, and too riskily for traditional media studies to produce flex-ible frameworks for assessing their personal, social, and cultural impact. Hence, as we noted in the previous chapter, William Merrin's call for a rethink of media studies as a discipline (2009). Alongside this, Paul Booth's (2010) argument that we see the relationship between media, audiences, technology and users as a holistic synergy and Fuller and Goffey's *Evil Media* (2012) which philosophizes how media *do things* in, through, to, for, with and without people in a digital economy of networked communication.

The problem is, of course, that the privileging of users and use through individuated studies of personal consumption may miss the dominant ideologies clearly at work within the affective economy of online culture. This is the reason that we have favoured close readings in Part II of this book, rather than individuated empirical tool-user anal-yses. When we look at and for the broader issues at stake, some key questions emerge. If globality, globalization, and global emotions do not provide the differentiated and complex conceptual frameworks for understanding our networked and distributed feelings, then what kinds of concepts do? Should we retreat back to the national, the local, the hyperlocal, or the personal? How do these capture 'the ways affect and emotions take shape through movement between contexts, websites, forums, blogs, comments, and computer windows, flooding us with words, and at times, leaving us speechlesss' (Kuntsman 2012, 1)? There is a theoretical tension between positivist discourses of online culture as universal, collective, sharing, caring, responsible, global, compassionate, connected, and those negative discourses of online culture as too personally, locally, and nationally fettered, irresponsible, uncaring, indifferent, hivelike, ignorant, bullying, and divisive. The theories surrounding this tension will inform the readings in Part II.

For now, it is useful to take two examples of research of online emotion that reinforce Zuckerberg's technologized faith in connectivity, sharing, and equalizing, but that may miss wider cultural determinants. First, we have early analysis of emotions online that notes changes in expression by mapping the use of emoticons across Usenet groups of same and mixed gender. Wolf's (2000) research into the use of basic, winking, and sad smileys noted a generalized upshift in expressiveness, with males online adopting more emoticons when they moved to a mixed-gender online discussion group. Wolf's rather generalized results, from a small-scale localized study, reinforce a dominant ideology of online groups as having a levelling or equalizing effect. Similarly, but with a different focus, we have more recent research on the use of algorithms to map suicidal feelings so as to identify at-risk bloggers, described in the findings of Huang, Goh, and Liew (2007). Their work suggests that online emotional content can be schematized into structured data through key words and phrases that can then be tracked and used to possibly save lives. Feeling the same and locating the same feelings online may obfuscate key differences in personal, local, and national circumstances that lead to suicidal emotions. Nevertheless, there is a powerful drive within these research methodologies of online culture to map, pattern, universalize, and track largely textual content into meaningful and controllable data that shore up the very notion of one's being online as connected and shared. This is the securitization of emotion online.

However, while maps, patterns, and mining are revealing homogeneous emotional content online, we also need to account for research into the individualized differences in feelings about and through technology. Thus, on the other hand, we have very specific and niche research on online gamers in China (Lindtner et al. 2009), on personal photographs used in national versions of Facebook, such as Russia's Odnoklassniki (Hutchings & Miazhevich 2010), on the mapping of offline/online social ties of married and single people in a US urban setting (Matei 2003), on the differentiated use of French diacritics in an online dating site (van Compernolle 2011), on the decoration of mobile phones by emotionally attached Japanese youths (Sugiyama 2009), and Amparo Lasén's (2011) empirical research on couples' use of mobile phones through negotiations, conflicts, and power relationships. In these examples, media technology provides spaces for specific, nuanced, and differentiated articulations of emotions. This suggests – as does Bella Dicks's (2011) four-volume collection of the fullest range of research methodologies for understanding life online – that research about emotion online needs to be multimodal. In fact, the differences in emotional responses are part of what makes researching emotion online fascinating for these researchers. Does this then belie the possibility of emotional connections online/offline and cross-culturally that could undercut such differences? At the same time, does our love of computers and their ubiquity in other devices suggest a universal seduction, need, and desire?

The representations of online culture as potentially democratizing, creative, connected, and sharing are noted by Seth Giddings and Martin Lister in their introduction to Tiziana Terranova's 'Free Labour' (2011):

> Almost from its inception, the Internet has been portrayed as a space characterized by free communication, collective intelligence, and by an alternative 'gift' economy based on the free sharing of time, communication, support, advice and virtual products or services online. (Giddings & Lister 2011, 350)

From crowdsourcing to flashmobs, blogs to instant messaging, to Twitter, Flickr, YouTube, to the online curation of likes and tastes with Pinterest, populist gurus of the Internet such as Clay Shirky (2008, 2010a) have found in online phenomena such as WikiLeaks counters to traditional media industries, precisely because they are not rooted in particular places and within specific economies with a fixed workforce. Traditional media empires, claims Shirky, have reached such a level of complexity and bureaucracy that they are unable to adapt their business to fully embrace an online culture of sharing and connectedness (2010b). For Shirky, this online culture is defined by its emotional(ized) content that appeals to and mobilizes groups. It has developed alongside our need to touch and hold objects that make us feel secure and loved, but it has mobilized our desire to find connections and share ideas and things that 'move' us with others:

> We are used to production of media [...] that has targeted individuals who have [...] long term consumption and long term reactions and we are increasingly moving to a media environment where we are targeting groups who have short term consumption and short term reactions [...] and that is swinging the role of emotion into a much more central position in the media environment. (Shirky 2009b)

Unlike collective memory, then, with its affordance of longevity, collective emotion is seen as fleeting. However, the previous chapters have provided the landscape for understanding the history of theorizations of emotion and affect within feminist theory, cultural studies, and media/ screen studies. Far from fleeting, we have sought to connect up the research of emotion with media studies to elicit an a priori interrogation of the concept of emotion culture as mediatized within our postbroad-cast ecology (see William Merrin's essay 'Media Studies 2.0' 2009). We assume alongside Lasén (2010b) that mobile culture may be shared but that does not mean it feels the same. There are multimodal possibilities and practices for the performance and consumption of emotion online and some of these will be afforded in our exploration of examples in Part II. Therefore, the 'trans-personalization' of media and communication devices may be a more useful way of bridging the gap between collectivity and individuation (see Lasén 2010b).

Globality, media, and emotion

In the 1990s, there was a tendency within the key literature on technology and society to underpin theorizations with notions of 'globality', defined by transnational flows, rapid communications, and more integrated political economies. 'Globalization' and 'global' became the most significant terms for understanding the spread of new information technologies and the impact they were having on other areas of life. On this basis, it is no wonder that the development of online media cultures is represented as eliding difference and offering universal, collective, or deterministic features. While one academic eye was busy critiquing the globalizing tendency of television (Barker 1999), film (Curtin 2007), advertising (Ciochetto 2011), journalism (McNair 2006), and popular culture (Crothers 2010) the other academic eye was keen on emphasizing the democratizing potential of the Internet (for example, Surowiecki 2005; Leadbeater 2010; Shirky 2008, 2010a; Gauntlett 2011).

Manuel Castells, in the first edition of his influential *The Rise of the Network Society* (1996), imagined the discontinuity between humans and machines as cancelled out by new technologies, 'fundamentally altering the way we are born, we live, we learn, we work, we produce, we consume, we dream, we fight, or we die' (31). He argued that although 'cultural/institutional contexts and purposeful social action decisively interact with the new technological system', it has to be remembered that 'this system has its own, embedded logic, characterized by the capacity to translate all inputs into a common information system, and to process such information at increasing speed, with increasing power, at decreasing cost, in a potentially ubiquitous retrieval and distribution network' (31–32).

In organizations like OneWorld (oneworldgroup.org), founded in 1994, we have such a decisive interaction. A transatlantic collaboration between UK and US pioneers of 'internet and mobile applications, which the world's poorest people can use to improve their life opportunities, and which help people everywhere understand global problems – and do something about them', OneWorld articulates a cultural myth of the world as limitless and borderless, comprising the first and third worlds.[2] This accords with Martin Lewis and Kären Wigen's insightful critique of the reiteration of spatial frameworks in their conceptualization of a metageography in *The Myth of Continents* (Lewis & Wigen 1997). Here we see that a world produced through the flows, connections, linkages, networks, and relations made possible by highly technologized cities that appear as pinpricks of light across the globe in nighttime images of the earth from space (see Beaverstock, Smith, & Taylor 2005 on 'world city networks'), is also a mythological construction that produces the urban Twitter user.

Such large-scale geographic and spatial constructs are created as ideological drivers of particular worldviews (for example, Zuckerberg's, at the beginning of this chapter). While globality falls into such a category, this concept of the global made up of overgeneralized world regions might actually be fundamental to understanding how our (online) world is put together (Lewis & Wigen 1997, 14). These metageographic constructs have a long history and, if 'recent history tells us anything', claim Lewis and Wigen, 'it is that globalization does not obviate such regional culture blocks; in some ways, it has even heightened their distinctiveness as a reaction to "Western" cultural hegemony' (1997, 14). Thus, acknowledging the mythical and cultural construction of world geography is actually very important to understanding how we encounter emotion online, as a global phenomenon of personal encounters highly situated in time and place.

Although the production and use of online media and new technologies have played a key role in 'calling for liberation from the myth of continents, the myth of the nation-state, and the imprisoning thesis of European priority', this does not mean that everything is now 'fluidity, contingency, movement and multiplicity' (Lewis & Wigen 1997, 15). If it did, then there would be no personal, local, regional, and national differences in how emotion is produced and consumed online. We would instantly know what to do, think, and feel when faced with YouTube videos of massacres in Syria. Our close readings in Part II will show up some of these differences, as well as the overarching cultural determinants that make mass disaffection a response to emotion online. The irony is that these differences are all articulated within a context of massive databases, dynamic multimedia, and vast information flows that propagate a desire to map, pattern, order, and securitize cultural and social data by emotion agents. Their aim, as was the aim of the 'old' media producers, is to produce what we will define here as *global emotion*, to be consumed by the largest media audience in the world.

Critics could easily dismantle such a concept as *global emotion*, for how can emotion be conceptualized as global when there is a growing body of research on emotion that is about Japan (Dasgupta 2011), Australia (Aveyard 2011), and Papua New Guinea (Hemer 2010), for example? Has not postmodernity's deconstruction of the grand narratives of History, Society, and Politics shown up the great regional, local, and personal narratives that run counterhegemonic to these big ideas? Yet, these big ideas persist, and they persist as metageographic concepts that can mobilize millions of people to share a link and hundreds of thousands of people to take on a cause, as in *Kony 2012*, even if they are mobilized for only the briefest of moments to passively consume. To dismiss the idea of global emotion as too overgeneralized in the face of diversity, difference, and nuance would be to miss one of the great ironies of Internet-based mass media and communications. They are still mass: they produce millions of passive consumers every minute of every day, passively reading and viewing (see Fuller and Goffey's [2012, 141] point that users may be 'transparent intermediaries'). Online media and commnications have the power to produce global citizenry as well as the power to be personally meaningful, memorable, and emotional. To the extent that how you are meant to feel about your body is integrated into global calculators that produce you as good (active) or evil (passive)[3] It is in the intersection between mass passivity and individualized interaction and participation that emotional online content is produced. In what follows, we explore in more depth the construction of this global audience as a community capable of sharing feelings.

Media torrents, global flows, and emotional resilience

Howard Rheingold, in *The Virtual Community: Homesteading on the Electronic Frontier* (1993), began his reflections on the new communities he was becoming a part of by describing his emotions. As a member of the WELL (Whole Earth 'lectronic Link, an Internet-based parenting community) in the 1980s, he had begun to understand the power of these communities to offer peace, solace, comfort, 'heart', and intensity as well as anger, fear and shame:

> Participating in a virtual community has not solved all of life's problems for me, but it has served as an aid, a comfort, and an inspiration at times; at other times, it has been like an endless, ugly, long-simmering family brawl. (Rheingold 1993, 9)

The overriding feature of such ideas on online individuality was that the commonality of interests and goals, not the accident of proximity, would lead to community and happiness (as predicted by J. C. R. Licklider & Robert Taylor in their landmark paper, 'The Computer as a Communication Device' in 1968, mentioned briefly above). Less dreamily, reflecting upon the 1980s, Nigel Thrift noted in 'Muddling Through: World Orders and Globalization' (1992) that mass media and communications had become significant and powerful through a 'quasi-mediated interaction' that 'is not impersonal or passive'. Rather it 'is a new kind of affective linkage which is only controlled to an extent by the media industries' (Thrift 1992, 5). These industries 'have become experts at the quasi-staging of public events, at managing their visibility [wars, climate change, terrorism]', and 'global responses to mass mediated events are becoming increasingly common' – Live Aid, the fall of the Berlin Wall, the Gulf War (Thrift 1992, 5–6). It is noteworthy that Thrift has since written extensively about the 'affective turn' in cultural geography (see Thrift 2004b, 2007, 2008). We shall return to this idea in Chapter 5; suffice to say here that globalizing emotions has long been a strategy of the old-media economy. While media messages are 'addressed globally to the communities of practice belonging mainly to the industrialized world or the fast-developing world' in fact 'the message is construed in such a way as to involve emotionally the individual viewer, by placing him or her in the position of being directly addressed by these voices' (Bortoluzzi 2009, 149).

Here, in Thrift's citing of John Thompson's *Ideology and Modern Culture: Critical Social Theory in the Era of Mass Communication* (1990), we can see the beginnings of a metageographically informed notion of new information technologies as carriers of affect. Unlike television, exclaims Thompson, technology can

> transform the life conditions of recipients in a more complicated, less evident sense. For it enables individuals to experience events which take place in locales that are spatially and temporally remote, and this experience may in turn inform or stimulate forms of action or response on the part of recipients, including forms of collective and concerted action. [...] It enables individuals in one part of the world to witness events which take place in another, and to respond, individually or collectively, to these events. [...] and the events themselves are subjected thereby to a new kind of *global scrutiny* which never existed before. (Thompson 1990, 17)

More recently, Alberto Ribes (2010) has deepened the interrogation of this scrutiny to focus on global media events as routinized (and increasingly autonomous), demanding collective awareness, remembering, recreation, and invention. Such events call for 'massive public attention with some regularity' as 'waves of cognitive, emotional and ritual performance engagement reach their climax at different spatial and temporal points'. Thus, in the context of online media, they are 'very much present in daily routines because they call our attention long before they occur, there are always people engaged in one of more of them, and finally when one event concludes another will begin' (Ribes 2010, 5). Although Princess Diana's death suspended the daily routine of television in 1997 to allow for engagement in ceremonial participation, today one hypermediated event bleeds into another with no suspension of daily life. Described as a media 'torrent' (Gitlin 2002) or media 'turbulence' (Csigo 2010), the intimate relations between viewers and media break down into a maelstrom of emotions and events. These are, as Peter Csigo argues, repaired through 'symbolic micro-practices of reconstituting coherence that is felt to be broken' (2010, 144). The Internet provides the platforms for such practices, as viewers are expected to exist in, around, before, during, and after broadcast media content (news, television, radio, films) to reestablish 'the sentiment that one's society is, after all, liveable and just' (Csigo 2010, 144).

Therefore, whether it be Ribes's global media events or Howard Rheingold's 'daily life in cyberspace' (1993, 25), globality has come to underpin much theorization of the Internet as a place where there appears to be no geographic limits in terms of scrutiny, witnessing, and affective/collective experience. This scrutiny has now fallen into the hands of the average Internet user, and it is up to him or her to reconstitute coherence that is felt to be broken. However, Tiziana Terranova has argued, in contrast to the restrictions of one-to-many television production, 'the cultural and affective production on the Internet' is decentralized 'to the point that practically anything is tolerated', because the Internet makes constraining feeling, behaviour, attitude, and opinions irrelevant (2011, 365). Rheingold would disagree, and in his most recent work *Net Smart: How to Thrive Online* (2012) his thirty-plus years of inhabiting online communities have taught him that the key media literacy skill of the twenty-first century is that 'empathy, friendship, and community [online] always have heart and soul if they are to be authentic' (2012, 225).

If we have moved from the individualism of media corporations targeting audiences to the collective 'quasi-mediated' interactivity of making our own media online, then how are our feelings about this process being understood? Sep Kamvar and Jonathan Harris (2009) in *We Feel Fine: An Almanac of Human Emotion,* alongside Charles Leadbeater's (2010) *We Think: Mass Innovation, Not Mass Production,* illustrate the globality of feeling and thinking with technology as collective and connective. Both have Rheingoldian underpinnings. In writing the code for *We Feel Fine,* www.wefeelfine.org – 'a computer program that would continuously crawl all blogs on the web and extract any sentence containing the words "I feel" or "I am feeling"' (2009, 15) – Kamvar and Harris sought to prove their thesis that a cultural shift is taking place. This shift is away from the Internet as a space for information and commerce and toward an online emotional space of interaction and collectivity (social, as the founder of Facebook would have it).[4] Combining freedom, connection, emotional intimacy, and personal memory, the blogosphere provides a new model for actively experiencing humanity, they claim (Kamvar & Harris 2009, 16). Globality, in the context of this research, is defined as 'a sense of empathy for people who we had never met, and at times we felt like we were looking in the mirror' (16).

On the one hand, such reinforcement of a 'caring community' can be easily problematized, as it was by the many critics of the viral campaign video *Kony 2012*. Michele White in *Buy It Now: Lessons from eBay* (2012) finds that eBay reinforces conventions of race, gender, and sexuality, not just in listings content but in directing users to 'adults only' parts of the site when searching for gay/lesbian items; eBay also allows narratives of racism to exist in black Americana listings. On the other hand, the notion of a globality of feeling or a community of caring preexists theorization of online culture in terms of memory and media as 'prosthetic' (Alison Landsberg, 2004). Like John Thompson, whose definition of global scrutiny is afforded by the affective proximity of technologically enabled media, Landsberg draws upon the commodification of memory in media and culture made 'portable and transportable' in a capitalist economy. 'Prosthetic memories are adopted as the result of a person's experience with a mass cultural technology of memory that dramatizes or recreates a history he or she did not live' (Landsberg 2004, 28). Thus, Kamvar and Harris (2009) have coded emotion to recreate an affective schema that they feel they have lived and are living but actually have not yet always lived through. To prove her point, Landsberg's book *Prosthetic Memory: The Transformation of American Remembrance in the Age of Mass Culture* (2004) draws upon literature from cinematic history that emphasizes cinema's emotional impact as a precursor to audience remembrance. In the previous chapter, we have explored this kind of literature on film and emotion, but the connections being made between prosthetic emotion, global media, and communications, and the audience's individual and collective response as the same though different (and at a distance) are worth reemphasizing here.

Globally mediated emotions

In thinking further about this idea of globally mediated emotions, we would do well to confront popular United States gurus of Internet culture such as Clay Shirky (2008, 2010a) before attending to the more nuanced research being done on emotions and online technology in the United States and United Kingdom. Although we do not cover them here, the reader would do well to explore the growing number of books published about the Internet from other regions of the world. Shirky has found in ventures like Wikipedia the exemplar par excellence of industrial participation freely given and openly shared, where experts mix with amateur enthusiasts. David Gauntlett (2011) has also argued that the Wikipedia model might translate into the real world to the emotional benefit of individuals and communities in more complex situations: 'Making and sharing your own things, rather than accepting mainstream manufactured or broadcast things, is positive in both political and emotional terms' (2011, 162). However, if we consider the Internet as homogeneous or forming a McLuhanesque global village, and if the new media landscape of social networking and mass collaboration has positioned emotion as important, then whose and what kind of emotions are being transmitted? Alternatively, if we consider the Internet as networked practices of cultural differences, then how does emotion go transnational and transpersonal?

Dorothy Kidd has argued that 'the majority of users' of the Internet 'are no longer the .orgs and .govs who operated among decentralized communications networks of many to many' during the 1990s. Rather, 'the traffic is now dominated by the .coms and the broadcast model, in which a small number of dominant global media giants control the distribution pipelines into the Net, online traffic, and much of the content, exploiting this resource through fees, advertising and subscriptions' (Kidd 2011, 412). If this is the case, then this is globally mediated emotion in the form of a sixth 'emotionscape', if we are to follow Arjun Appadurai's (1996) five '–scapes' of the new global cultural economy ('ethnoscapes', 'mediascapes', 'technoscapes', 'finanscapes', and 'ideoscapes'), whereby emotion is no longer simply inside the 'individual actor' but is actually now 'navigated by agents' (Appudurai 1996, 33). The *emoscapes* (as we might term them) of our new global cultural economy (alongside the other five scapes) are what make up our imagined communities, 'the multiple worlds that are constituted by the historically situated imaginations [and emotions and memories] of persons and groups spread around the globe' (Appadurai 1996, 33).

Thus, while we have come to understand globalization as determined by phenomena such as transnational flows, rapid technological development, and competing political economies (see Kellner 2002), we have experienced globalization as consumers of low-cost goods and have seen the opening up of new markets and the increased demand for natural resources. As Scott Lash and Celia Lury note in *Global Culture Industry*, 'What the global culture industry does is use play and mimicry, use this emotionality – this affect – for the accumulation of capital' (2007, 191). Realization that workers across the globe are exploited, images of hitherto unknown lands destroyed, and fears over energy shortages in the future have affected us. Globalized media forms, practices, and content have been repeatedly critiqued as centred upon distributing ideologies of the West (see Li 2003). Online communities may also form around these globalized forms, practices, and content, but in the face of any universalizing discourse, counterhegemonic interventions inevitably emerge, as they have done for decades with the long history of alternative and radical media. As Carpentier and Scifo (2010, 115) have reminded us:

> The success of the new generation of media technologies – in combination with their presupposed interactive and even participatory nature – feeds the assumption that we are living another new communication revolution. With the advent of 'new' internet-based media, the discourses on the democratization of the media regained strength. At the same time, this very welcome attention for the media democratic processes became burdened with amnesia and myopia. Through the focus on the participatory potential of new media, the participatory capacities of 'old' media were forgotten. Moreover, also the long history of 'old' participatory media, like alternative and community media, became ignored.

Therefore, the emotional attachments, ceremonies, rituals, pilgrimages, and memories that viewers, readers, listeners, users, and consumers have to old-media forms and practices serve as reminders that communities of consumption, practice, and use preexist the Internet. As Nick Couldry argues in *Media Rituals: A Critical Approach,* these always 'stand in or appear to "stand in", for something wider, something linked to the fundamental organizational level on which we are, or imagine ourselves to be, connected as members of a society' (2003, 4).

From global to local to cyborg emotion

Within the last few years, the representation of emotions online as becoming universalized and standardized through ideologies of online culture that promote connectedness, (over)sharing, transparency, and homogenization has been critiqued by figures such as Jaron Lanier (2010), who claim that we are at risk of overshadowing individuality. In *You Are Not a Gadget: A Manifesto,* Lanier (an early virtual reality designer and consumer) bemoans 'the romantic appeal of cybernetic totalism':

> Those who enter into the theatre of computationalism are given all the mental solace that is usually associated with traditional religions. These include consolations for metaphysical yearnings, in the form of the race to climb ever more 'meta' or higher-level states of digital representation. [...] This is about aesthetics and emotions, not rational argument. (Lanier 2010, 178)

Again we can hear the urgent demand 'Are you on Facebook yet?' while recognizing that users of the Internet all over the world do receive mental solace and are consoled at and by their consoles. Along these lines, Henry Jenkins, at the annual 'Console-ing Passions Conference' (a conference on television and gender studies), reminded the audience to be careful of proclamations on 'good' or 'bad' online culture (2006b, 9–10).

Early research on digital architecture (such as multi-object oriented and multi-user domains) by Sherry Turkle analysed the relational and emotional interactions between avatars in *Life on the Screen: Identity in the Age of the Internet* (1997) and asked whether through these encounters we can better understand our real emotions, which cannot be switched on and off. In the context of Fredric Jameson's dystopic 'waning of affect' (1991) in postmodern culture, Turkle sought to understand the new cyberculture as one of real and practiced emotions. More recently, in *Alone Together: Why We Expect More from Technology and Less from Each Other* (2011), Turkle has discarded altogether the distinction between real and technologized emotions and fallen for our love of technology as emotionally driven. Critiquing our relationship with technology as respite, seduction, amusement, relaxation, optimism, salvation, and romance, she finds the old 'anxieties' about too much technology have been replaced by putting our 'hope' into 'an enduring technological optimism' of 'machine-mediated relationships' (2011, 11).

Such ideas have been played out in the literature that has emerged on online relationships. Aaron Ben-Ze'ev's (2004) *Love Online: Emotions on the Internet* extols sharing and trustworthiness as the key features of successful online and offline relationships. Like much research in this area (e.g., Baker's 2005 *Double Click*; Whitty & Carr's 2006 *Cyberspace Romance: The Psychology of Online Relationships*; Whitty et al.'s 2007 *Online Matchmaking*), it is inspired by those early foundational theories of online community from Sherry Turkle (1997) and Howard Rheingold (1993, 2002). Thus, the relationship between user and online media is whittled right down to the universalizing notions of love, intimacy, and romance, as Sherry Turkle observes:

> It is striking that the word 'user' is associated mainly with computers and drugs. The trouble with that analogy, however, is that it puts the focus on what is external (the drug). I prefer the metaphor of seduction because it emphasizes the relationship between person and machine. Love, passion, infatuation [...]. If one is afraid of intimacy yet afraid of being alone, even a stand-alone (not networked)

computer offers an apparent solution. Interactive and reactive, the computer offers the illusion of companionship without the demands of friendship. (Turkle 1997, 30)

Here, Sherry Turkle sets the stage for how online communication has been theorized since then, which culminates in her most recent work, which proposes the contradiction of feeling alone together and chimes with the journalistic approach of Adam Gopnik in the *New Yorker* at the beginning of this chapter. The theories of emotion and intimacy drawn out in Chapter 1 and reiterated in Chapter 2 will be applied in Chapter 4, where we focus in more depth on social media and happiness.

However, 'techno-optimistic discourses', as Nico Carpentier and Salvatore Scifo (2010, 115) term them, have a habit of making new the long histories of powerful corporations controlling communication infrastructure and downplaying the personal, local, alternative, creative, and community-based applications of authentic, life-affirming engagements within traditional media (see the continued production of hard copy handmade fanzines, for example). That aside, we are concerned here with how people feel about these technological dreams and the economic realities that they bury. 'Determined technologies' as Raymond Williams (1974, 7) described them, are both emotionally charged and can be used to emotionally charge communication in a multitude of ways. It is this conjoining of global technologies and personal, human emotion that has also been rather destabilizing to the technological dream of participation and democracy.

Therefore, from one manifesto (Donna Haraway's *Cyborgs: A Manifesto* in 1991) to another manifesto (Jaron Lanier's *You Are Not a Gadget: A Manifesto* in 2010), online technology continues to be a contested space where views of how we should feel, behave, and communicate dominate our engagement with new media. For Haraway it was the irony 'of contradictions that do not resolve into larger wholes', 'of holding incompatible things together because both or all are necessary' [read organism and machine, intimacy and technology, globality and emotion] that generated the rhetorical strategy needed to understand our modern world (1991, 150). She takes 'pleasure' in confusing boundaries – we are all 'cyborgs' according to Haraway, and emotion is key as technology and biology become confused. As she argues in *Cyborgs: A Manifesto*:

Late twentieth-century machines have made thoroughly ambiguous the difference between natural and artificial, mind and body, self-developing and externally designed, and many other distinctions that used to apply to organisms and machines. Our machines are disturbingly lively, and we ourselves frighteningly inert. (1991, 153)

On the one hand, the confusion, according to Haraway, is both dangerous and liberatory when the technologies themselves become so miniaturized and close to the human body that they are invisible and ubiquitous. On the other 'a cyborg world might be about lived social and bodily realities in which people are not afraid of their joint kinship with animals and machines, not afraid of permanently partial identities and contradictory standpoints' (Haraway 1991, 155), standpoints such as Turkle's *feeling alone together*. Clearly, there is a need to explore the physiological understandings of affect, because online communication has shifted from the early days of text-on-screen interfaces to haptic, interactive, augmented, and predictive technologies that require proximity to our bodies, intimacy, and touch: theorizations we explored in Chapter 1. The question is whether these shifts offer universal or individualized possibilities. The Internet, the World Wide Web, browsers, search engines, and cloud computing have been and are presented as technological and universalizing principles that seem to ignore the soft 'individual' centres (Castells 1996) of emotional experiences of human beings in the world. How different people(s) actually use these technological developments and devices for exploring emotion will be addressed in the close readings in Part II.

Extensions of emotion

Thus, we come to the notion that media function as 'extensions of man' in Marshall McLuhan's ([1964] 1994) sense of the phrase, as technologies (from pens to computers) mediate our communications, with a focus upon form rather than content. Form in the context of mediated extensions of a human's physical capabilities could be printing (hand), cameras (eye), audio recorders (voice), telephones (hearing), and digital archives (memory) such that it was 'not the machine but what one did with the machine, that was its meaning or message' (McLuhan [1964] 1994, 7). Those media forms that record, produce, and deliver emotional content and emotional responses are vital to explore because of the 'psychic and social consequences of the designs and patterns as they amplify or accelerate existing processes'. For the 'message' of any medium or technology is the 'change of scale or pace or pattern that it introduces into human affairs' (McLuhan [1964] 1994, 8). In his later polemic *The Medium is the Massage*, McLuhan is both prophetic and clear:

> The medium, or process, of our time – electronic technology – is reshaping and restructuring patterns of social interdependence and every aspect of our personal life. It is forcing us to reconsider and re-evaluate practically every thought, every action, and every institution formerly taken for granted [...] Societies have always been shaped more by the nature of the media by which men [sic] communicate than by the content of the communication. (1967, 8)

Here, McLuhan emphasizes modes or modality, and this is important to our book because not everyone feels the same, yet they seek out shared emotions online. It is this incompatibility of collectivity and individuation that is at stake in an idea of 'global emotion'.

Hardt and Negri (2000) accord with this in that 'tools have always functioned as human prostheses, integrated into our bodies through our labouring practices as a kind of anthropological mutation both in individual terms and in terms of collective social life' (217). Prosthetic emotions are again being suggested; this leads us to understanding the flow of communication over individuals as an integrative force and process. As Anna Gibbs has argued in reconceptualizing media as 'biomedia':

> But the distinction between things of a technological kind and human beings has become extremely problematic, as the technology we incorporate into our lives begins to modify us – our capacity for attention, our desires, and the way we remember. (Gibbs 2011, 252)

Therefore, whether it be Marshall McLuhan's 'extensions of man' (1994 [1964]), Donna Haraway's 'cyborgs' (1991), Michael Heim's 'erotic ontology of cyberspace' (1993), Virginia Nightingale's 'non-anthropomorphic cyborgs' (1999), Clough's 'teletechnology' and 'autoaffection' (1998, 2000), Erik Davis's 'techgnosis' (1999), or, more recently, Bernard Stiegler's (2012a) 'technics' and forces of metadata, there remains an important question. Under what circumstances are these incompatibile elements smoothed over and who by? For Fuller and Goffey (2012, 4), 'media' play a pivotal role as 'irreducible elements in the composition and configuration of affect' for '[d]elight, terror, geeky enthusiam, midly hypnotic euphoria, ugly feelings, and paranoid rage find their conditions in the objects and objective forms that make up their environment'.

Thus, it is less the question of whether human emotions and globalized online media are inseparable or not and more the question of media power, as Bernard Stiegler eloquently puts in an interview at the World Wide Web 2012 conference:

> The Web radically modifies public and private spaces and times – and deeply alters public-private relationships. This technological framework became a new public space and a new public time – with the growing danger to be privatized.
>
> The question first and foremost is political: within the Web a new process of psychic and collective individuation is appearing [...] the individual's psychic transformation is never only psychic, and the relationship between psychic individuation and collective individuation works always through technical mediations. (Stiegler 2012a)

In the light of Stiegler's stark assessment, we would do well to extend the reach of Anna Reading's conceptualization of the *globital* (2011), built upon her previous neologism of the *globytal* (2009), for understanding the convergence of technology (mobile phone camera images) in terms of memories (witnessing the 7/7 bombings). With regard to emotion online, it is worth rearticulating Reading's concepts of globytal and globital time for exploring the ways in which the personal/local and the global converge to form globital emotions, a concept that is mindful of the specificity of personal and local conditions and the continua of history in the face of technological innovation. We shall return to Reading's concept at the end of this book and, although its application pertains to memory studies, it is the inclusion of the digital that may be useful for future explorations of emotion online. Similarly, Andrew Hoskins's (2011) treatment of the 7/7 bombings posits a framework of 'connective memory' as a form of interactive remembering in a 'post-scarcity culture'. Considering the emotional (personal, collective, local, national, and international) impact of the 7/7 bombings in 2005, it makes sense to see these new frameworks emerging in the synthesis of memory and technology studies, as played out in the encountering of emotion online, as both increasingly pervasive and mobile.

Mobile and pervasive emotions

Global emotion, then, is a key concept we use to understand the two driving tensions that underpin what is at stake when interrogating and encountering emotion online as it is performed and encountered across a range of globalized media forms: television, film, photographs, advertising, text, and audio. The globality of metadata, the privatized infrastructure of digital space, and the increasingly deep rootedness of online worlds into real times and places (for example, through museum archives, citizen journalism, photo witnessing, microblogging, social networking, geocaching, and video diaries) mean that real individuals and places are becoming anchors[5]. However, this anchorage is mobile, with varying degrees of reception, depending on levels of wiredness. Digital sites are never still or stable: sound and image are mashed up, photos are un/tagged, text is remixed, e-mails go viral, links are shared, pages disappear and move, postings and repostings are edited on social networks, and many other examples of circulation all call our attention to the work of emotions *as they move.*

Research into emotion and affect has begun to converge with the fast-paced mobility of the technological changes we have seen in the media, creative, and communication industries. Maxine Sheets-Johnstone's (2011) expanded interdisciplinary work on movement as having primacy in communication is very useful for thinking about emotion and affect in the context of mobile, pervasive media and ubiquitous computing. Hitherto, studies of emotion and media have assumed a static viewer/body, which is no surprise, considering the passive cinematic/televisual consumption of online media. It is the 'tactile-kinaesthetic body', says Sheets-Johnstone, that experiences affect: that turns toward what attracts it and moves away from those things that do not (2011, 505). Kate Crawford's (2009a) research on 'mobile emotions' and attentive listening in social media (2009b), Lasén's (2010a) work on mobile media and 'affective bandwidth', Kathleen Cumiskey's (2010) attention to women's fear in public places without their mobile phone, and Ingrid Richardson's 'pocket technospaces' and the 'bodily incorporation of mobile new media' (2007) all demonstrate a growing recognition that 'affective computing' (in terms of design) needs to be emotionally, socially, and experientially accountable within a variety of spaces (see Boehner et al. 2007). When mobile technology is encountered, enacted, and performed in real spaces, it involves a tactile-kinaesthetic body that is globally networked but emplaced and emotionally charged. As Sadie Plant has noted on the simple act of making and receiving mobile phone calls in public spaces:

> Certain conversations can induce emotional and bodily responses which may be quite incompatible with [phone users] perceptions of their physical location. Their participants often look as though they

don't quite know what to do with themselves, how to reconfigure the tones of voice and postures which would normally accompany such conversations. The mobile requires its users to manage the intersection of the real present and the conversational present in a manner that is mindful of both. (Plant 2002, 50)

Therefore, the most recent findings in Ling and Campbell's edited collection, *Mobile Communication: Bringing Us Together or Tearing Us Apart* (2011), explore the same tensions as Sherry Turkle's intimacy versus solitude dilemma. How can we be in two different affective domains at once? The wearability of technology (in our ears, in our hands, on our wrist) now ensures a 'corporeal intimacy with the handset or portable console' that 'renders it an object of tactile and kinaesthetic familiarity' (Richardson 2005). We touched on this in the previous chapters, but it is worth extending further here. While the 'materialities of human bodies and nonhuman bodies are often in ontic conflict', there are design 'enablements that encourage frequent use and thus practised dexterity' and these 'vitiate against mobile-body "disincorporation" and issues of poor usability' (Richardson 2005). Thus, argues Richardson in defining her concept of 'mobile technosoma':

The contrivances of the body are quite literally *built into* the blueprints and specifications of any technical device or assemblage (the arrangement of keys, hands-free usability), just as the body is manoeuvred and disciplined by the procedures of the apparatus ('typing' with the thumb, the 'space-making' or 'blue-toothing' on-the-mobile pedestrian).

As bodies become built into human-computer interaction (HCI) and computers become ubiquitous in our physical space and pervasive to our physical selves, we are corporeally and psychically individuated into globalized and networked apparatuses. This intimacy is not just confined to users, audiences, and consumers.

In the last decade, researchers of the social and cultural impact of the Internet have become very intimate with their objects of study – not only with the technological apparatuses and their impact on their/our lives, but with the multinational global companies that fund the research on these tools and their social application. Have they, as we noted in the introduction, fallen in love with their research? It is interesting to note that three of the key theorists of these phenomena, Nancy Baym (2010) Kate Crawford (2009 a/b) and Mary Gray (2009), have joined social networking theorist danah boyd (2010, 2005) to be part of Microsoft Research's (MSR) Social Media Collective in recent years to research just such sociotechnical issues; the work is funded by Microsoft. Having invited numerous scholars to MSR 'from fields that haven't commonly been in conversation with industrial researchers', boyd conveys her joyous feelings about this collective:

> ::bounce:: I am *ecstatic* to announce that Nancy Baym, Kate Crawford, and Mary L. Gray are all joining Microsoft Research New England, MA [...]
> ::bounce:: [...] Nancy, Kate, and Mary are three leading scholars in this arena and I'm ecstatic that they'll be coming to MSR to advance this line of inquiry. [...] Each of these phenomenal scholars has a long history of helping us understand the relationship between technology and society and I'm sooo soooo soooo excited that they're coming to MSR. As all of you who know me now, I love MSR. I also love Nancy, Kate, and Mary. So the combination makes me feel like a kid in a candy store. (boyd 2012a)

We can see the emotional intimacy being conveyed here from a researcher who often presents her self as close to other researchers, close to the reader, and close to the technologies she is researching. Nothing unusual there; yet, more concerning, she is close to Microsoft Research, and that emotional attachment may impact upon how a talented group of researchers interpret Microsoft's relation to research, to globality, and to emotion. However, while it is important to recognize these affective dimensions of the new media research landscape, of HCI and of the metadata being gathered about our human lives, the main thrust of our close readings focuses on the ordinary and everyday emotional encounters we have online.

In Nancy Baym's *Personal Connections in the Digital Age* (2010), she makes the simple but reiterated point (made since the early days of Rheingold and Turkle) about how people use emotions online:

> As people appropriate the possibilities of textual media to convey social cues, create immediacy, entertain, and show off for one another, they build identities for themselves, build interpersonal relationships [...]. Our expressions of emotions and immediacy show others that we are real, available, and that we like them. (62)

It remains to be seen what MSR's Social Media Collective produces in terms of research that has impact (social, academic, public, industrial, economic, policy), and what this impact says about the relationship between globality and emotion or industry and research. One thing is very clear: even the academic researchers of online media communications get very emotional about their objects of study.

How the global gets inside us

As *New Yorker* critic Adam Gopnik tried to understand how the Internet gets inside us at the beginning of this chapter, he would do well to acknowledge the Internet as geographically rooted rather than as cyber-cognitively displaced. In her research of 'globalized fear', Rachel Pain identifies a 'powerful metanarrative that is currently popular in analyses of the relation of fear, terror and security'. She continues:

> There are two senses in which these metanarratives of fear can be considered to be 'global'. The first is the idea, more often implicit than worked through, that emotions are being produced and circulate on a global scale: this has become prominent within much recent political analysis of security and terror, including work in human geography. The second sense in which these explanations and processes are 'global' ones is that they tend to be prioritized and discussed as though they apply to everyone all of the time. (Pain 2009, 469)

Not only this, 'globalized fear' invites the notion that emotion is trackable online in the sense that webometrics (see Mike Thelwall et al. 2010, 2011, 2012) could produce large-scale data analyses of sentiment: *big data* on and of emotion. The European CyberEmotions Project (2009–2013) upholds that metanarrative of globalized emotion and defines its remit in terms of determining 'collective emotions in cyberspace' and 'the role of collective emotions in creating, forming and breaking-up e-communities'. With none of the partners from the humanities, the nine research organizations involved in the project take an informatics approach to emotion by integrating this with psychology. Put simply (or rather not) the project combines

> psychological models of emotional interactions and algorithmic methods for detection and classification of human emotions in the Internet with probabilistic models of complex systems and data driven simulations based on heterogeneous emotionally-reacting agents. The theoretical foundations will be mainly based on statistical physics applied to the study of the emergent properties of

many-object systems interacting in self-organized evolving networks. (CyberEmotions website)

What is striking about this is its positivist inflection: 'We concentrate on the issue of how to support and maintain the emotional climates of security, trust, hope, and freedom in future techno-social communities and how to prevent or resolve conflicts within them' (CyberEmotions 'Objectives'). Moreover, the project's delineation of 'sentiment analysis', in the context of our research on online public sentiment and our focus on ordinary spaces of emotional communication, is useful for understanding the drivers for the emerging research into the next generation of socially and emotionally intelligent ICT services. The need to statistically and psychologically delineate emotions as collective is indicative of the drive to make sense of the media plenty, media torrent, and media turbulence that characterizes our individuated experiences of being online. In the close readings that follow, we deliberately take an arts and humanities approach to individual and social emotion online in order to challenge any notion that 'emotional climates of security, trust, hope and freedom' are fully realizable and mappable.

Part II
Close Readings

4
Social Media, Happiness, and Virtual Communities

We share therefore we are: likes, retweets, acceptance, followers, friends, connected, linked, networked, gifting, and *everything is connected to everything.* These are just some of the buzzwords and phrases of our socially mediated economy, which circulates around notions of 'open happiness' (Coca-Cola), your 'happy place' (Campbell's Soup), or 'make room for happiness' and long-standing messages of 'I'm lovin' it' and the Happy Meal (McDonald's).[1] From the installation of a Hug Machine in Singapore in 2012, which delivers a free can of Coca-Cola in return for a hug, to the development of digital out-of-home technologies that seek to engage consumers in gesture-based marketing, our bodies are being drawn together into emotional markets, audiences, and crowds.

This chapter focuses on the sense of community established through socially mediated crowds, found on and through social networks and through the sharing and sending of viral media such as flashmobs. It is particularly interested in the construction of happiness online, how it can be contagious, and how it seeks to efface cultural, social, political, historical, geographic, and religious differences. We draw upon the theoretical work on emotion and affect discussed in the first half of the book, but put particular focus on the concept of happiness, as it is a dominant emotion and an affective feeling that surrounds social media, which is built upon positive concepts of community, networking, relationships, and sharing. It questions the affective and political dimensions of social media by using three online case studies – Facebook, flashmobs, and online self-help – to think through the ways in which people engage emotionally (and happily) in virtual communities.

Happiness as a concept has received a great deal of attention, particularly since 2005 (see Ahmed 2010, 3), within cultural work on emotion and affect as well as in journalistic accounts, and, as the opening of this chapter showed, in social media marketing strategies. There are 'happiness tests' where you can gauge your happiness, a 'happiness project', indices of global happiness (the Happy Planet Index), and even an academic journal, *Happiness Studies* (see Ahmed 2010, 4). A BBC report in 2006 noted a decline in British happiness, and stated: 'The proportion of people saying they are "very happy" has fallen from 52 per cent in 1957 to just 36 per cent today' (http://news.bbc.co.uk/1/hi/programmes/happiness_formula/4771908.stm). Indeed, in many of the happiness studies, the conclusion is that wealth does not equal happiness, echoing the colloquial expression that 'money can't buy you happiness'. Happiness research websites reproduce top-ten lists of the key features of corporate, individual, and social happiness. One of the reasons for this 'happiness turn', as Ahmed refers to it, is the influence of self-help and therapeutic cultures, particularly within popular culture in the United States. The rise of positive thinking gurus and self-empowerment rhetoric has meant an increase in the notion that it is within an individual's power, and even a moral obligation, to be happy (See the film *Eat Pray Love* (2010), based on Elizabeth Gilbert's 2006 memoir, as a good example of this rhetoric).

In *The Promise of Happiness* (2010), Ahmed continues the work she started in *The Cultural Politics of Emotion* (2004) by maintaining an interest in the ways in which feelings are attributed to objects (2010, 14). In so doing, she argues that: 'Feelings do not then simply reside within subjects and then move outwards towards objects. Feelings are how objects create impressions in shared spaces of dwelling' (2010, 14). As we shall explore in the next chapter, this notion is important for thinking about feeling *in place,* because 'the ability to attend to and make meaningful any banal, everyday, embodied experiences of ongoingness is highly situated in time and place' (Horton & Kraftl 2012, 41). Thus, Ahmed interrogates the ways in which we are 'directed by the promise of happiness' (2010, 14). This notion of happiness is particularly useful to studying the patterns, flows, distribution, and communities of happiness and happiness-making online. It allows us to think about the ways in which happiness directs us to certain sites, encourages us to construct profiles in particular ways, to blog about particular subjects, and to share certain forms of social media. Even when the myth of a future or promised happiness is debunked in popular academic culture (no doubt in the light of media representations of apocalyptic futures) it is replaced by a rhetoric of happiness that has more in common with our present Internet culture (and memories of a Hollywood ending).

This can be seen in Daniel Gilbert's *Stumbling on Happiness* (2006) or Nic Marks's research for the New Economics Foundation (NEF) on true contentment through connections with others and through positive feedback loops (see TED Talks' *The Happy Planet Index*, August 2010, by Nic Marks and http://www.happyplanetindex.org). Such ideas signpost to our next chapter on climate change (wherein the West becomes a synonym for environmental shame), because the new Happy Planet methodologies discover social connectivity and economic learning from countries where *happy lives do not cost the Earth*. Thus, Nic Marks proposes five ways to be happy, based on his research for the UK government's Office for Science: connect, be active, take notice, keep learning, and give. It is these kinds of happiness concepts that we interrogate in this chapter.

Virtual communities

Virtual communities can be understood as 'shared spaces of dwelling' (2010, 14) and Howard Rheingold's *The Virtual Community: Homestead on the Electronic Frontier* (1993), focused upon in Chapter 3, is an early and yet still resonant study of the ways in which people emotionally engage with Usenet groups. Rheingold defines 'virtual communities' as 'social aggregations that emerge from the Net when enough people carry on those public discussions long enough, with sufficient human feeling, to form webs of personal relationships in cyberspace' (1993, 5). However, he describes his own entrance into the virtual community of the WELL (Whole Earth 'Lectronic Link) as 'discovering a cozy little world that had been flourishing without me, hidden within the walls of my house; an entire cast of characters welcomed me to the troupe with great merriment as soon as I found the secret door' (1993, 1–2). His personal description exposes the wonderment and excitement he finds in this secret community and explains his emotional attachment to the community he discovers online. Indeed, his experience shares many similarities to Broughton's (2011) account of Spaghetti Western Web Board users covered in Chapter 2, who later meet up 'in real life.'

As Rheingold writes: 'I can't count the parties and outings where the invisible personae who first acted out their parts in the debates and melodramas on my computer screen later manifested in front of me in the physical world in the form of real people, with faces, bodies and voices' (1993, 2). Rheingold's experiences exemplify the messy border between feeling as if you know someone through the emotional exchanges online and then actually meeting the person in the flesh, 'in real life'.

Although we might imagine someone alone at his desk on the computer as an alienated and lonely position, from Rheingold's point of view, this was a very comfortable and reassuring experience, which provided him with a deep sense of friendship and belonging – of community (1993, 2). As Rheingold states: 'People in virtual communities do just about everything people do in real life, but we leave our bodies behind' (1993, 3). Rheingold's statement has been very provocative and opens up many questions, such as, What does it mean to 'leave our bodies behind'? What does the absence of bodies allow for and prevent? And how does the notion of community change without the bodily presence of its members?

Furthermore, Rheingold points out that 'Community is a matter of emotions as well as a thing of reason and data' (1993, 15). His definition is very apt for the work in this book, in the sense that emotions function as a kind of glue that binds groups of people together, regardless of whether they are online or offline. However, as Rheingold suggests, there needs to be some balancing between these two positions – between sharing online and actually meeting face-to-face offline (1993, 23). What he suggests, however, is not to dismiss the opportunities that both situations offer – some people share better without having to 'see' someone else and others enjoy the sense of anonymity that computer-mediated communication allows in wholly different ways than previous experiences of community have enabled. We will focus upon this in more depth in Chapter 6, in which we tackle the rise in cyberbullying, flaming, trolling, and hate online. For now, it is important to note the tension that exists; as Rheingold states, 'It's a way of both making contact with and maintaining a distance from others' (1993, 26). The use of flashmobs online provides a useful of example of community at a distance.

Flashmobs

Flashmobs are leaderless gatherings organized by cell phone, e-mail, and the Web. The mobs usually do something silly, demonstrating only that a floating connection can flash into flesh. In 2003, at a Toys "R" Us store, a flashmob stared at an animatronic *Tyrannosaurus rex* for three minutes and then fell to the floor with screams and waving of hands before quickly dispersing. In New York, participants assembled at the food court in Grand Central Station, where organizers (identifiable by the copies of the *New York Review of Books* they were holding) gave mobbers printed instructions regarding what to do next. Shortly after 7 p.m., about two hundred people suddenly assembled on the mezzanine of the Grand Hyatt Hotel next to Grand Central Station, applauded loudly for 15 seconds, then left (Stewart 2007, 67). International pillow fight days, water fights, mass choral performances, and dance and musical routines (many inspired by popular music and television) have erupted into public space in many major cities around the world.

In her work on 'ordinary affects', Stewart suggests that flashmobs are an affective, collective, and somewhat silly gathering, not always aiming to do much more than wave hands or collapse in giggles. They are organized through cell phone, e-mail, Facebook, and other forms of social media. However 'silly' they may be, Stewart's decision to place them within her collection of affective moments signals their emotional and affective resonance, particularly within popular American culture. Their extension to other major cities is seen to connect crowds across difference by events such as in International Pillow Fight Day or provide unsettling performances of difference, making the banal deeply felt, such as in pregnant women break-dancing in London in 2008. It is their interruption of the flow of everyday life, the video recording of that interruption, and the posting of those videos on YouTube as a form of witnessing that interests us most.

Flashmobs imply a sense of humanity and togetherness that is perhaps a nostalgic construction of an imagined past where people in specific communities came together to help and support each other. Yet, at the same time, people are viewing these expressions of collective together-ness on the highly individualized space of their computer screens, and social media marketers are witnessing these collective expressions as a visual display of the market itself. Thus, the convergence of screen, product, emotions, and everyday life provides that vital mix for digital out-of-home technologies and gesture-based branding strategies to flourish in our media ecology.

One of the first 'commercial' flashmobs – 'Sound of Music' – took place in Central Antwerp Station on 23 March 2009. This was not a piece of performance art or unregulated street performance, but a promotion stunt for a Belgian television programme where they were looking for 'Maria' for a production of *Sound of Music* (based on the UK television format – 'How Do You Solve a Problem Like Maria?' (BBC1, 2006). Not unlike the marketing of *Lost* in 2004 through the placing of messages in bottles left on beaches where people in the United States went on vacation, the 'Sound of Music' flashmob provided an early example of the synergy of mediated forms and formats that was quickly and crea-tively engaged with by audiences. In the United States, the sharing of 'flashmob' clips became so prevalent and popular that a new television show was created called '*Mobbed*' (Fox, 2010–), a clever remixing of *Candid Camera* and reality television.

The series, which received unprecedented ratings, follows the 'real-time' construction of flashmobs, including one where a man proposes to and marries his fiancée in a matter of minutes. The website [www.fox.com/mobbed] asks 'Do you have big news or know someone worthy of being MOBBED? This message alternates with the statement 'Changing lives in a flash!' These taglines speak to the programme's promise of being able to transform lives and affect people in significant ways. 'Mob' becomes a verb meaning 'to transform, affect, radically alter' as opposed to its dictionary definition, which is to 'crowd into' or 'surround and attack'. 'Mobbed' in the television programme is a positive phenomenon, as opposed to a negative experience.

In one of the first episodes, a man prepares to 'mob' his girlfriend and not only propose to her, but also marry her, all before the episode ends. One of the prerequisites for a mob is to have the person in a public place but under false premises. In this case, the woman who is to be mobbed by her boyfriend believes that they are just out for a romantic meal. The first sign that things are not as they appear happens when a woman approaches the boyfriend and dumps a glass of water on him, warning the woman to be mobbed that he has been cheating on her. The boyfriend exits for the toilet (to get ready for the flashmob), leaving the woman confused and upset. A waiter comes to talk to her and soon breaks into song, along with other participants (including the woman who dumped the glass of water). The relatively frightened and very surprised woman is then dragged outside to find a huge crowd anticipating her boyfriend's proposal. There are fireworks, objects juggling in the air, explosions – it is clear that this is meant to be a spectacle. The woman, now crying and holding her hands to her face, watches the crowd part to reveal her boyfriend. He does some kind of rap dance, which we, as viewers, have seen him rehearse, and then asks her to marry him. Confused and bewildered, the woman says yes, and he then suggests that they do it now. He tells her that her family is in the crowd, and once she says 'yes' to the marriage proposal, an enormous white dress is thrown over her. Everything moves fast and the woman ends up getting married in a dress that is not even fully fastened. As viewers, we are excited and happy for the chance to participate in their celebration.[2] The episode demonstrates the power of the crowd to generate a happy feeling and reiterates notions of community, collectivity, and togetherness. Celebrations such as marriages and proposals are easy fodder for flashmobs and, as the programme's tagline suggests, the dominant theme in the series.

Parodies of flashmobs and their 'happy' atmosphere appear in popular US sitcoms such as *Modern Family* (abc, 2009–). In one episode, two of the central characters, Mitchell Pritchett (Jesse Tyler Ferguson) and Cameron Tucker (Eric Stonestreet), a gay couple in their early thirties, enter an outdoor shopping complex with the pretence of shopping for a birthday gift. Suddenly, on the lower courtyard, a flashmob starts to take shape. When Mitchell pretends not to be interested in the flashmob, Cameron tells him,'This is joyful' and gets excited, clapping his hands and jumping up and down. Mitchell unexpectedly starts to participate in the flashmob, while Cameron unsuccessfully tries to keep up with the choreography. In a mock interview scene, Mitchell explains that his participation in the flashmob is his 'love letter to Cameron' – his way of showing Cameron that he is not as rigid as he thinks. And yet the scene ends with Cameron's exasperated 'How could you, Mitchell?' referring to his feeling of betrayal for not including him in such a 'joyful' experience, suggesting that Mitchell has denied him of some happiness. In each of the examples above, the flashmobs are a sign of joy, happiness, and give us a sense of togetherness, but, as Stewart implies above, not much more.

Flashmobs are very much part of popular culture and are mostly designed either to promote something or as a stunt to draw people's attention. They are not, in themselves, political, but could be read as such. In his early work, Rheingold draws on Mark A. Smith's 'recipe' for virtual communities: 'social network capital, knowledge capital, and communion' (1993, 13), which he returns to later in *Smart Mobs: The Next Social Revolution: Transforming Cultures and Communities in the Age of Instant Access* (2003). Mark A. Smith, who was a graduate student when Rheingold first knew him, became Microsoft's research sociologist (until 2008) and built software that maps social networks (2003, 30). The question on Rheingold's mind a decade later is, 'What happens when virtual communities migrate from desktop computers to mobile phones?' (2003, 30). In other words, how do instant access and the use of a more 'public' form of communication change/alter earlier conceptions of virtual communities? What happens when bodies get emotional and create public spectacles of that emotion (as in the numerous witness videos of hateful rants aboard uploaded for critical commentary)? In many ways, the answer to these kinds of questions lies in theoretical analyses that are embedded in more conventional forms of media such as television; hence, our insistence on drawing attention to the convergence and synergies among media formats.

Rheingold distinguishes 'social mobs' from flashmobs. The notion of collective power is very germane now, with occupations taking place across the world in demonstrations against capitalism and greed. The democratization of online media means that it is open and available to all; you do not have to be a professional writer or filmmaker to express your views. Conversely, however, as Rheingold points out: 'The disappointing news about virtual communities is that you don't have to be civil, capable of communicating coherently, or know what you are talking about in order to express yourself to others' (2003, 121). He goes on to argue that 'Online media that support social communication have a defensive capability that face-to-face socializing lacks' (2003, 121).

There is a tension here between the sharing, collective sense that online media, particularly social media, allow for and the alienated participation in such media. You can comment, *snark, troll,* or *flame* (that is abuse, provoke and enrage) in ways unallowed in face-to-face interaction, as we will interrogate in Chapter 6. In their work on emotion communication in video-mediated communication, Antony S. R. Manstead, Martin Lea, and Jeannine Goh (2011) argue that

> It is apparent that physical presence is not a necessary condition for facial communication of emotion to occur – emotion communication occurs even in the absence of any possibility to communicate it directly to another, and is more influenced by the quality of the relationship between the communicators and the cultural norms for the expression of emotions than by the kind of communication medium that is available (169).

Of course, that is not to say that facial communication does not heighten the emotional response, but it is very interesting to note that it is not an essential condition of such a response. What is more important, as Manstead et al. point (2011, 169) out, is the 'quality of the relationship between the communicators and the cultural norms for the expression of emotions', criteria we find in abundance in social media. And so, in studying emotion and affect, it seems important to reconsider the political dimension of such sentimentality on sites such as YouTube and Facebook and to consider their affective influence within 'friendship' circles.

In his early work on online activism, Rheingold provocatively asks: 'Are virtual communities just computerized enclaves, intellectual ivory towers?' (1993, 261). Although he goes on to interrogate this assumption, the idea that online activism is relatively removed from any real sense of political action remains at the heart of the scepticism regarding political action online. This is important for those initiatives such as

The Happy Planet Index (NEF) mentioned above, whose five tenets for achieving personal, community, national, and global well-being bear all the hallmarks of discourses of online culture. Notably, Evgeny Morozov, a specialist in social media, recently coined the term *slacktivism* to define 'feel-good online activism that has zero political or social impact. It gives those who participate in 'slacktivist' campaigns an illusion of having a meaningful impact on the world without demanding anything more than joining a Facebook group' (cited in Jones 2011, 80). This point is certainly illustrated through the example of *Kony 2012*, discussed in the introduction to our book. 'Awareness' makes up a significant chunk of Invisible Children's fund raising and suggests that much money is spent in drawing attention to the charity and its aims, rather than in 'real' political action. The result is that people can make themselves 'aware' by 'liking' the charity on Facebook, or wearing a bracelet, and feel that they have participated in a form of political action. This is not unique to *Kony 2012* of course, and it is not uncommon for the most charitable observer to view such awareness campaigns with dispassion.

Similar campaigns, such as 'USA for Africa' and 'Band Aid' in the mid-1980s, used celebrity and record sales to make people feel as though they were connected to broader social movements, while actually contributing to the charity's proceeds. In his work on social media and social movements, Jonny Jones compiles an excellent overview of the positions both scholars and journalists have taken with regard to social media. He cites Jodi Dean (2005), for instance, who argues that 'often people can "believe they are active, maybe even making a difference simply by clicking a button, adding their name to a petition, or commenting on a blog"' (cited in Jones 2011, 80). He also draws attention to Malcolm Gladwell's (2010) argument that the 'revolution won't be tweeted' because some media generate networks with 'weak ties', 'while involvement in risky, radical action is predicated upon "strong ties"' (cited in Jones 2011, 80).

Therefore, while there is scepticism that such media can actually be revolutionary or even political, we would argue that they do carry a moral and ethical responsibility that is often couched in sentimental and popular discourses of happiness, such as the five tenets from The Happy Planet Index, cited above: connect, be active, take notice, keep learning, and give. In her work 'On Affect and Protest', Deborah Gould (2010) interrogates theorists on emotion, to question the divide between rational/irrational and also scholars of social movements, to encourage them to recognize the importance of emotion in protests. She argues that: 'Movements, in short, "make sense" of inchoate affective states and authorize selected feelings and actions while downplaying and even invalidating others' (Gould 2010, 33). The collective power to 'make sense' of emotions while also selecting certain feelings and actions can be witnessed online in the ways people troll and snark and in their comments, whether in response to a news item, a film, or a Facebook post. Gould's suggestion that social movements can be a 'guide for what and how to feel and for what to do in light of those feelings' (2010, 33) should be extended to think about social media and its ability to guide and direct its users to particular feelings, and actions to take on behalf of those feelings, particularly when it comes to happiness. We shall return in Chapter 6 to the social movements that were informed by early work on moral panics when we closely read about the increase in trolling.

Facebook me

Social networking and microblogging sites such as Facebook and Twitter are also apt examples of the 'shared spaces of dwelling' that Ahmed refers to (2010, 14). They exist virtually and yet are an archive for people's intimate everyday feelings and thoughts. Launched in 2004, Facebook has grown from 150 million users in January 2009 to almost one billion at the time of writing (as of December 2011 Facebook had 483 million daily active users). The typical user spends around 20 minutes a day on the site, and two-thirds of users log in at least once a day (see Ellison et al. 2007, 1144). 'Facebook helps you connect and share with the people in your life' (www.Facebook.com). This life is contemporaneous and *of the now*, with numerous dormant friends and memories lurking, which are perhaps better served by the recently relaunched Friends Reunited. The tagline's emphasis on 'connect and share' evokes notions of community and collective experiences. The format is designed like a community bulletin board, and the notion of 'posting' fits with this image. As Meikle and Young define it: 'Facebook is a complex space, a site of multiple convergences and modes of interaction, and one that offers keys to understanding our converged media environment' (2012, 59).

Posts about new babies, work frustrations, political views, and parenting advice abound. In a random moment of logging on, we found an article that a friend of a friend of a friend had posted from the *New York Times,* written by a woman whose 18-month-old son is suffering from Tay-Sachs disease and will die before he reaches the age of 3. In her status, she urged anyone reading the article to remember the importance of *the here and now,* and suggested people give their children an extra hug today. Comments followed about loving unconditionally, seizing the moment, and enjoying the happiness we find without expectations. This both accords with the popular theorization of happiness as something one stumbles upon in the present and acknowledges that Facebook is an archiving of that *here and now* and is not necessarily about reaccessing the past. It is a moment that is replicated almost daily on these forms of social media – whether shared through a status update or through a flashmob clip. Generally these are sent or posted with an emotional tag – 'You'll love this' or 'This made me cry'. The sharing extends the 'promise of happiness', as Ahmed refers to it, bound in the act of communal expression: 'The promise of happiness is what makes some things promising, as if to share in things is to share in happiness' (2010, 30). It accords with conceptualizations of sharing, giving, liking, and taking notice that are becoming increasingly germane to happiness as presentist and thing/idea/object-related. You experience the joy yourself and then pass it on, with the hopes of sharing this experience and the promise this experience conveys. As Ahmed suggests: 'If happiness creates its objects, then such objects are passed around, accumulating positive affective value as social goods' (2010, 22). We trust those who have posted the most; we take notice of those with the most friends, followers, tweets; we learn from those who have accumulated the most videos, photos, podcasts, clips, 'toons and links; and we purchase goods that have the most trustworthy reviews. We even follow a reviewer's reviews to other goods, not because we need or even want those items, but because we want to follow that reviewer's pursuit of the happy object. This is the curation and archiving of happiness objects by digitally literate citizens who are seen to be the best measurers of emotion online (their own emotions as well as the emotions of others that are 'like' theirs).

In other words, you are sharing your hopes that this kind of collectivity exists and is possible. But there is another side to it, as Ahmed discusses, where there is an expectation that you find these moments transformational. We are invited to reply, but the expectation is that you will say something in line with what has been said to maintain your presence in a particular community of 'friends' or fellow purchasers. In other words, in the example offered above, all the comments were approving and supportive of the message this woman was promoting through her post of the article – that is, they all reiterated the need to appreciate life and to go give our children, if we have them, a hug. Most of the comments included a reference to crying when reading the article – which again, is a sign that they understood and responded, as they should, emotionally. No one wrote: 'My kids are driving me crazy, so no hugs tonight', for instance. Ahmed points out that 'happiness can be promised as a return for investment in social norms' and that 'such optimism does not originate from a subject, but is generated through promises made to the subject, which circulate as "truths" within public culture' (2004, 196). So the happiness is there in some way to return the promise of being a good citizen, which leaves us questioning the affective nature of such interactions online and their emotional expressions.

One of the interesting things to note in social network sites such as Facebook is the dominance of happy faces. People often use these sites for posting photographs – generally of their children, holidays, or weddings.[3] Inevitably, this means a lot of smiling faces: smiles over the birth of a baby, smiles at the altar, smiles on the beach – people generally post photographs in which they look happy, and this is often signalled by the smiling face. Facebook is largely about happy, smiling faces and the presentation of our lives as we would want to live them: to be seen by others as happy lives or at least offering the promise of happiness. These are still Annette Kuhn's 'imagined communities' of *Family Secrets: Acts of Memory and Imagination*, preexisting public faces whereby 'every effort' is made 'to keep certain things concealed from the rest of the world' while at the same time opening out the security, intimacy, and safety of family lives to an online network (Kuhn 2002, 1–2). When such levels of family intimacy are made public, the pressure to maintain the representation of happiness is distributed among a growing and increasingly dormant (but still present) audience within one's network.

Of course you will sometimes find the sad, unhappy status offered by a 'friend' who has been given bad news or just had a bad day. For the most part, negative emotions are filtered and premediated such that Facebook users shore up the positivity structured into the corporate memory of the company, its data architecture, and its representation as a force for social good (see Garde-Hansen 2009). Facebook is used as a means to celebrate the happiness in our lives with others. Posting happy faces is part of how a user on Facebook develops a visual profile; and yet, as research has pointed out, one of the crucial differences between Facebook and Web pages is that people other than the 'user' can post on the Facebook walls. So 'friends' can (and often do) post an undesirable photo of someone for everyone else to see on his or her 'wall'. This dimension of Facebook has prompted researchers to ask whether we 'are known by the company we keep' (Walther et al. 2008, 29), thus initiating provocative questions regarding community and intimacy online.

Indeed, the format of Facebook encourages its users to believe there is some form of intimacy that has been established. Our contacts are referred to as 'friends', we have a 'home' page, and one listed by our name. As Garde-Hansen (2009) has argued, friendship is 'key to Facebook's security, community building and trustworthiness':

> In particular, the maintenance of existing friendships in an increasingly globalised world, the development of existing friendships within a restricted work/study environment and [...] the additional benefit of rediscovering old friendships through alumni networks all focus upon friendship and by extension [on] memories. Even giving Facebook 'gifts' of friendship, poking (nudging potential or past friends online, who can accept or reject 'the poke') and joining or creating new networks speak clearly to a discourse of fraternity, homogeneity, belonging and community that Derrida questioned as conventional and undifferentiated in *The Politics of Friendship* (2005).
> (Garde-Hansen 2009, 145)

Yet Facebook is constantly under criticism over the way in which it lists relatively unsecure settings as 'normal'. It is up to the individual to go through the security settings, for example, and to edit them in such a way that they are not available to the public, as if to suggest that one should have this kind of openness with a 'global community'. Users are too often lulled into thinking that it is acceptable to advertise their birthdays or post personal information without the fear of hackers or outsiders trying to use this information in identity theft or credit card fraud. As Meikle and Young observe: 'Rather than being a third form of communication, social network media create a tension between broadcast and personal communication, between messages intended for someone in particular and messages intended for whoever comes across them' (2012, 68).

Nevertheless, Facebook continues to fiercely defend rules, codes, and behaviours (and the homogeneity of its architecture) in light of early attacks upon social networking sites such as Friendster by Fakesters. In her research of Fakesters, danah boyd found that:

> Through the act of articulation and writing oneself into being, all participants are engaged in performance intended to be interpreted and convey particular impressions. While some people believed that 'truth' could be perceived through photorealistic imagery and a list of tastes that reflected one's collections, the Fakesters were invested in using more impressionistic strokes to paint their portraits. If we acknowledge that all profiles are performative, permitting users to

give off a particular view of themselves, why should we judge Fakesters as more or less authentic than awkwardly performed profiles? (boyd 2008, 153)

These weak profiles that boyd considers just as significant and legitimate as strong ones resonate with the weak and strong ties associated with the tensions between online versus offline communities. However, just because the term 'weak' is applied does not mean to say that these communities are not dynamic or productive. Strong ties use more and multiple media to reinforce those ties, such that the stronger the bond, the more the connection is produced. Yet, the weak ties in one's Facebook network have a predetermined inference of social and emotional communication, because they are paired to us as 'friends' rather than as (potential) work colleagues as in Academia.edu, potential clients/employers as in LinkedIn, or as potential fans/consumers/collaborators as in MySpace. On the surface it may appear that a user has a thousand friends; however, in reality, as Facebook sociologists concede, a network is constantly expanding and contracting with the difference between 'all friends' and actual 'maintained relationships' that in themselves are maintained by 'one-way' or 'mutual communication' (see Marlow et al. 2009).

Caroline Haythornthwaite's research into weak and strong ties online concludes by stating, 'Online participants themselves report strongly held, close ties with others that are just as important to them as offline ties' (Haythornthwaite 2005, 135). There is a difference between using social media and using online media as a means for continuing existing intimacy, or even building it to some extent. Early work on social media assumed that the direction of communication was online to offline; however, as Ellison et al. (2007) observe that 'the assumed online to offline directionality may not apply to today's SNSs that are structured both to articulate existing connections and [to] enable the creation of new ones' (1144). Indeed, many people we have asked about their Facebook usage describe meeting someone briefly at a social occasion and then 'friending' that person online. Often communication or subsequent social events are then facilitated by their new Facebook connection.[4]

While we were writing this chapter, the press released new information regarding Facebook's renewed effort to help prevent suicide. Facebook added a feature that allows users to connect with a counsellor online.[5] If a post is upsetting to a user, he or she can use the drop-down menu to report feelings of 'self-harm' or 'suicidal content'. Facebook's safety team can then send this to Lifeline, and send both a message and a link to Lifeline's live confidential chat to the user. Part of the reason for this interaction is the 'suicide notes' people have left as their status updates. In September 2010, for example, an American college student wrote 'jumping off the gw [George Washington] bridge', and in Christmas of 2010 a UK woman, Louise Back, posted 'took all my pills be dead soon so bye bye every one'. It was the inactive and dismissive posts of her 'friends' in response to this suicide note that caused popular criticism (see the *Daily Mail*'s 'Woman Commits Suicide on Facebook...and none of her 1,082 online friends help', 6 January 2011). These desperate acts have encouraged the company to take some responsibility to safeguard their 800 million users, to stand in as a 'real' friend while 'so-called friends' remain passive and dispassionate. Thus, Facebook acts *in loco fraternis,* we might say. The flip side of happiness, of course, is unhappiness, and suicide is the most desperate of all expressions of this emotional state. The idea that someone can use the status update to announce anything from the birth of a child to his or her own imminent death is evidence of the significance of social network sites as documenters of everyday life as emotionalized, and evidence of our need to study the emotional and affective relationships people have with such sites.

Although extreme views and desperate moments do appear on Facebook (we shall cover this in more depth in Chapter 6), the majority of status updates are about the domestic: for instance, a child refusing to eat anything but fruit; or a husband who is praised by his wife because he watches the kids while she nurses a hangover; or a woman resigning from her job; or a party you must come to, are enjoying right now, should have been at. These events are very rooted in the banal, everyday, and the domestic and are reminiscent of the kinds of things that fill what was known as 'kitchen-sink drama' in television terms and is still the fodder for popular British soaps such as *Coronation Street* and *EastEnders.* Habitual users of SMSs start to construct a narrative about their lives, and each update is a mini-episode of what comes next. In a sense, users construct themselves as characters: the happy housewife, the frustrated but contented mother, the political thinker, the lad on the lookout, the confused teenager, or the 'with-it' pensioner. As Nancy Thumim argues in *Self-Representation and Digital Culture*: 'The common-sense assumption is that Facebook is primarily a tool for socializing and yet profile pictures do largely consist of amateur portrait snaps and the website is set up explicitly to upload and "share" photos of "me." This means creating representations of "me"' (2012, 153). However, what is difficult to say is whether the users posting these snaps and updates believe what they say about their identities or feel that it accurately reflects their lives. What is more likely is that it captures one side of them, as the characters on soaps do. They are relatively two-dimensional and are designed to be 'open' enough to appeal to as many people as possible. Unlike soap opera characters, we are not screenwriters entirely in control of our own character, and this has prompted the rise of online reputation management tools as found on Google's dashboard. The *Me on the Web* feature recognizes the economic and social risks of being online and provides a tool for managing social media identity and one's writing into being. Such management is becoming increasingly premediated as parents, schoolteachers, and citizens vigilantly manage all mediated events (from sports days to birthdays) as potentially threatening. Controlling your own clickability is about managing yourself as a brand. Watchwords of consistency, commitment, and authenticity all suggest that a strong and intimate relationship with online media is required.

Theorists of soap operas have argued that soaps make the 'ordinary appear extraordinary', and this can certainly be applied to our thoughts about domestic drama online (see Geraghty's *Women and Soap Opera*, 1991). Ordinary, everyday events are posted as though they are extraordinary enough that everyone will want to know about them; some people log in and read these mini-stories with the interest of a soap viewer. Parallels can also be drawn between our interest in the pictures we see online and those we find in celebrity magazines or in the sidebar of the UK's *Daily Mail* website, for example. What we want to see is the humanity of the other: the messy banality of their lives and their (in)ability to be happy. We want to know that we are not alone in our suffering, our happiness, and even in our boredom. Most people want and search for some sense of connection while at the same time seeking to compete. As Thumim points out: '"Community," like "ordinary person," is both an emotive and a slippery concept' (2012, 24); they are both cultural constructions that are becoming increasingly valorized as 'good' and 'authentic'. This sentiment is echoed in Rheingold's own experience of using the WELL (Whole Earth 'lectronic Link) and his research into virtual communities, or what he later terms 'technologies of cooperation' that sit alongside conflict and competition in the smart mob (Rheingold 2002, 46).

Public sentiment

Facebook and flashmobs are largely about sentiment and the construction of the self in the public domain. Through them 'reciprocity, cooperation, reputation, social grooming, and social dilemmas all appear to be fundamental pieces of the smart mob puzzle' (Rheingold 2002, 46). They involve people's feelings, intimate information, and emotional well-being, and are posted, followed, and tweeted around the world, because the discursive representation of the Internet is predicated on the concept of commons whereby content does not come from one single broadcaster, institution, or company (even though in many cases content is coming from a single source). With that in mind, the viewer, reader, and user are seen to be on their own. To return to the example offered earlier, an individual story of a woman who is losing her son to a rare and yet vicious disease is used as a platform to remind people to value what they have, instead of a call to action to seek greater understanding and research around the disease. Each user logs into this example and leaves feeling happier about his or her lot in life, whilst not contributing to the struggle this woman faces. The consumption is no different from the passive reading of a print article from a woman's magazine, a news report on 'real-life' tragedy, or a soap opera storyline of a main character's demise. We take happiness from her unhappiness: she has fulfilled the promise of happiness by giving us her tragic content. We are allowed, even encouraged, to feel better about our own lives at the expense of and in the face of another person's misfortune, and we are expected to do nothing. Marshall McLuhan's scathing attack on passivity in *The Mechanical Bride* resonates:

> The ordinary person senses the greatness of the odds against him even without thought or analysis, and he adapts his attitudes unconsciously. A huge passivity has settled on industrial society. For people carried about in mechanical vehicles, earning their living by waiting on machines, listening much of the waking day to canned music, watching packaged movie entertainment and capsulated news, for such people it would require an exceptional degree of awareness and an especial heroism of effort to be anything but supine consumers of processed goods. (McLuhan 1951, 21)

Thus, the supportive posts might be seen as the cards and flowers that grace public sites of mourning that Denise Riley (2005) refers to in her work on sentimentalism in the public sphere (discussed in Chapter 1). The posts, like the cards and flowers, ask 'Why?' but do little more. People are willing to offer their sense of injustice for the other, but not as willing to take action that might prevent the injustice from happening in the future. Similar to Jodi Dean's observation of online activism that people '"believe they are active, maybe even making a difference simply by clicking a button, adding their name to a petition, or commenting on a blog"' (cited in Jones 2011, 80), people who post their sadness about someone else's grief are effectively doing the same. There is a difference between the relatively simple act of clicking a button or writing a brief post and actually participating in the complex messiness of a demonstration or going to someone's house and offering your sympathy or preventing the person from taking his own life. We are encouraged to feel better, even to feel happy for having done something for someone else, and yet very little 'real' action has taken place.

Illouz's suggestion, raised in Chapter 1, that the Internet 'presupposes a psychological self that can apprehend itself through texts, classify and quantify itself, and present and perform itself publicly' (2007, 108) is made manifest in social media such as Facebook. People construct their selves as they want to be seen and, perhaps at times, perform a kind of happiness they think others would like to have: passing on the promise of happiness as it has been passed to them. This construction is drawn from a wide variety of media and cultural forms: the television soap, cinematic romance and, increasingly, the wider industrialization of therapeutic self-reflexivity: the road to contentment as personified in the television series and films of *Sex and the City* (HBO 1998–2004, 2008, 2010).

Spiritual cyber gurus: happiness at your fingertips

In her work on television, therapy, and the social subject, Mimi White argues that: 'The new therapeutic dynamics of consumer culture embrace a wide range of strategies, encouraging people to manage problems, emotions, and fantasies. In conjunction with new technologies, a new sense of social subjectivity begins to emerge' (2002, 313). The notion that the Internet can be seen and used as a therapeutic space is illustrated in particular by a new generation of women and men who offer their spiritual guidance online. On 18 September 2009, the *New York Times* 'Style' Section announced that 'there is a new role model for New York's former Carrie Bradshaws – young women who are vegetarian, well versed in self-help and New Age spirituality, and who are finding a way to make a living preaching to eager audiences, mostly female' (Salkin). Salkin's piece, 'Seeing Yourself in Their Light', described the lives of five women (Sera Beak, Gabrielle Bernstein, Meggan Watterson, Kris Carr, and Jennifer Macaluso-Gilmore) who are all making a living from telling women how to find their 'soul voice'.

Salkin's article begins with Bernstein and explains that a few years ago, she would have been busy in her very 'Carrie'-like career, drinking cocktails at fashionable bars and dressing the part, whereas she can now be found on a yoga mat, spiritually guiding women into a better life. Bernstein has written two books *Add More ~ing to Your Life: A Hip Guide to Happiness* (2010) and *Spirit Junkie: A Radical Road to Discovering Self-Help and Miracles* (2011). The first book features Bernstein on the cover, dressed in a short, white 'angel' costume standing on a skateboard in the middle of a Manhattan street. The image is very much linked to the opening montage of *Sex and the City*, which featured Carrie Bradshaw (Sara Jessica Parker) in a pink tutu, walking the streets of Manhattan. Each woman is white, attractive, young, and privileged enough to be paying the bills by promoting herself. It is easy to imagine an episode of *Sex and the City* in which Bradshaw meets Bernstein and attends one of her 'yoga-empowered' nights.

Bernstein states that 'the purpose of this book is to help you shine light on the darker areas of life and create positive change' (2010, 19). Her work can be seen as part of the 'positive psychology' that dominates America's self-help market and that forms the basis of happiness economics more generally, as outlined at the beginning of this chapter. Ahmed argues, 'Positive psychology is positive about positive feeling; it presumes the promissory nature of its own object' (2010, 8). The suggestion that Bernstein's readers 'create positive change' implies this 'change' will be for the good of the person. In other words, 'Happiness becomes a form of being directed or oriented, of following "the right way"' (2010, 9). This 'right way' in Bernstein's formulation involves 'Rethink*ing* + Mov*ing* + Receiv*ing* x 30 days = Chang*ing*' (2010, 19). Bernstein promises, 'The *~ing* Equation will bulldoze negative thought patterns and create positive change so you can move forward and live an awesome life' (2010, 19). Her solution, like that of many self-help books in positive psychology, involves taking 'negative feelings and rethink[ing] them into positive feelings of self-love' (2010, 38). This process of inversion, of taking the bad and making it good, appears simplistic and straightforward – surely anyone should be able to do it? But it also implies that feelings are negative and positive, that there are good feelings and bad ones, and that the bad ones must be banished in order for good ones to emerge. Bernstein, like many other positive thinkers, draws on individual stories as both example and evidence. 'Carolyn', for instance, is an example of someone who became addicted to perfection. Bernstein's solution was to get her to bounce on a trampoline and let loose of control. Soon enough (5 minutes, in fact), Carolyn 'shouted joyfully, "I choose balance!"' and left her high-powered job in the fashion industry to enroll in a graphic design program (2010, 71). Carolyn's 'journey' stops rather abruptly. We know that she has enrolled in a new course, but why will this mean happiness for her? Did the bouncing really resolve a lifetime of being a perfectionist? Bernstein asks: 'With Twitter, Facebook and Blackberry messenger, who has a chance to chill out?' and declares that she is 'bringing serenity back' (2010, 71). Bernstein's self-help is focused on the construction of self as not only happy, but without any negativity (with technology as problem and saviour in one). As Ahmed notes, 'Happiness becomes, then, a way of maximizing your potential of getting what you want, as well as being what you want to get' (2010, 10). Bernstein's motivational lectures and inspirational messages on her website and 'gabby B tv' are about realizing one's potential by finding happiness in one's 'truth', but what if one's 'truth' is about the very negative things Gabby urges people to change?

Kris Carr has published several books, most beginning with the words *Crazy Sexy* (e.g., *Crazy Sexy Diet*), but ending with phrases like Cancer Tips, or 'Cancer Survivor.' Sera Beak's *The Red Book: A Deliciously Unorthodox Approach to Igniting Your Divine Spark* is more consciously focused on the project of the divine, as opposed to explicitly being about self-help, though her messages embrace much of the discourse within self-help literature. All these women rely on social network sites such as Facebook, Twitter, and YouTube to promote their vision and, to a certain extent, themselves 'as brand.' Many offer newsletters and some have their own TV channels. Bernstein's 'Gabby B TV' and Kate Northrup's 'Glimpse TV' broadcast their personal words of wisdom to the general public. In Bernstein's repertoire you can hear keynote lectures, motivational speeches, and advice on stretching, all free and downloadable. Her mini-podcasts show her speaking to an audience and telling her devotees that they can find happiness in their lives by letting go (though not clear whether letting go of technology is one solution).

These 'spiritual gurus' are not alone; many other authors and self-helpers have picked up the cause of happiness as a life project. Gretchen Rubin's *The Happiness Project: Or, Why I Spent a Year Trying to Sing in the Morning, Clean My Closets, Fight Right, Read Aristotle, and Generally Have More Fun* (2011 [2009]), which has been on the *New York Times* bestseller list, is an excellent example of Ahmed's claim, 'Not only does happiness become an individual responsibility, a redescription of life as a project, but it also becomes an instrument, as a means to an end, as well as an end' (2010, 10). Rubin's book takes happiness as a project, as something that can be achieved through a variety of lifestyle changes, including organizing your closets, getting more sleep, not expecting compliments, and exercising better. Rubin organizes the chapters over the course of a year (note that Daniel Gilbert's 2005 *Stumbling on Happiness* has twelve chapters covering twelve weeks) – so there is a clear timeline and expectation about *when* you will be happy (provided you take the necessary steps). Each month has a project title such as 'Boost Energy', 'Lighten Up', and 'Make Time for Friends'. As the titles suggest, the advice is very straightforward and common-sense-oriented, but it is peppered throughout with quotes from writers and thinkers as well as personal anecdotes designed to assure the reader that following this project will lead him or her to happiness.

The corresponding website (http://www.happiness-project.com) continues the 'project' of happiness where the one-year structure of the book ends. People are encouraged to sign up for a free monthly newsletter, which highlights the best material from the Facebook page and blog, and an e-mail service that sends a free happiness quotation to your inbox every morning (see website). There is also an opportunity to join or start a 'happiness group' in your local area, where you can enact this operations management approach to happiness on others. Interested people are asked to e-mail Gretchen for a starter pack, and existing groups and e-mail contacts are listed on the site. The notion of community is fostered here in the promise of people coming together with the purpose of being happy. The convergence of e-mail, blog, Facebook, and Web interaction is common with many of the spiritual/happiness self-helpers online. They use a combination of online media to get their messages across, to build their 'brand' image and, of course, to make money. They appear to attract very devout followers. When Rubin goes 'offline' for a week's holiday, for instance (site accessed 26 March 2012), she writes: 'Are you thinking, *"But, oh, Gretchen, what will I do without reading a daily post about happiness?"* Don't worry! To read more about happiness in the coming week, you can read the paperback of *The Happiness Project'*, as if to preempt the loss her followers will experience. The Happiness Project is another example of the way in which happiness is seen as an individual responsibility and moral obligation. Rubin writes: 'Working on my happiness wouldn't just make me happier, it would boost the happiness of the people around me' (2011, 14). Although her statement sounds altruistic, as it is designed to, it is also about justifying why she thinks it is acceptable to devote a year to her own self-fulfilment and happiness.

In framing it as something that will bring greater good to those around her, she avoids the obvious criticism that she is being terribly self-indulgent in allowing herself to focus only on herself. This evasion means that others can happily turn inwards and focus on 'me' time as a means of making sure they are doing and being what they want to be. This individualistic logic not only perpetuates the notion that we are all responsible for our own happiness, but also means we are not responsible for the happiness of others. It breaks down notions of community, humanity, and solidarity and disallows inertia, dispassion, or disconnection as therapeutic possibilities. As Angela McRobbie suggests in *The Aftermath of Feminism*: 'Self-help guides, personal advisors, lifestyle coaches and gurus and all sorts of self-improvement TV programmes provide the cultural means by which individualization operates as a social process' (2009, 19).

It also leads to individuals that espouse knowing the secrets of happiness being held up as celebrity/cult figures. On Facebook, for instance, many self-healers, such as Marianne Williamson or Dr. Wayne W. Dwyer generate a substantial amout of 'likes' (Dwyer has over 600,000), which suggests a certain level of celebrity, and certainly of devotion. They usually offer daily status updates that read like spiritual mantras and generate a series of 'likes' and comments from their followers. These self-help gurus are not only seen as celebrities, but also function as 'brand' names for publishing houses and keynote lectures, which generate a significant amount of money.

Are their followers to be considered fans? One of the key differences between the people who 'like' the statuses of self-help gurus and the fans discussed in Chapter 2 is the lack of production from the former. They are *followers* as opposed to *fans* in that they follow the work, ideas, and movements of their spiritual gurus instead of creating new texts based on their work. And yet the ways in which people embrace the work of these spiritual gurus and incorporate their suggestions or practices into their own everyday life mirrors some of the behaviours of media fans.

The example of self-help on the Internet fits with Jenkins's (2006a) description of convergence outlined in Chapter 2, insofar as several forms of media are used to draw people in – advice is offered through podcasts, social media networks, websites, printed material, and DVDs. It allows people to have advice, or access to the advice, at any time. This functions as a reassuring mechanism, but also as a potent example of happiness consumerism. So, for example, people might begin the day by reading an 'affirmation' in a book or an affirmation sent by e-mail to their handheld phone. They might drive to work with a coffee mug labelled with their favourite mantra or saying. Then during the day, they might check and 'like' the statuses of their various gurus. Thanks to the Internet, the emotional wellness one might get from self-help advice is readily available and accessible, and therefore the responsibility for being happy is increasingly shifted towards the individual (and away from others who might once have been responsible).

Social media and networking plays a key role in distributing notions of happiness, in branding individuals who become 'happiness experts', and in creating opportunities for people to blog, e-mail, and interact with others about their own 'happiness projects'. But most of these 'happiness projects' are focused solely on the individual, rather than lending themselves to a sense of community. At the same time, the followers of these experts must find some sense of community in the notion that they are participating along with others – or must find a sense of solidarity with other people who attend the public lectures and talks that these self-helpers offer. But the underlying focus is still on one's *own* happiness, not on a sense of responsibility for the happiness of those around the user nor on any deeper interrogation of hyperlocal conditions that may be preventing happiness (pay, work/life balance, housing, family dysfunction, body image). In this way, the online distribution of happiness can be seen as fairly one-directional and individualistic. Although this chapter has focused on positive constructions of the self through social media such as Facebook, as well as the sending and sharing of flashmobs of happiness and a new generation of spiritual healers and self-helpers, this does not foreclose the use of online media and culture for creating global communities of care. In the next chapter, we read more closely on the subject of just how caring we can be in and about our world.

5
Emo-Techno-Ecology: Fear and Anger about Climate Change

Towards an emo-techno-ecology

In her book *A Paradise Built on Hell: The Extraordinary Communities that Arise in Disaster* (2009), Rebecca Solnit does not hold back on her anger at what she describes as the fear-mongering US news reports of gangs, marauders, looters, and rapists (read 'black', she claims) that were seen to underwrite disaster reporting about Hurricane Katrina in 2005. According to Solnit, the rescue operation became a state and civilian armed kettling to save private property rather than lives, and the criminalization of those involved in this disastrous extreme weather event (1833 confirmed dead) was produced by racist fears. Six years later, the weather-war dyad with racism as a key public sentiment continues to permeate ordinary online discussions, as this extract of a conversation posted on YouTube's *Earth Hour*, September 2011, bears out (all errors in original):

> perfect hour for niggers to break into ur home and steal shit, 1 hour doesnt do fuck all to the planet. *CryptWarrior69*
>
> @CryptWarrior69 that isnt at all what it's about, its about finding people who care about the environment to celebrate a fucking hour without technology together, together to send a message that if we fuck over this planet, we're fucking ourselves, just care a little more, is that so hard? *xdoods*
>
> @xdoods We are already fucked over anyways, I'll bet in a few decades our species will be extinct because of our own stupidity (we'll probably start using our nukes on each other at some point, leaving the Earth burnt out and radioactive and humans non existent). The Earth has been through a lot worse, turning out a few lights won't

contribute to much of anything. The character of human beings needs to change, because we only have ourselves to blame. *dchains*

Racism and conversations about race are prevalent and proliferating online from citizen journalism to massive multiplayer games (see Lisa Nakamura & Peter Chow-White's collection *Race After the Internet* 2011). Racist fear is also rife in topics that are totally unrelated to race, as the extract of dialogue above from an online climate change campaign shows.

In fact, while anger is articulated in the second posting in response to the racist fear of looting, fear and self-hate undermine action in the third comment, as blame is attributed to humanity as a lost cause in the context of crisis events in geological time. In his reading of the post-Katrina response, Brian Massumi makes reference to George Bush's 'armies of compassion', spearheaded by the National Guard, recently returned from Iraq (2011, 19). Massumi draws extreme weather and war into a discursively connected 'threat-form' of 'the suddenly irrupting, locally self-organizing, systemically self-amplifying threat of large-scale disruption' (2011, 20). War, weather, and the racist fear of looting conjoin to produce a climate of intangible threat that explains summer riots as much as summer flooding. Therefore, in terms of such a 'war climate', as Massumi terms it (2011, 20), the postings above are a very typical exchange of views on climate change.

Fear, shame, and anger find a perfect home online (distributed, uncentred, deterritorialized, networked, untroubled by broadcasting standards, censorship, ethical communication, common sense, and family viewing contexts). This is what freedom to express fear looks like, and it adds more evidence to Barry Glassner's *Culture of Fear: Why Americans Are Afraid of the Wrong Things* (2009 [1999]). It is also how ordinary affect performs the fabric (and sometimes glue) that binds and connects 'ideas, values, and objects' (Ahmed 2010, 30), as we explored in Chapters 1 and 4. More than this, as Fenton (2008) states: 'At the same time, we live increasingly under conditions of globally and systemically engendered insecurity and uncertainty, which belie the promise of assertive individuality not only for the "excluded" but for many of the "included" (242)'.

Understanding the online articulation of emotion about climate change can help us appreciate the continua of old ideas and old representations that permeate this mixed-mediation of emotion online. For the Internet, as Chris Atton argues, is not 'an unproblematic force for social change': to think so would be to ignore the old 'political and economic determinants that shape the technology' (2004, 24). Attention to these old determinants can also help us understand the pleasures that online users derive from the performance of such emotions, which may have more in common with film and television viewing than with active online global civic engagement.

That fear exists transmedially in relation to climate change, in opposition to hyperlocal articulations of regional weather extremes, suggests that we need to understand our mediated ecology along two wavelengths simultaneously: local and global emotions (the latter explored in depth in Chapter 3), or as local and global *emo-scapes*. If the global is a set of processes that connect localities (see Friedman & Friedman 2008), and transnational cultures are shaping media content (see Löffelholz 2008), we need to develop a multiperspectival approach to our 'new social geography', as Stephen Reese has termed it (2008, 241). This approach, as we shall read it in this chapter, should take into account the relationships between human beings as feeling individuals and affective bodies, as well as technologically enabled infotainment producer/consumers. In either case, people are affectively connected to their environments. Online media provide an important space for the performance of multiple constructions of climate change, both as lived and projected. In fact, climate itself is constructed differently by individuals and communities (in contrast to climatologists) and is premediated:

> Living in particular places and particular cultures, climate is constructed as a function of their experiences and memories of past weather events, and what is socially learned from previous generations. These climates may often be reified through paintings or photographs of physical markers, such as [evidence of] a flood, drought or a rare snowfall (Hulme et al. 2009, 198).

In her research on environmental issues, Kay Milton explored why some people were committed to protecting nature while others were indifferent. Rather than seeing the reason as residing only in the cultural, Milton 'became aware of the emotional character of people's connections to the world, and came to the conclusion that emotions are what link us, as individuals, to our surroundings' (2005, 25). Like Teresa Brennan in *The Transmission of Affect*, we see here affect as a 'vehicle connecting individuals to one another and [to] the environment' (2004, 19). Importantly, Milton does not limit environment to our interaction with human others; 'It can be anything with which the individual organism engages, for emotion is part of that engagement' (2005, 35). Thus, as we showed in Chapter 2 with our focus upon screening emotion, the *emo-techno-ecology* we will propose in this chapter of those in rich nations consists as much of television, radio, cinema, mobile phones, and computers as it does of family members, pets, or other animals.[1]

The extension of the domestication of urban space and the urbanization of domestic space with technology are the threads woven together to create what is one aspect of our concept of *emo-techno-ecology*. With this concept, we are not undermining Gregg and Seigworth's point that there is 'no single unwavering line' (2010a, 5), but rather, we are asserting that there is a desire to produce such a through line that connects bodies, emotions, and technologies around a notion of care and attention. At issue then in our mediated emotional ecology is how we enact climate change positions through fear and anger online. How these emotions are expressed (textually, visually, and corporeally) may well dovetail with the universals in Patrick Colm Hogan's (2009) sense of 'narrative universals' in *The Mind and Its Stories: Narrative Universals and Human Emotion,* with human emotion as patterned through narrative constants. That these 'universals' are grounded or anchored in personal and local places demonstrates that the two wavelengths of local and global emotion are being technologized. That this technologization has become routine and excessive (tweeting terror on a daily basis) compels individuals' attention back (to their) home (oikos or eco). It is in our increasingly technologized homes that emo-techno-ecology works profoundly. In the home we care, we take care, we pay attention, we watch out for humans and non-humans, and it is from the home that our attention is being captured (see Stiegler 2012b).

For Catherine Brace and Hilary Geoghegan (2011), writing in the context of human geography, climate change is encountered holistically, not just as it is understood top-down through the communication of scientific discourses, but as it is understood relationally at a local level:

> Climate change can be observed in relation to landscape but also felt, sensed, apprehended emotionally as part of the fabric of everyday life in which acceptance, denial, resignation and action co-exist as personal and social responses to the local manifestations of a global problem. (Brace & Geoghegan 2011, 284)

This emotional aspect to understanding human geography is vital, because it draws 'the body' into the individual's learning and participation in climate-change debates. Weather is, of course, felt every day, and Massumi makes the point above that so is war, when it is discursively connected to weather. Hence, it is no surprise that research is emerging on the affective dimensions of meteorology, forecasting, atmosphere, landscape, and climate, indicating that affective dimensions are critical to how we feel in daily life.[2]

In thinking about individuals and communities facing environmental challenges, we are aware that emotion and affect are built into their responses before they have even engaged with the science or posted their opinions online. Those living in areas prone to flooding may engender a 'watery sense of place' while those living in areas with mundane weather systems may be known for their minute observations of weather (see Trevor A. Harley 2003 in Strauss and Orlove's *Weather, Climate, Culture*). It is becoming clear that private individuals are turning to online media as a way of sustaining communities, networking 'care' packages, and expressing their shame and fear about environmental changes. They are also thrashing out the climate-change debate in forums such as YouTube, where discussion message posters shame and enrage each other on the causes and effects of climate change. They are critically engaging with climate change through audiovisual media created for online distribution, and they document and archive their emotional and affective responses to the environments they inhabit through geo-tagging carbon crimes. They are also spreading fear and hate.

The emo-politics of climate change

It should come as no surprise that the very concept of climate change is loaded with ideological meanings that make it ripe for the emotionalized responses we will read about later. Brace and Geoghegan (2011, 285) acknowledge 'the inconsistencies and ambiguities that stalk the phrase' and 'the assignment of cause, the attribution of blame and the patina of doubt that surround the term'. Climate change is then 'simultaneously a reality, an agenda, a problem and a context' (Brace & Geoghegan 2011, 285). Much like globalization or war, climate change has been presented as a global-scale problem affecting the whole planet, when in fact, regional, local, and personal encounters with landscapes as well as regional, local, and personal encounters with technologies inform and determine how individuals emotionally respond to this global threat.

We are not very interested here in unpacking the loadedness of 'climate change'. There is much debate about the causes and effects of changes to our local, regional, and global climates; continuing scientific developments in this area will inform those debates (see Anthony Giddens's *The Politics of Climate Change* 2011).[3] There is also a good deal of research on how local and global media cultures intermingle in the viewer's aware-ness of climate (see Szerszynski, Urry, & Myers 2000a/b, who explored ideas around the 'banal globalism' of the consumerist global citizen). Cottle and Lester's (2009) empirical research on the ubiquity of images of climate change as a 'global threat' so as to produce 'ecological citi-zenship' is informed by Ulrich Beck's point that 'tangible, simplifying symbols, in which cultural nerve fibres are touched and alarmed, here take on central political importance' (2009, 98). Mediations of climate change slot into preexisting audience empathy practices and can connect across deep time with past cultural reactions to climate (see Wolfgang Behringer's fascinating exegesis of the Little Ice Age in *A Cultural History of Climate* 2010). Beck argues that a 'globalization of emotions' is produced when people imagine themselves connected to others 'as parts of a fragmented endangered civilization and civil society characterized by the simultaneity of events and of knowledge of this simultaneity all over the world' (Beck 2006, 6, 42).

This early research lays the foundations for how online media are being discursively practiced as a form of affective mediation of global responsi-bility and care. In this chapter, we do not select one media form or one approach to online culture. Rather, we are more interested in how the term 'climate change' broadly triggers emotional responses and affective (re)actions online and how these are performed with/through online media as part of global networks in discursively produced emotions. These emotions may elide any possibility of coordinated and construc-tive political action by even well-informed and well-meaning ecolog-ical citizens. In fact, in the early findings of the *Report on the Global Citizenship and the Environment*, Szerszynski, Urry, and Myers showed that global citizenship was broadly understood as being open to other peoples, environments, and cultures rather than as having shared or universal norms in any sense. They also noted that global citizenship was conceived by respondents 'less in terms of abstract rights and duties, and more in affective terms of care and compassion' (2000b, 10).

In the policy context, recent work in this area has acknowledged the role emotions play in shaping responses to climate change. In *Communicating Climate Change to Mass Public Audiences* (2010), the Climate Change Communication Advisory Group (CCCAG) advised the UK government to understand the thorny issue of arousing emotions:

The impact of fear appeals is context- and audience-specific; for example, for those who do not yet realise the potentially 'scary' aspects of climate change, people need to first experience themselves as vulnerable to the risks in some way in order to feel moved or affected. [...] The danger is that fear can also be disempowering – producing feelings of helplessness, remoteness and lack of control. [...] Similarly, studies have shown that guilt can play a role in motivating people to take action, but can also function to stimulate defensive mechanisms against the perceived threat or challenge to one's sense of identity (as a good, moral person). http://www.pirc. info/projects/cccag/

The CCCAG does not consist of media or communication technology researchers, and the messiness of affect is clear in their paternalistic recommendation to policy makers and communicators:

> Overall, there is a need for emotionally balanced representations of the issues at hand. This will involve acknowledging the 'affective reality' of the situation, e.g., 'We know this is scary and overwhelming, but many of us feel this way and we are doing something about it'. http://www.pirc.info/projects/cccag/

It is the distribution of fear, shame, and anger that creates *emotional geographies,*[4] whereby emotions become landscapes or spaces we inhabit or move in and out of, and *geographies of emotion,* whereby the planet becomes carved up into regions/peoples that are seen to care and regions/ peoples that appear not to. A key issue that arises out of this CCCAG advice is how fear, care, and responsibility are gendered in the context of how climate change is enacted emotionally online (e.g., see YouTube's *Supermodels Take It Off for Climate Change,* 2009, with over one million views) and then how those emotions are dealt with by authorities (see www.climatecrisis.org).

If a great deal of effort is going into making citizens feel strongly about 'climate change', how is this being done and through what mechanisms? In 2010, the UK government saw two of its three advertising campaigns about climate change withdrawn ('Climate change "exaggerated" in government adverts', BBC News, 17 March 2010), because of exaggerated claims and fear mongering. The television and print advertisements mashed up fairy tales and children's storybooks with climate-change messages of human pollution, extreme weather, and the destruction of the planet for future generations. As a father reads to his daughter, the pages of the storybook become animated into a mini-disaster movie with no hero and no resolution, only the question from the daughter: 'Does it have a happy ending, Daddy?' No promise of happiness here.

Not unlike the television campaigns to raise awareness of AIDS in the 1980s, this campaign does not take the advice of the CCCAG. Rather, it domesticates climate change as fear, disaster, and vulnerability, with the future of the environment in the hands of an audience divided into those with parental responsibility (expected to care) and those in infantile positions (ignorant or incapable of caring).[5]

The adverts are couched in the domestic sphere (balancing the authoritative voice of the loving father with the sweet innocent voice of the vulnerable little girl) and produce convergence of the cherished hard copy storybook with digital animations, placing climate change action between two realms: the home and technologized space. However, the dilemma, as we later show in this chapter, in terms of online participation in environmental issues, is that gendered discourses of fear, anxiety, and hysteria can often be matched by rational, instrumentalist, and pragmatic approaches that dismiss the whole climate-change agenda as emasculating. Note that the emphasis (as in Chapter 4's use of *The Happy Planet Index*) is upon care, giving, and paying attention: all feminine attributes. Moreover, there are geographies of emotion being territorialized online in response to unsettled and unsettling debates about climate change, and these geographies are anchoring shame and empathy into specific places.

Costa Rica ranks first for greenness by *The Happy Planet Index,* because it is successful on a low resource. However, the United States should be more ashamed than Japan because of its carbon footprint to population ratio and its dismissal of the Kyoto Protocol. Denmark should not be ashamed, because it is perceived as an environmentally friendly country and hosted the Climate Change Conference in 2009. The United Kingdom should be ashamed because private e-mails from the East Anglia Research Institute were released and were used by sceptics as evidence that anthropogenic climate change may be exaggerated. The developing countries should not be ashamed because they do not have the finances to 'green' their economies.

While these geographies of shame are being carved out, so too is 'humanity' itself presented in terms of shame, not only as ordinary polluters, but also as online polluters of Internet transparency. As the Internet-based newspaper *Huffington Post* stated on 27 February 2012: 'It's a sad time for the climate. It's enough to make an iceberg melt. That's because everyone is stealing emails from everyone else. [...] There is no winner in this email war. Mother Earth and her inhabitants are the losers.'

Thus, we want to argue that the emotions around this debate affirm Stewart's work on 'ordinary affects' (presented in Chapter 1) as 'expressions of ideas or problems performed as a kind of involuntary and powerful learning and participation' (Stewart 2007, 40). It also chimes with the ongoing attention to the 'ordinary' in the work of Graeme Turner (2010), John Hartley (2009), and Ben Highmore (2010b). What is striking in the *ordinary turn* (to rephrase the notion of an *affective turn*) within cultural studies and sociology is the idea that attention to the ordinary explicitly requires acceptance of pervasiveness, because no part of contemporary life is untouched by media and cultural phenomena.

In line with the theories presented in Chapter 1, ordinary responses to climate change produces those 'structures of feelings' that can 'be funny, perturbing, or traumatic', that 'can be seen as both the pressure points of events or banalities and the trajectories that forces might take if they were to go unchecked' (Stewart 2007, 2). Ordinary affects about climate change are 'public feelings that begin and end in broad circulation'; they perform affect as public sentiment, but 'they are also the stuff that seemingly intimate lives are made of' (Stewart 2007, 2). Yet, ordinary celebrities, ordinary people, ordinary citizens, and ordinary identities make up the 'demotic turn' says Turner, and in the context of information technologies this does not necessarily lead to democracy (2010, 174). As Natalie Fenton has argued:

> Being political and enacting citizenship have become assimilated into and absorbed by the modes and contents of entertainment – personalization, dramatization, simplification, and polarization, a potentially antipolitical civic privatism of individuals. (2009, 56)

Online postings on climate change are so entertaining to read that they follow Fenton's adumbration and thus, as in the case of *Kony 2012*, may serve only to provide 'kitchen-sink' drama out of geopolitical issues.

Before we attend to the ways in which shame and anger are being enacted online, it is important to understand the mediatization of climate change within the context of emotional geographies of everyday fear that centre upon the body. We shall focus in more depth upon the production of fear around narratives of embodied terror in Chapter 6. For now, though, it is important to understand what Massumi (1993, viii) describes as '*low-level fear* – naturalized fear, ambient fear, ineradicable atmospheric fright', which has a very long history (see Massumi's edited collection *The Politics of Everyday Fear*, 1993, and Barry Richards's *Emotional Governance: Politics, Media and Terror* 2007). As we noted in Chapter 1 regarding Eric Shouse's use of Massumi to think about feelings as personal, emotions as social, and affect as prepersonal (Shouse 2005), we can see here a premediated return to the body. It also has a purpose in that 'the materiality of the body' is 'the ultimate object of technologies of fear, understood as apparatuses of power aimed at carving into the flesh habits, predispositions, and associated emotions – in particular, hatred – conducive to setting social boundaries, to erecting and preserving hierarchies, to the perpetuation of domination' (Massumi 1993, viii). In the case of climate change, fear is reproduced at an ecological level with human self-destruction performed through media representations on an everyday basis as a form of traumatic entertainment.

In what follows, we carve out just how climate fear has been and continues to be mediatized as an everyday spectacle, undermining attempts at global campaigns and thus ensuring cognitive dissonance. In much the same way the graphic images of disease as health warnings on cigarette packets may be proven to be initially shocking or fear-inducing, everyday emotional engagement with climate fear images may have no impact on risk-takers surrounded by a multitude of everyday fears and dangers in their emo-techno-ecology.

Emotional geographies: climate fear

In their introduction to the collection *Geography and Memory* (2012), Jones and Garde-Hansen draw together the new conceptual and empirical emphases upon performative and embodied practices of everyday life through their attention to the work of Nigel Thrift (1999, 2004a, 2004b, 2008). As noted in Chapter 3 of our present book, Thrift's early ideas on globalization (1992) have developed into an application of affect within cultural geography that has been very important for resituating global concerns as not simply abstractly social-constructionist. Rather, 'care, risk, fear, responsibility, contentment, self-control, anger, shame, desire and hate' come to reemphasize 'affective personhood' and to address 'local, national and global calls for individual and connected practices that are creative, sustainable, open, shared' (Jones & Garde-Hansen 2012, 5). Thus, emotional geographies should be understood as, first and foremost, the affective dimensions of home, space, place, landscape, area, environment, and atmosphere as a priori experiences that move us, and that we move in and through. This is another return to the body, but it is not devoid of mediation.

For communities to come to terms with grief, loss, and fear as a result of extreme weather events (floods, heat waves, tsunamis, hurricanes) in the places they live requires a rethinking of the discourse of sustainability that was couched solely in the sciences in order to include the mediatization of emotional and human security in risky environments (see Roeser's edited collection *Emotions and Risky Technologies* 2010).[6] This happens vertically through intergenerational communication (oral histories, newspaper archives, family narratives/albums, museums) and horizontally through 'event' representations (television news reports, blogs, Flickr photos, and word of mouth). Just as the relationship between media and war has been so thoroughly scrutinized by academics (Baudrillard 1995 [1991]; Dayan & Katz 1992; Maltby & Keeble 2007; Hoskins 2004, Hoskins and O'Loughlin 2010), so too the mediatization of climate change in mixed-media ecology needs special attention. Security and resilience is possible when we understand the everyday emotions produced around ordinary spaces and places and then understand how 'climate change' or extreme weather is made highly emotional in those contexts. Hence, we should first recognize that representation of an abstract future risk has a long history within media history and popular culture. Sociologist Anthony Giddens argues in *The Politics of Climate Change* (2011):

> Giddens' paradox holds. For most of the time and the majority of citizens, climate change is a back-of-the-mind issue, even if it is a source of worry. It will stay that way unless its consequences become visible and immediate. In the meantime, no strategy is likely to work which concentrates solely on provoking fear and anxiety. (2011, 108)

What he misses in his primary focus upon politics and the Green movement is how emotion and affect operate around climate change in the mediatized discourses, forms, and practices that make up our emo-techno-ecology. Thus, while it is less 'back-of-the-mind' (cognitive) and more felt (affective), this does not mean the latter should be ignored or played down. This would be to miss the pleasure audiences receive (perhaps even need) from the mediation of tragic events (as noted in Chapter 2) – that is, the promise of happiness in and from the tragic content. The mediatization of fear and anxiety (necessary or unnecessary) has been developed through a variety of media formats in the last decades, particularly film.

While Giddens (quite rightly) points to the weak communication of science by journalists or by a government's scare-mongering tactics as too negative (see the advert mentioned above), he does not cover in any real depth the affective mediation (film, television, photography, journalism, and online media) that enacts emotional geographies that are mapped by tragic pleasure. There exist *strong ties* between audiences and jeopardy/impending doom that structures public sentiment, as the postings at the beginning of this chapter bear out, from narrative cinema (*The Day After Tomorrow* 2004, directed by Roland Emmerich), to documentary film (*An Inconvenient Truth* 2006, directed by Davis Guggenheim), to photos of polar bears on melting ice (simply search 'climate change' in Google Images), to the journalistic norms that have powerfully shaped how climate change is (mis)represented in US mass media (print and television). As we saw in Chapter 2, the 'tragic structure of feeling' (Ang 1985) that underlines the viewers' appreciation of the text is important for mediating any sense of pleasure; climate-change narratives (from fictional to factual) offer just the emotional ups and downs that audiences desire and expect. We should not be surprised then to read time and again the online-posted refrain 'We're all doomed anyway', with its explicit acceptance of future disaster and self-hate that implies human penance. In many ways, this total annihilation of the human body from the Earth's ecological system is a narrative underscored by Platonic precepts of the unreality of the material world versus the true form of universal truths accessed by the soul and intellect. This sense of unreality made real and felt by cinematic representations has been enjoyed and distrusted by audiences for decades. As Maria Bortoluzzi argues in '*An Inconvenient Truth*: Multimodal Emotions in Identity Construction':

> In the case of a real threat for humanity, the interdiscursivity of fiction used to enhance the impact of promotional communication on wide audiences might have both the positive effect of attracting the viewer and conveying to large audiences the alarming message put across by the film, as well as the effect of *déjà vu* and fiction. (2009, 157)

Rightly, Giddens's paradox states that climate change appears to people as neither visible nor imminent, so they do not take action; or, as Bernard Stiegler would argue, the 'hyper-attention' of the disaster narrative disaffects and destroys the ability to pay attention and care (2008). It is only when the threat is real that action is taken and by then it is too late, with only a chink of hope that it might not be. This is the paradox at the heart of the environmental disaster movies *2012* (2009), *Sunshine* (2007), *Armageddon* (1998), *Deep Impact* (1998), *Earthquake* (1974), and *The Day the Earth Caught Fire* (1961) for example. Giddens's reproduction of his own paradox in the context of the politics of climate change tells us more than anything that if the debate creates heightened emotions in the audience, it will be engaged with (as we identified in Chapter 2) for the bodily pleasure this brings. If we put the emotional or affective relationship to the climate-change text at centre stage (rather than either ignoring or manipulating it), we can see just how emotional geographies are mediated and paradoxically enjoyed at the expense of discourses seeking to explain 'universal truths' about our Earth and its climates.

From the perspective of compassion, there is the positioning of celebrities as centres of 'empathy' that create peripheries of concern around environmental issues (Angelina Jolie, Bono, Al Gore, Sting, Leonardo DiCaprio, Cate Blanchett, to name but a few). In the context of environmental narratives, Hollywood celebrities (many of whom may have acted out Giddens's paradox on screen, to the delight of audiences) slip seamlessly into the fear-arousing and empathic appeals of mediations of risk. These celebrities (mostly Western, mostly from the United States) function, as Carolyn Calloway-Thomas shows us in *Empathy in the Global World: An Intercultural Perspective* (2010), as empathy creators (read *emotion agents*) who distribute credibility to the cause. This is not only because of the global attention they garner. Henry Jenkins's work on fan cultures (as noted in Chapter 2) has shown this is because celebrities create emotional geographies around themselves, so that audiences not only empathise with them as human beings, but also feel intimately (beyond empathy) what the celebrity feels. Audiences may also leave the celebrity to do the heroic work on their behalf, as they are used to doing through cinema.

Misha Kavka argues, with regard to television (as noted in Chapter 2), that the 'affective power of the mediated image' is in its 'ability to bring out feelings where the real world may leave us cold' (2008, 1). Narratives of fear and anxiety may be just what are needed in the face of cold, scientific, and undramatic facts of climate change. The narratives encompass the fear of catastrophe as everyday, but this fear is invisible, and this invisibility is what marks it out as very close to our fears about being online. Hence, Massumi has stated in his 'Introduction to Fear':

> What society looks toward is no longer a return to the promised land but a general disaster that is already upon us, woven into the fabric of day-to-day life. The content of the disaster is unimportant. [...] In its most compelling and characteristic incarnations, the now unspecified enemy is infinite. Infinitely small or infinitely large: viral or environmental. [...] In the infinity of its here-and-to-come, it is elsewhere, *by nature*. It is humanly ungraspable. It exists in a different dimension of space from the human 'here,' and in a different dimension of time [...]. In a word, the enemy is the virtual. (Massumi 1993, 11)

Vitally, Massumi focuses upon the body as a 'fright site' (1993, vii), and on the fear as 'virtual'. Thus, in the context of emotion online, climate fear is shot through with mysterious affects that are made ordinary: invisible crowd technologies, arbitrary geological time, and the alien universe become domesticated and pathologized. Such fears and anxieties are enacted in the most banal of online spaces. The researcher of online emotion about climate change can trawl thousands of websites, online newspapers, blogs, and homemade videos on YouTube for small selections of discussion and interaction about climate change (between 20–100 postings). However, the most productive online discussions revolve around 'old media' campaigns, so we would like to turn to how cinemagoers negotiate the climate change debate online.

An inconvenient emotion of active disengagement

Qualitatively more distinct online commentary about mediations of climate change can be located on the Internet Movie Database (IMDb)[7] of the film *An Inconvenient Truth* (2006), directed by Davis Guggenheim and produced by Participant Productions. In fact, film and television review cultures online open up a public sphere for deeper political engagement than most news sites. There is much research to be done on product review comments: their content, emotional register, intellectualism, and the way readers use them in making decisions and engaging in the contextual debates the products rest in.[8] In the case of this climate-change film, it had 497 user reviews on IMDb (far less than the 1 per cent rule) as of early 2012 and was rated 7.7/10 by 42,077 users. Of these reviews, 313 loved the film while 143 hated it; 100 reviews were posted by 'prolific authors' (20 per cent of user reviews by those who have posted over 100 reviews). Like all film review sites, IMDb functions as a platform for reviewers to detail likes and dislikes. In online review cultures, the verb *to like* has transmogrified into a noun; 'likes' are now both quantifiable (e.g., this company, event, product, film, book, friend, blog post, comment has 100 'likes') and are coveted by commerce. We explored the positivity of 'liking' in Chapter 4, but here it is interesting to note that danah boyd, a key researcher of social media *homophily* (which is 'liking' and friending those who we 'like' and 'friend') has begun to explore the contribution of social media to the production of a culture of fear as an instrument of an *attention economy*.[9]

In the six years since the release of the film *An Inconvenient Truth* and the archiving of reviews, the emotional engagement in the reviews has shifted considerably. The 2009 and 2011 leaking of climate research e-mails, the world economic downturn, shifts in American politics, and the increase in online interest groups have produced a clearer division between 'believers' and 'sceptics'. The reviews archive and hold in tension those who are seen to 'trust' Al Gore and 'care' about the planet and those who hate Al Gore and disbelieve climate-change science. For the non-US audience member, the affective connection between climate, politics, and the film is thin or weak, but for people in the United States it is thick or strong. Torn between them, the ordinary film review reader is placed in a position of impotent dispassion toward the Americanization of the debate and toward climate-change politics as whole when mediated through this film.

The early IMDb reviews on *An Inconvenient Truth* clearly note the emotional engagement of the film. Here from a UK viewer:

> It's an impressive science lesson, but if that doesn't sound exciting enough to get you out of your armchair and along to your multiplex on a Saturday night, maybe look at it from a different angle. Will it inspire you? Will it move you? Will it give you something to discuss as you come out of the cinema? And will it give the thrill of emotion that you feel you deserve, having coughed up the price of an admission ticket? The answer to all those questions is, probably yes. (IMDb Author: Chris Docker from Scotland, 15 September 2006)

Many of these reviews either mention 'fear' in the post title or in the body of the text. Whereas in early posts (2006–2008) fear is articulated in the context of how the film is a real-life disaster movie showing climate change to be a real and present danger, the later posts (more inflected with scepticism) pose fear in another light:

> This film scares me because it so blatantly uses emotion rather than science to lead the viewer into believing in AGW [anthropogenic global warming] and yet most of the world somehow believed it, and even in light of recent evidence of how skewed the information was, people still refuse to revisit their opinion on the matter, especially amongst the educational establishments where they force kids to watch it. (IMDb Author JCR-4 from Rome. 15 February 2011)

Cutting across believers and sceptics is fear: fear of impending doom and the guilt and shame associated with mass consumption, as well as the fear of control by an elite group of emotion agents (filmmakers, governments, and liberals) who produce shame and anxiety in order to socially control and capitalize. Most of the reviews date from within a year of the release of the film (it was released 28 May 2006 in the United States). Between the date of the first review, posted on 16 April 2006, and 28 May 2007 there were 387 comments. We analysed the chronologic and geographic data provided by the posters (making the assumption that this was authentic) to produce the following insights into geographies of emotion being enacted online (see Table 5.1).

Notably, before 2009 (the year of the Copenhagen Accord and the e-mail leak scandal) over 54 per cent of posters were from North America and they 'trusted' both Al Gore and the theory of anthropogenic climate change; 18 percent of 'believers' were from outside North America. They trusted the film so much that many posts designated the film a 'must see', a 'wake-up call' or a 'truth'. It is no surprise that the comments are dominated by North Americans. Many of the comments from Europeans define the film as more about and for the United States than for themselves. It is notable that 'rich' countries are mostly represented here. While online reviews from Africa, India, Asia, South America, and the Middle East are in the minority, those posters are also firm 'believers' prior to 2009. The region of the world with highest scepticism ratio (2.5:1) is Europe. Comments from Europe (mostly from the United Kingdom, Ireland, France, and the Netherlands) were anti-American in their scepticism and were deeply critical of the documentary in terms of its structure, style, and disregard of the genre. They also were fearful of it as propaganda.

Table 5.1 Comments on *An Inconvenient Truth* at Imdb.com. From the 497 comments on *An Inconvenient Truth* (film released 2006) at IMDb.com we were able to see the ratio of 'trust' in the documentary versus 'distrust' before/after 2009

Area	Believers (pre-2009)	Sceptics (pre-2009)	Ratio believers to sceptics pre-2009	Believers (post-2009)	Sceptics (post-2009)	Ratio believers to sceptics post-2009
N America	270	53	5:1	15	11	1.3:1
S America	6	–	–	–	–	–
Europe	47	19	2.5:1	1	5	1:5
India/Asia	10	–	–	1	–	–
Africa	4	1	4:1	–	–	–
Australia	18	2	9:1	2	1	2:1
Middle East	1	–	–	–	–	–
Not stated	4	4	1:1	2	2	1:1

The ratio of North American 'believers' to 'sceptics' until 2009 is approximately 5:1. However, after 2009 this changes. While the quantity of postings has fallen off due to the film's having been released some time earlier, the ratio of North American and European 'believers' to 'sceptics' has altered dramatically, with the latter having reversed.

This is only a snapshot of a shift in the ordinary debates of what seem to be ordinary reviewers of a climate-change film over a fairly short period of time. It is, of course, not possible to extrapolate beyond these postings or to prove definitively that later postings act homophilically by not disrupting or disputing the emerging consensus. However, there are two emotions that permeate most if not all of the postings: fear and shame. In many postings, the two are wrapped together, and specific reference is made to the geographic context of viewing. For example,

One need not spend hours searching the Internet to come to grasp the subject matter of global warning. [...] I saw the film in Owensboro, Kentucky, with my wife on the opening Saturday night. Owensboro is Kentucky's third-largest city. The parking lot at the multiplex was filled to capacity. I'd never seen such a collection of trophy SUV's and pick up trucks in my life. [...] What film did all those people with the gas guzzlers go to see? I can't imagine. [...] The film was scary and probably close to 100 percent accurate in its predictions of gloom if huge changes in human behavior are not undertaken immediately. Even scarier to me is the fact that my wife and I were the only ones in the theater tonight. (posted 24 June 2006 by nbineurology)

It is wrong to assume that online messages, reviews, and posts are devoid of a sense of place and time. It is also wrong to dismiss them as dispassionate, apathetic, banal, or devoid of intellectual critique. Although much of online discussion/debate is circulated in topic-focused, corporate-owned, or personally owned domains, review comments on IMDb, Amazon, or TripAdvisor, for example, provide a certain freedom for ordinary commentary (notwithstanding moderation).

In fact, our research has shown that with increasing frequency those contributing to such discussions and reviews anchor their online presence to a specific time and place in order to materialize an emotional geography. Identity, place, and becoming are key dynamics that permeate our emo-techno-ecology and position differentiated online interactions. What is clear is that regardless of these geographies, we need to pay attention to what people are saying online. This is not idle chatter to be tuned in and out of; rather, we should be the attentive lurkers and be attentive to lurkers that have received so little attention in scholarship on the Internet due to the focus upon the expression of voice (see Crawford 2009a) or on the creative acts of fans. With this in mind, if fear has a long-mediatized social and cultural history that disaffects citizens from caring about the 'environment', how is shame being technologically mobilized to create action?

Geographies of emotion: geo-shaming

There are localized uses of online media to shame individuals and organizations in the name of climate change. As the posting from IMDb, quoted above, shows, the poster draws attention to his geographic location, the car park at the multiplex full of SUVs, and the 'reality' of media consumption that surrounds his/her viewing of the film. Real computerized geo-tagging and mapping have now replaced this *textual geo-tagging* by the film reviewer, so individuals have the tools to witness and document shameful acts against the environment with the power to broadcast them online. For example, in the United Kingdom, the National Union of Students' Snap It Off campaign, in which photographs taken by students of over-lit university campuses or of lights left on in empty rooms were uploaded to a website and the named university was shamed into resolving the matter. Therefore, it is important to understand how global empathy, compassion, and care are being collectively produced, using pervasive computing along horizontal and vertical axes.

Like the UK's Snap It Off campaign, the World Wildlife Fund's (WWF's) Earth Hour produces a larger but equally effective transregional community that seeks to shame the world into acting (for one hour) to save energy. Both examples use online media and mobile networking to perform emotions around climate change. In what follows, we analyse the emotional debates that rage around Earth Hour. WWF's annual *Save the Planet for 60 Minutes* Earth Hour video campaign is archived on YouTube and produced 4,762 comments in 2009; 1,956 comments in 2010; and 13,051 comments in 2011. Earth Hour and its postings on YouTube respond to the climate-change debate with a 'global' switching off of lights for one hour every year in major cities worldwide. This is a global flashmob (see Chapter 4 for definitions of flashmobs), created and networked through the Internet, in which 'the Earth' is collectively 'celebrated for one day per year'. Each major city has its own 'Earth Hour' in its own time slot. The campaign, begun in Sydney in 2007, defines the event as having 'grown into a global symbol of hope and movement for change' with '128 countries across every continent coming together to celebrate an unambiguous commitment to the one thing that unites us all – the planet' (*Earth Hour* 2011 on YouTube). It is a response to the critique of *political slacktivism*, but it is mired in a *feel-good-factor* therapeutic approach to climate-change politics.

The Internet plays the most significant part in this campaign for, 'with the power of social networks behind the Earth Hour message, we hope to attract even more participation so we can build a truly global community committed to creating a more sustainable planet' (www.earthhour. org). The switching off of lights across major cities has a visual impact, and the production of annual promotional videos for YouTube (as well as for other platforms) ensures that the message is engaging and emotionally charged. Scenes of many major cities plunged into darkness are edited together with footage of people from different countries lighting candles. In the 2010 video, Coldplay's song 'Fix You' provides the soundtrack, while numerous black screens with text are edited to display statistical evidence of the impact of Earth Hour as a global movement. We are moved, or at least we are meant to be, in the same way that *Kony 2012* is meant to move us, and thus it becomes symbolic rather than political. The music, the visuals, and the narrative work together to perform an affective plea.

YouTube provides a vital online public sphere for the articulation of cross-cultural views and socially un/acceptable discourses about audio/visual images. When we focus upon the 2011 Earth Hour official video (with 1,683,226 views, 19,044 likes, 1,187 dislikes, and 13,051 comments at the time of writing), we find a three-minute film that espouses a narrative of universality, in which individuality is replaced by global collectivity; it is addressed to you personally: 'You don't need to be an expert', states the opening voice-over, 'You just need to be you and do your part'. While images of individuals and mass groups are edited together, so too are images and footage of different locations around the world; the voice-over defines the event as 'the biggest grassroots environmental movement in history'. A variety of presenters, speaking different languages, are drawn together by the narrative, which announces that 'people of the world are speaking with an unmistakable message: that this is the time and action must come'. Footage that shows numerous important buildings around the world shutting off their lights is juxtaposed with flashmobs, crowds with candles, and celebrations in the street. The video reiterates collective emotion through archiving and mashing up the previous year's footage, and again an emotional song is used as the soundtrack: Temper Trap's 'Sweet Disposition' (2011), with the bridge refrain: 'A moment, a love, a dream, a laugh/A kiss, a cry, our rights, our wrongs'. It is worth emphasizing that we found it impossible to locate academic research that had calculated the levels of electricity saved by Earth Hour across the world, compared to typical consumption. Nor were we able to find opinion leaders that reflected upon the levels of energy needed to power the social networks that required Earth Hour to be globally coordinated each year.

So far, so 'old-media' campaign, and so very similar to other well-financed awareness-raising videos, such as *Kony 2012*. However, the 'event' is controversial and is charged with online emotional responses that encapsulate the public debates raging in the early twenty-first century around climate change. Early research on text-based computer-mediated communication in the early 1990s showed that lack of consensus and polarization on issues of controversy were common, because users found it hard to tell how others were really feeling (see Lee Sproull and Sara Kiesler's *Connections: New Ways of Working in the Networked Organization* 1991), thus challenging the idea of collectivity. Yet the intention to create an emotional collective on a global issue through a personalized media campaign is ideal for the kind of webometric analysis undertaken by Mike Thelwall of the Statistical Cybermetrics Research Group (webometrics.wlv. ac.uk), who is also part of the CyberEmotions consortium (2009–2013).

From a data-mining perspective, the work of Thelwall could be applied to the 13,051 comments. Thelwall et al. have produced webometric analyses of public sentiment in social web texts, with case studies based on MySpace (2010), Twitter (2011), and YouTube (2012). These consist of visualized diagrams produced by their free-to-download web analysis software, which readily display the communication bonds, directions, and frequency of comments. In terms of YouTube, Thelwall, Sud, and Vis (2012) provide benchmarks against which research on the comments can be compared. Thelwall, Sud, and Vis's research showed that 'YouTube comments are predominantly short, with a median of 58 out of a possible 500 characters (about 11 words). This suggests that comments are deliberately kept short, rather than being constrained to be short'. More importantly, benchmark sentiments were established with this quantitative method:

> Although negative sentiment was uncommon, it was more prevalent in comments for videos attracting many comments [...] conversely, positive sentiment was disproportionately common in videos attracting few comments. Thus, it seems that negativity can drive commenting – perhaps through long-running acrimonious comment-based discussions. (Thelwall et al. 2012, 625)

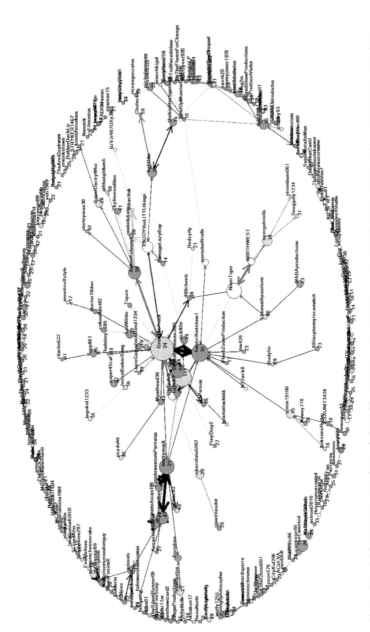

Figure 5.1 Webometric snapshot of the 580 posters commenting on the Earth Hour 2011 video provided by Professor Mike Thelwall of the Statistical Cybermetrics Research Group, University of Wolverhampton, UK. We are very grateful to Mike Thelwall for offering this statistical insight

More notable from their analysis of videos that produced 999+ comments is that these topics show how audiences use media to support personal goals, and that YouTube does host 'genuine audience discussions' and functions as 'a significant public space' for 'engaging in debate and exchanging opinions' (Thelwall et al. 2012, 619).

In 2012, the authors presented to Mike Thelwall the 13,051 comments posted to Earth Hour 2011; he quickly produced a webometric snapshot (see Figure 5.1) and returned it to the authors. This showed us immediately that the comments came from 580 posters (average 22.5 comments per poster).

Figiure 5.1 provides a network analysis diagram to illustrate the strength of interlinking between the posters; we can easily visualize that the vast majority of comments posted are one-offs (see the periphery). The only denser two-way communication occurs between a few pairs of posters (see the middle and thicker arrows). This image is a diagrammatic snapshot of a public space that allows us to quickly select the key posters engaged in dialogue (for example 'mattymuck', 'pyramidhead156', 'UltimateAsian199', 'GrowTheTruth', 'AntonKolesnyk', 'NinerTiger', 'NORTHWEST', 'lispokill' 'Stickittotheman7891', and 'franticflinstone1'). This minority of posters are emotionally engaged in the climate-change debate; no doubt we would find that they post in other online spaces too if we search their handles elsewhere. They unintentionally create a temporary public sphere (see William Outhwaite's 1996 *The Habermas Reader* for explorations of the concept of public sphere) in the comments for Earth Hour 2011. A webometric analysis is unlikely to delve much deeper than revealing that public sentiment in the opinion-exchange phase is expressed by a minority and is largely driven by negativity (in line with Thelwall et al.'s benchmarks for other YouTube postings). A more detailed textual analysis may well accord with Judith Donath's (1999) observations regarding identity and trust online (the use of flaming and trolling to assert dominance or evoke free speech). However, Earth Hour 2011 is not a community but an open platform upon which anyone can speak on any unrelated topic, or off topic completely. Thus, it functions as a mixed mediation of affect.

In the following exchange on 20 April 2011 between two posters, it is clear that they are creating denser texts of antagonist dialogue in order to thrash out their interpretations of climate science (all written errors are as quoted):

> @*UltimateAsian199* yo gay wad are you mental. A volcano eruption causes more pollution-CO2 than all of our fossil fuels burning in the

air combined for every year. Anyway without Co2 in_ air we would die Die you fuking liberal pig. You are just a gay freaking hippy. *pyramidhead156*

@pyramidhead156 Volcanoes emit around 100,000,000 tonnes of CO2 a year. Compare that to man-made emissions of CO2 which comes to about 10,000,000,000 tonnes of CO2 per year. So volcanoes emit around 1/100th of CO2 that we do and are therefore insignificant in terms of global warming. Please, do your research before_ using an ignorant statement. A little CO2 is beneficial for plants to convert the molecules to O2, which humans breathe in. Yet too much can kill us all. Please, use a legit argument. *UltimateAsian199*

@UltimateAsian199 were are u _ getting this false infotmation. *pyramidhead156*

@pyramidhead156 this information is offered everywhere bud; encyclopedias, online resources, etc. If you think I'm_ lying, because apparently I'm a "liberal" willing to save the human planet, then check it out yourself. Think before you speak; words become actions bud. Lets not get ahead of ourselves. UltimateAsian199

@UltimateAsian199 I will stop if you_ fuking stop fightying. *pyramidhead156*

@pyramidhead156 I'm not fighting; just proving my own thoughts. You questioned my beliefs, which are important within my life, and countered with my philosophy. You don't_ have to believe it, but don't go around raving others about their mindset. Those looking for trouble, receive trouble. *UltimateAsian199*

@UltimateAsian199 wth are you even talking about! I dont fight with a keyboard..............…. your freaking awkward.............…..
.. ...you are no phylosopher at age 15..... i study are solar system and stars which yo idea is_ nonsense. btw im 19 kid you live in what Asia I live in Tamriel. *pyramidhead156*

@pyramidhead156 You said, and I quote, "I will stop if you fuking stop fightying". So therefore, you claimed this conversation as a "fight" and told me to "stop". I'm no *philosopher, but I do have good intentions for the benefit of the general public. I never claimed to be a philosopher, nor_ do I intend to become one. Stop using arguments with no evidence to support your statements. Opinions only become facts with proof. *UltimateAsian199*

What is striking about this exchange is the differentiated emotional and social register of the two posters (who are both anonymized and anonymous to each other). On the surface we could dismiss this as trolling and the feeding of a troll. However, trolling is far more innocent than this, contrary to popular media representations. Trolls ordinarily have a history of laying down bait for newbies to bite, but in this case there are no newbies. It would be better to define it as flaming, but again the posts (while hateful) are reasonably knowledgeable with the intention being to argue (or fight, as they term it) each for his own cause. This is Massumi's weather-war dyad textualized as increasingly emotional writing (displayed through increasingly ungrammatical nonsense and hyper punctuation) alongside a determination to appear rational (through grammatical correctness and incorporation of the other's position).

Certain words suggest they believe each other to be relatively young males ('bud', 'gay wad'), and national identity seems American in the case of *pyramidhead156* who claims he is 19 years old and lives in Tamriel (this is a fictional continent in the action role-playing open-world video game *The Elder Scrolls* [1994–present]) and later he wants to know 'why do we have snow in very hot areas such as the united states explain that'. Such simplistic questions do in fact represent the kinds of questions that ordinary people ask climate scientists. The altercation between the two posters is entertaining and informative. Perhaps this is still a troll, but then all the users are too digitally literate to be hooked by the bait. The reader gets a sense of knowledgeable passion being conveyed by both parties with a self-reflexive recognition that this emotional communication is taking place online in a mixed media world ('I don't fight with a keyboard......your [sic] freaking awkward'). However, they are not examples that shore up the notion of online collective emotion. Rather it seems clear from searching for their profile handles (and their likes, playlists, uploads, and comments) outside of Earth Hour 2011 that while they are drawn to each other through common registers of place, age, and gender, they convey aggressively divergent opinions on climate change.

If we were to simply extract the negativity from the exchange by a statistical method, we might dismiss these messages as immature and meaningless flaming or bashing (hostile and insulting interaction by Internet users). Likewise, if we were to assume that the thousands of one-off postings mapped around the periphery of the debate are statistically positive, we might miss that many of these one-off comments are asking what the soundtrack to the video is, presumably because they like it and want to purchase it. (This would, ironically, make climate-change media content a consumer lifestyle choice rather than a politically activating campaign.) We can see that *pyramidhead156* uses his anonymity to insult *UltimateAsian199* in terms of repeated expletives, his perceived national identity ('you live in what Asia'), his sexuality ('gay wad', 'You are just a gay freaking hippy') and his politics ('Die you fuking liberal pig'). His use of language suggests he is young, male, North American, conservative in politics and possibly religious. However, a flame war does not ensue and *UltimateAsian199* responds with considered and well-meaning information designed to enlighten *pyramidhead156*. This is because YouTube is not a safe space that has to be maintained as safe. All users know and accept it is not moderated and there is no higher authority to appeal to. There is no need to maintain netiquette as per Susan Herring et al.'s (2002) research into managing trolling in a feminist forum. Thus, *pyramidhead156* is not without knowledge, and the debate continues when they are joined by *mattymuck*, who attacks *pyramidhead156*'s spelling and belief in God (an entertaining interjection for the reader) and increases the level of knowledgeable information on carbon and isotopes. While *mattymuck* explains that North America's proximity to the sun during winter is 'due to our orbit, our "perihelion"', *pyramidhead156* disappears with '....dear Lord u talk nonsense nonSense aklshfdslahfklasdifiaselj'.

Interestingly, *pyramidhead156* does not really disappear at all (neither do any of the other contributors) and this is what 'sentiment analysis' of Earth Hour 2011 could miss. *pyramidhead156* is all over the Internet, as are the others (in forums, on review sites, on blogs, channels, and social networks). A Google search of his handle confirms that he is now (at the time of writing) 20 years old, North American, and an avid online gamer. To *pyramidhead156*, being emotional online is context specific; he is fully aware that living in a mixed-media environment means mediating emotion in terms of modularity. Whether he is trolling video forums, stealing videos from others and uploading them as his own, insulting posters on reviews of new games, or excitedly waiting for Marvel to release new material, *pyramidhead156* represents a mediated mix of modulated sentiments depending on forum, context, content being debated, and the online behaviours of those he is commenting with. While a pattern of online behaviour can be discerned when we take the time to qualitatively track *pyramidhead156*'s sentiment, just as troll hunters hunt trolls[10] and present dossiers of evidence to law enforcement agencies, we have to acknowledge that such 'folk devils', as we will define them in the next chapter, cannot be simplified as one-dimensional just because they are using text-based CMC to perform emotions.

This is important when analysing how online debates rage on key global issues, because we either create the spaces for debates to rage and users to bash and flame or shut down such dissension because our assumption is that such spaces should be collective/community driven for the benefit of the global campaign. It is no surprise to us that the *Kony 2012* video was released on YouTube with a disabled comments system. Not in the spirit of YouTube interactivity, *Kony2012* sought an old-media economy model to disseminate the video through a new-media platform so as to disallow the *pyramidhead156*s from bashing the video. What *pyramidhead156* achieves in the context of Earth Hour 2011 is a critical questioning, and his responses are provocative so that the readers learn something about climate science that they did not know before (even if it is simply a new word like *perihelion*) in an entertaining way. In the introduction to this book, we noted that danah boyd has argued that 'social technology support[s] homophily [birds of a feather flock together] in a new way' such that people extend their communities into online worlds, seek out opinions like their own, and 'find social support and validation' (2005, 201). On YouTube, we can observe these homophilic communities emotionally engaged in diverse and heterophilic ways.

Read between the lines of Earth Hour 2011 and we find that 'differences can be seen amidst similarities' (2005, 201). While the video campaign seeks to unite people toward a common goal through a coordinated 60-minute action once every year, the comments attached reveal quite the opposite. YouTube archives a long running, often abusive, international, divisive argument that is fuelled by negative emotions of hatred and anger expressed as racism, homophobia, partisan politics, and antireligious sentiment. This ongoing spectacular and at times entertaining argument is produced by ordinary people. At the same time, it provides a space for love, care, shame, and self-hate to be expressed. It is perhaps in these comments systems that we witness antihomophily in practice, which fundamentally explains why such global awareness campaigns often dilute online-solicited action. As we noted in the introduction to this book, the bystander effect can be seen in operation here. The more an online-mediated campaign creates emotional awareness of a tragic event or situation, the less likely it is that consensus and action will result. As King et al. (2008) used *Second Life* to test the bystander effect, finding that users defer, in a Foucauldian sense, to an invisible higher power, so too do many comments tacitly refer to others as responsible for causing and/or solving the 'climate-change' problem. Governments, previous generations, God, Mother Nature, Al Gore, the West, and the Earth itself are named and shamed, but rarely does the individual consumer accept full responsibility. Our close reading of the mediation of mainstream online climate-change activism finds it is deeply connected to a continuum of old-media campaigns that seek to broadcast a single message. The Internet is being used in the same way that film, television, and popular music have been used: to raise global awareness and to mobilize action. The ordinary consumer (rooted in a specific time and place) presents an emotional response to the fear and shame that does not shore up the discourses of collectivity and creativity that globalized media campaigns seek to harness. Therefore, it is little wonder that such campaigns may have limited resonance beyond that one hour per year.

6
The Hate and Shame of Women's Bodies Online

Getting emotional about *nudz*

Beverley Skeggs (2001) has argued that women (and especially working-class women) use femininity and the female body as a form of cultural capital. Without the ability to gain capital in other arenas, their bodies and their appearance are their main resource. From a feminist perspective, this goes some way towards explaining the predominance of a culture of consumption around the aesthetics of female body parts, from body modifications and the cosmeceutical industry to the transmediation of the porn aesthetic into the mainstream televising of young working-class women in the United Kingdom (*The Only Way Is Essex*, Channel 4, UK) and women's bodies online (Rate My Vajazzle). Even the popular (non-working-class) feminist Naomi Wolf (2012), in reclaiming the term of shame *vagina* for her recent book *Vagina: A New Biography* (2012), has found new markets in which to accrue cultural capital. On the one hand, her book has joined the trend to remarket this female body part as no longer shameful/hateful. On the other hand, it has repoliticized the biology of the vagina as transcendental (with a nod to William James). That she incites notions of the Goddess, the female soul, and sexual healing alongside neuroscience as a solution to the feeling of being demeaned for writing about the vagina demonstrates (as we showed in Chapter 4) the new discourse of emotional empowerment that mixes science with spirituality. Wolf's book, a classic personal-is-political approach to the female body, is one that revolves around affect and dealing with her guttural responses to how she feels about her vagina and its functions in the context of history, culture, science, religion, and an increasingly open, misogynistic culture. In this chapter, we explore how that context exists online, in a mixed-media exchange of ordinary women's sexuality and bodies as shamefully visible and shareable *nudz*:

> *Nudz* short for (or code for) Nudez – getting nude pictures off a girl online.
>
> *Josh: "Guess what?"*
>
> *Greg: "Yeah?"*
>
> *Josh: "I totally scored Nudz from that girl I was Skyping last night"*
>
> *Greg: "Awesome! Come on bro', sharing is caring!"*
>
> (definition by by Peruvian Flute Band on
> The *Urban Dictionary* website, 20 November 2011)

Alongside the increasing emphasis upon the importance of online self-portraiture of women's breasts and images of ordinary sexuality (see Schwarz 2010a/b/c) there has also been a rise in friendship photography (see Schwarz 2009; Garde-Hansen forthcoming), celebrity practice online (see Marwick & boyd 2011a), increased audience management (see Marwick & boyd 2011b), and the self-branding of the individual when seeking love online (see Gibbs et al. 2010). It may not be surprising that *nudz,,* as they are termed,, have become an online currency. They reveal the integrated sense of sharing built into this everyday photography, but with the added question for feminist theory of with whom the images are shared, to what ends, with what impact upon women in their everyday lives, and how that impact is being represented, They also show how oversharing or even stealing profiles to undermine online public identities (*fraping* or Facebook raping, the hostile takeover of another's social networking profile) highlights that one's online self is hackable by emotion agents (by Facebook itself or by trolls[1]).

Whereas in past centuries women – their bodies and dowries – were exchanged between men, and still are in many societies today, it is now the images of their ordinary (often white and young) bodies and body parts that have accrued an online cultural capital that is used to create social bonds between men, between men and women, and between women and women. This exchange is not new within our Western media economy: from glossy magazines to pornography, images of the female body continue to create powerful, objectifying gazes (see McRobbie 2008; Clough 2007, 2009; more recently on women in fashion blogs by Agnes Rocamora 2011). What is new is the proliferating ordinariness of such images, captured by ordinary young people in ordinary places who may themselves be submitting the body to what Hall et al. (2012) define in their study of MySpace.com as self-sexualization into subordinate and stereotypical notions of gender and sex roles. Online, they are a form of visual gossip, provoking that confessional intimacy we noted in Chapter 2 as fundamental to the warts-and-all television talk show. Without a strong critical history of the cultural and mediated exploitation of women's bodies, young people trade the images online as if they were literally trading cards, thus creating a fan culture around them. In anchoring comments and conversations, such images function, as Leopoldina Fortunati (2008) has argued of 'mediated gossip', to 'express a series of emotions such as pride, contempt, resentment, envy, jealousy, relief, fear, anxiety, uncertainty'.

Yet nudz also have an economic function in online culture; they attract page clicks and that attracts advertising revenue, and thus intimacy and economics are produced as co-constitutive rather than as intimacy contaminating rational economic behaviour or vice versa, as we noted in Chapter 1. Viviana Zelizer (2005) has asked in *The Purchase of Intimacy*, 'When dealing with disputed forms of interpersonal intimacy' (for our purposes here, fraping or sharing nudz) do we have the right to insist 'that public policy [...] insulate household relations, personal care, and love itself from an invading, predatory, economic world?' (3). The mixed mediation of our intimate spheres for many decades has undermined attempts to insulate us and perpetuates the low-level and daily-reiterated fear that our online selves and families may be fraped. In this chapter, we investigate how the mixed-mediation of images of young women's bodies online portrays intimacy as female and private and portrays male online users as publicly invasive and predatory. This portrayal shores up gender stereotypes and effaces 'how all of us use economic activity to create, maintain, and renegotiate important ties – especially intimate ties – to other people' (Zelizer 2005, 3).

Although online images identifiably belong to an individual known by his or her own small offline or online network, they also anonymously belong to the rest of the globalized network once they become uncontrollably dis/liked, tagged, and shared. It should not be surprising that online spaces also provide such 'shared spaces of dwelling' (Ahmed 2010, 14) for shame, hate, and rage to be performed and contested. The intimacy of the private sphere and the intimacy of women's bodies are opened out in online culture for both public/private scrutiny and enter-tainment. As the *Guardian* newspaper highlighted in 2012, 'creepshot' images posted online are joined by

> hundreds posted by group members of women waiting for trains, packing groceries, standing on escalators; the camera homing in on their bottom, crotch or breasts. And they joined thousands more on creep websites as a whole, a large, thriving online subculture. The point is to catch women unawares, lay claim to something off-limits, then share it around for bragging rights and comment. (Cochrane 2012)

As theorists of media, we need to be concerned that the new norms of sociality and connectivity that José van Dijck (2012) has character-ized as produced by social media platforms are also being used to shame and hate women's bodies as a global mode of exchange. That bloggers, posters, and citizen journalists can track this exchange and critically interrogate the representation of women's bodies is important, but these are minority voices compared to the masses of ordinary and vitriolic emotions expressed about women, their bodies, and their sexuality.[2]

The anonymity that is afforded to hate on the Internet is well researched, from Sherry Turkle's early findings in *Life on the Screen: Identity in the Age of the Internet* (1997), to Antonio Roversi's *Hate on the Net: Extremist Sites, Neo-Fascism On-line, Electronic Jihad* (2008), to the more recent focus upon weighing and balancing the freedom of expres-sion with evidence of online hate speech (see Daniels 2008; Banks 2010). As we suggested in Chapter 3, the emergence of the popular notion of a 'global psyche' is certainly being packaged as one to be feared as well as celebrated, for it reignites a *hostile worlds* view, whereby the private and intimate is seen to be in danger of corruption from outside global forces. Chapter 4 interrogated communality and collectivism in terms of the less threatening (but perhaps more insidious) social conformity of happiness, but Barbara Perry and Patrik Olsson have suggested in 'Cyberhate: The Globalization of Hate' (2009) that the Internet has enabled a global racist subculture to share its values and ideologies. We might also extend this hate to include the hatred of women and disgust at women's white bodies.

Thus, we would like to argue that the online practice of sharing nudz is being represented as a form of everyday terrorism upon young women's everyday lives. The notion of a *tool of terror* might not be an overstatement, considering the everyday fears that permeate women's relationship to the

Internet as a space where intimacy may be violated.[3] Yet, at the same time, nudz reveal an affective 'involuntary and powerful learning and participation' (Stewart 2007, 40) for men and women to discover ordinary women's bodies in their intimate spheres. At stake are emotional and affective capital and the role of digital media and communications technologies, which are influencing how we should take account of the exchange of online images of women's bodies in everyday life. For instance, recent literature has covered the use by teenage and young women of digital cameras (see Lee 2005; Hjorth 2009) and the visualization of young people's gender and sexuality with mobile phones (see Ravindran 2009 for a case study in India; see Schwarz 2010a for a case study in Israel, and see Hjorth 2010, 2011a/b for a range of case studies). This research has sought to critique the representation of the Internet as an anonymous fantasy playground, of 'a kind of mentally nude commune' (Ben-Ze'ev 2004, 18) and seeks to understand the value accrued to the locally and ethnically specific representation of gendered identities and bodies online. Yet, in the context of their introduction to *The Spam Book: On Viruses, Porn, and Other Anomalies from the Dark Side of Digital Culture* (2009), Parikka and Sampson would categorize nudz as a form of pornographic exchange that serves digital sociality and community, and yet such sociality is political. As the special issue of *Feminist Media Studies* on 'Mobile Intimacies' has recently argued, such debates around mobile technologies, media and intimacy demonstrate gendered practices prevailing. Thus, 'mobile intimacy is a feminist issue' (Hjorth and Lim 2012, 477).

Crucially, the focus on mobile camera phones for fuelling the production of nudz is symptomatic of a haptic-affective economy we identified in Chapter 3, which, unlike mass media and networked media, is individualized media that personalizes public space (see Campbell & Park 2008). For, as Jane Vincent argues in 'Emotional Attachment and Mobile Phones', her contribution to the *Thumb Culture* (2005) collection: 'The very act of using a mobile phone involves the simultaneous engagement with more senses than we use for other computational devices as we simultaneously touch, hear and see via the mobile phone in order to keep in touch with our buddies' (2005, 120–121). For Larissa Hjorth, mobile phones and ICTs are defined by the 'various forms of labour and intimacy' that produce them and 'have become part of the emotional landscape of the Internet' to form 'imaging communities' that 'demonstrate unofficial forms of reterritorialization that counteract the bounded territorialization of "imagined communities"' (2008b).

Whether these are 'tribes' or 'communities' of shared emotions, Michel Maffesoli argued early on that we are 'witnessing the tendency for a rationalized "social" to be replaced by an empathetic "sociality," which is expressed by a succession of ambiences, feelings and emotions' (1996, 11). If so, then women should do well in these newly emotional landscapes, considering centuries of relegation to the domestic sphere of intimacy, empathy, and messy emotional labour. However, when we consider the current value accrued to images of ordinary women's bodies among the online tribes that share them, it would seem that nobody cares about these shared bodies and to whom they originally belong, outside of the close-knit community of young people who upload them. This is largely because their economic value is seen as very separate from or hostile to their intimate, everyday life value.

Recent research of self-portraiture online by sociologist Ori Schwarz in his insightful article 'On Friendship, Boobs and the Logic of the Catalogue: Online Self-Portraits as a Means for the Exchange of Capital' (2010b), has shown that digital photographs of the user's body and body parts have become ubiquitous because they reflect the question, 'Who do I want to be and how do I want to be seen by others?' This can be recast in the light of the ongoing research by Amparo Lasén (2010a/b, 2011) and Lasén and Gomez-Cruz (2009), as noted in Chapter 3, which reveals that mobile phone users are emotionally attached to their phones and that mobile culture may be shared, but that does not mean it feels the same to those within the network. Thus, multimodal possibilities and practices for the performance and consumption of emotion online are afforded through the 'trans-personalization' of media and communication devices that bridge the gap between collectivity and individuation (see Lasén 2010b).

Therefore, while the intimacy of online communications is designed to gain local interest (friends, comments, 'likes', and ratings), it is important to emphasize affective value as the key driver, for 'following the logic of the field and based on their lack of other resources', online users of self-portraiture render 'corporeality a main resource' (Schwarz 2010b, 180). While women taking control over how they are represented visually can be seen as emancipating (especially in the light of early screen theorizations of the male gaze), there is the danger that women will reify conventional versions of femininity, which are traditionally valuable to online markets. Regardless of women's own responses, or other women's emotional responses, to such intimate images in the public domain, such images are socioeconomically valued for the affective charge that draws online crowds. We would not be so attracted to and easily absorbed by the UK *Daily Mail's* web page sidebar of exposed intimate moments of celebrities if economic value were not one of the key drivers. Thus, 'affects and emotions present a particular kind of information' about mobile media as 'intensities, passions, encounters, and experiences performed and elicited [...] present complex power dynamics involving individuals, collectives, institutions and commercial interests' (Lasén 2010a, 154). For Larissa Hjorth in her research of women's use of social networking and ICTs in Asian-Pacific countries, such new online intimacy is economic, because these women were once the low-paid menial workers within the telecommunications industries:

> Through the lens of online communities such as SNS, we can consider how this produces a tension between, on the one hand, new emotional grammars of propinquity, intimacy, creative expression and female empowerment, and, on the other hand, the increasing exploitation and naturalisation of gendered reproductive and social labour. (Hjorth 2008b)

Thus, young women online, newly empowered toward caring and sharing, may naively ignore the long histories of their own economic exploitation and may not see their bodies in terms of the 'technosocial dynamics of the distribution and consumption stages, i.e., the emergence of new audiences for lay photography' of their ordinary nude bodies (Schwarz 2010b, p. 165).

On the one hand, women may personally and socially *learn* from their private camera phone images: what they look like from the back, from the side, semi-nude, fully nude, in sexually provocative poses, or even in sexual liaisons with others Such images all operate within a regime that sees any evocation of sex in ordinary life as potentially promiscuous. On the other hand, this 'involuntary and powerful learning and participation', which is so affective (Stewart 2007, 40), may be overridden by the online lay audience's demand from within a mediated market of such body imagery. While the mobile publics that create (and are created by) these images seek to challenge the notion of the 'social' as 'good' they do so by producing the 'intimate' as 'bad' for ordinary women. Hence, female celebrity bodies are protected and framed by front covers, web page sidebars, studio production values, and paparazzi shots. Whereas ordinary women's bodies come with no securitization. The online lay audience has itself learned a great deal from television and celebrity magazines in terms of the commercial and entertainment value of intimacy to a wider public. We suggest it is the notion of *jeopardy* demanded by television producers of characters, scripts, and reality TV contestants that moves such an audience (see Hearn 2006; Andrejevic 2004). It is that exploitation of 'an intimate shared shameful moment, which is aired for all to see' that makes emotions catchy and contagious (Probyn 2005, 85–86) to this premediated online and mobile public, which seeks out objects of affect.

As we explored in Chapter 2, Ahmed reminds us that 'even when we feel we have the same feeling, we don't necessarily have the same relationship to the feeling' (2004, 10). This is vital when thinking about nudz, because while women may construct intimate moments through images of themselves, as Probyn describes of television's intimacy, this does not necessarily mean that viewers will experience that intimacy or *catch* that emotion in the same ways – the boyfriend may desire, his friends may laugh, her mother might cry, and the rest of the network will 'like' (which in the context of nudz online implies objectifying the image in order to build a relationship with the poster). Therefore, as Schwarz suggests, such images offer corporeal (or in our context here, sexual) capital, which can be exchanged/converted into social online capital (2010b, 166): what we have earlier called *strong ties* that produce hierarchies/tribes within social networks (more friends, more likes, more emotional attachments for the often male user who is sharing without caring).

Schwarz notes the productive value of self-portraiture online in terms of the 'image-entrepreneur' and 'site-operators' capitalizing upon social bonds and gift exchange (note the reference to sharing and caring in the definition of nudz at the beginning of this chapter), but it is important to emphasize that he assumes that the control of the image remains with the Self or, at least, very close to the Self. He is wary of autotelic explanations of self-portraiture online whereby women, for example, might photograph their bodies and body parts for the purposes of self-exploration, regardless of the means of production, distribution, and consumption. Yet Schwarz does not explore the emotional fallout from images of ordinary women's bodies over which the users lose entire editorial control.[4] Thus, the logic of the field, the social capital of the network, and the emotional demands of a lay audience for nudz effectively steal from the gift-giving economy. The hard, rationalist argument of *it's the Internet baby, deal with it* becomes the determiner of how, why, and to what ends vernacular photography of female bodies is put. It also allows traditional media (such as television) to steal this logic, reaffirm its own confessional history, and morally uphold itself through the production of 'right' and 'wrong' intimacies. We shall focus upon television in more depth later in this chapter.

If this photography produces the female self as a valuable corporeal commodity in one arena of trusted intimacy, we have to be mindful of Ahmed's ideas around 'emotional contagion', which, we argued in Chapter 2, now permeate online culture. It is *de rigueur* to take that televisual intimacy that audiences have passively consumed for decades and turn it into a personal/social intimacy of loves, hates, secrets, confessions, and memories shared with the world. Such spiteful commentary upon female body parts has permeated celebrity magazines that 'out' bad bodies and spread the contagion of celebrity body snarking (see Gorton & Garde-Hansen on Madonna's ageing body [2013]). That emotional contagion is crucial, because the circulation of the corporeal commodity takes on different meanings as it meets with others who have no intimate connection with that original self but see the economic potential. Thus we may ask, How are ordinary female bodies becoming archived and remembered as *with* economic value but *without* moral values? As we noted in Chapter 3, in reference to Bernard Stiegler's focus upon power: 'The Web radically modifies public and private spaces and times – and deeply alters public-private relationships [...] within the Web a new process of psychic and collective individuation is appearing' (2012).

Larissa Hjorth (2007, 2009) has extensively researched the positivity of the gift-giving economy imbued in camera phone practices, whereby the sharing of moments between intimates becomes commonplace privately and publicly. This accords with the therapeutic discourses we discussed in Chapter 1 and analysed in Chapter 4, but it is now extended to the notion of the visual. It is good, healthy, and liberating to open up the intimacies of the (female) body/psyche for the world to see. Naomi Wolf (2012) has certainly done this with *Vagina: A New Biography,* in which she explores her diminishing lack of orgasm in her forties. The concept that *we are all friends online,* the proliferation of the domestic sphere into online spaces, and the technologization of the home in real spaces serve to reinforce the notion that what is private is also, by rights, public. Interestingly, Hjorth asks, 'Will, for example, female users turn around mass media's objectification of women? Or will users perpetuate the same images, same stereotypes'? (2007, 228).

It should be clear by now that we see powerful ideological continua between the histories of the old media economy and the carving out of social spaces in a new-media economy. Chapter 4 explored the 'happiness' associated with the phenomena of social networking sites, online archives, dating sites, flashmobs, and websites, which all underpin the notion that the visualization of one's self should be communicated, shared, and understood in ways that produce positive public sentiment. Chapter 5 approached the mixed mediation of the war/weather dyad as practiced on and offline as a highly politicized, geographically specific but multi-perspectival phenomenon. Here, we approach the logic of the happiness and the positivity associated with the 'social good' of online presentations of the self from the perspective of a very old economy of industrial demands for images of women and their bodies as objects of desire, shame, and disgust. We understand the online cultural exchange of these images in the context of theories of emotion: shame, self-hate, revenge, and anger. Although Schwarz notes that photos act as currency exchanged between users in order to be more 'liked', he also assumes that such photos *belong* in that exchange and are *showable*. In many cases the images are not *at home* (in their original place of production/consumption), and the women they represent are absent from their editorial/directorial control. For the smash-and-grab underbelly of a free culture relegates copyright as 'old-media' thinking, in favour of nonexclusive, transferable, sublicensable, royalty-free, worldwide license to use any content (phrasing taken from Facebook's terms and conditions). Moreover, the logic of the network demands what cannot be shown just as much as what can be shown. Therefore, in this chapter, as female academics of media and communications, we get emotional about nudz.

Hostile intimacy and fraping bodies

The logic of the field of television 'creates the illusion of intimacy' (Gibbs 2005) and, as we highlighted in Chapter 2, the set leans forward, in toward the viewer, disallowing passive consumption. In the same way, we lean forward into computer and mobile phone screens to read text and images with a much deeper engagement and proximity to any other screen. It is this intimacy that we will explore in more depth here, because it challenges us to reconsider that emotion and economics are inimical to one another. In fact, fraping makes fruitless the preservation of a sacred, private sphere of families, intimate relations, and friendships as opposed to an online public sphere. For it is, in fact, *only* those most intimate with us (the trusted ones) who are close enough to frape us (i.e., people in the room during the short time that our computer is on and our social networking page is logged into). It is the fraping of young female bodies and how this hostile intimacy is played out online and in the mixed-mediatization of a moral panic to which we now turn.

As we explored in Chapter 2, the logic of the television or of the film screen requires emotion markers. During the television broadcasting of UK Channel 4's documentary *True Stories: My Social Network Stalker* (20 February 2012), Ruth Jeffery, a victim of fraping and nudz by her own boyfriend, Shane Webber, is produced as an embodied emotion marker, whose body is produced as displaying affects. This is not a documentary to lean back and passively consume. Rather, it displays and produces an emotional response in the audience to the online exploitation she has endured for three years, a response that may be different from Ruth's state. As we see camera closeups of Ruth's nervous tics, her tightening faucets and feeling light switches to see if they were truly off, her shaking and stammered speech, Ruth recounts the clearly traumatic memories of this everyday terrorism.

Her boyfriend had been taking nude photographs (nudz) of her, for their private consumption; unbeknownst to her, he posted them on low-rent porn sites. Their journey through online media was then exponential and uncontrollable. We are at once transported out of Teresa Brennan's 'private fortress, personal boundaries' of the 'Western individual' and terrorized by 'the unsolicited emotional intrusions of the other' (2004, 15). Ruth emerges as an intensely private young woman who has no control over the version of her Self now projected in online profiles set up in her name and the MSN messages sent from her account. Neither could she control the total breakdown between the online and offline worlds that occurred when a stranger seeking sexual favours arrived at her door, thinking the online Ruth had been soliciting him through e-mail.

Palpably, the divide between online identity and real, lived life was being systematically destroyed, and we could clearly see Brennan's 'transmission of affect', not simply from media text to audience, but in the 'bodily changes' in Ruth, as this new 'atmosphere' of everyday online terrorism 'gets into the individual' (Brennan 2004, 1). Denying culpability, her boyfriend helped Ruth track and remove the images before they destroyed her reputation. Trust and empathy were at the heart of the retelling of this story, which is *an old story being moved in new ways by new technologies* and rehashed by television – the subtle, loving, and coercive control of a naïve young woman by the one man she thought she could trust. Such a scenario, played out in millions of heterosexual relationships across the world, behind closed doors, in Facebook news feeds, on married women's social networking sites, and using images of egalitarian sexual promiscuity, was being made transparent and networked. The added advantage was that we could all post our comments about the programme on discussion boards as it played out on our TV screen. The anonymity of online communication and trust that Shane Webber had established in everyday life had protected him for three years, and the information overload of the Internet meant his everyday terrorism went unnoticed by many until UK television nationally broadcast the documentary as a standard confessional (in which Ruth's mother admits she did not come to her daughter's side because she drank in the evenings). We have here the 'public sphere' of the Internet brought into 'the private spaces' of Ruth's life (and vice versa), brought into the private space of the television audience's homes: thus, 'binding public discourse to the interested, invested *Intimisphere*' (Kavka 2008, 49–50). Television steps in to effectively convey the emotional torment that we are not able to access in the 2011 online news articles about the case.

In fact, a brief inputting of 'Ruth Jeffery' in Google Trends finds that during the trial in October 2011, search traffic was moderate and was confined to this period only, with little if any notable traffic in the years preceding, during which her hyperlocalized stalking took place. It is only at the time of the UK television broadcast in February 2012 that the name Ruth Jeffery spikes to almost three times more traffic than when the trial of her boyfriend was completed the previous year. Thus, camera close-ups of red and wringing hands, tears of a sister (also a victim), anguished faces of troubled parents, disturbing soundtracks, pixellated scenes and surveillance-effect montage sequences are produced to create audience anxiety. The emphasis at all times is upon faces, hands, and screens such that, as Gibbs has argued, the television functions as an amplifier and modulator of affect 'which is transmitted by the human face and voice, and also by music and other forms of sound, and also by image' (2002, 338).

Perhaps most affective for the audience, and something that they would intimately identify with are, as Smith defines them, the emotion markers (1999, 118) whereby the documentary produces what are in this context the 'money-shot' images that have so undermined Ruth's self-esteem. As we noted in Chapter 2, Smith's further (2003, 12) delineation within film of an invitation to feel can be here reproduced in television by virtue of the invitation to the viewer into the private, domestic sphere of Ruth's home (see Figure 6.1 below).

The camera focuses on Ruth seated on her sofa with her laptop balanced on the chair arm, with its screen turned toward the viewer. We are invited to sit with Ruth, to lean forward as she points to her laptop screen that depicts photographs taken by male online porn users of their own erect penises positioned over printed-out copies of the nudz of Ruth. On some of the erect penises, the words 'Fuck me Ruth' and 'I love you Ruth Jeffery' are written in ink. The television camera captures Ruth's discomfort at seeing these images archived on a number of different sites. The increase in traffic at the time of the broadcast

Figure 6.1 Still of Ruth Jeffery sitting on her sofa showing the audience the screen shots of her nude images and how they were creatively used online. *My Social Network Stalker*, Channel 4, broadcast 20 February 2012 (Rize Films)

suggests a high probability that online users go searching for the images, adding to Ruth's shame as they extend the moral jeopardy beyond the television screen.

Ruth's body is resituated by television as an emotionally affected (but digitally illiterate) personhood in the privacy of an ordinary domestic space (note the teddy bear in the background). Her home and the Internet are produced as separate, hostile worlds. We are watching Ruth consuming the multiple fragmentation of her own naked body: fragmented by the disembodied male erections that cut across her private images. This layering of image (original nudz) within screen (porn user's laptop), within image (printed copy of photo with penis), within screen (Ruth's laptop), within screen (viewer's television) comes to signify the fracturing of Ruth's identity. Yet, it also demonstrates television's 'moral' role in negotiating this mixed-media ecology of bodies and screens.

We are disgusted but attracted as we watch the proximity of a clothed Ruth, abjectly viewing her own nakedness within the proximity of a stranger's penis. It is this visual object to which disgust 'sticks' as Ahmed states (2004, 92). As we noted in Chapter 1, disgust works performatively 'not only as the intensification of contact between bodies and objects, but also as a speech act' (Ahmed 2004, 92). The computer screen image of a photo of a penis over a photo of Ruth's naked body is just the level of contagion through proximity and distance to configure her body online as disgusting and shameful. We (if we are female viewers) are expected to *feel for* Ruth, to feel her shame on her behalf because the sacredness of the intimate sphere has been despoiled and fraped but, as Ahmed reminds us above, people do not always feel the same way about the same object, as we explored in Chapter 5.

Feelings about nudz

What is striking about the documentary are the different emotional performances in the real-time online commentary that surrounded the broadcast. While Smith suggests that film viewers are invited to feel and 'must possess some level of understanding [of] emotion cues and markers' (2003, 12), we must counter this with the question, What if that heightened emotion only serves to disaffect audiences as much as affect them? What if, as we explored in Chapter 5, audiences inoculate themselves against the emotion contagion and use the affective content to learn, participate, but not care? The differentiated television audience online can post comments about Ruth Jeffery's situation that may undermine the purpose of the documentary, if that purpose is to raise concerns about nudz and fraping. This raises some critical questions. Do the online users want to engage more in Ruth's pain? Are they attracted to and repulsed by her body? Do they seek out the images to determine her desirability or their disgust? Or perhaps they wish to learn more about such sexual cyberabuse, to make doubly sure they are not victims. Viewers are shocked, fearful, and mesmerized by Ruth's story and wish to share those feelings with others online as part of their extratextual pleasure. They also need to participate with others in order to reach decisions about their own relationship with the Internet. Again it is the tension between proximity and distance from the fearful and disgusting visual object that motivates the comments we draw upon below.

As noted in Chapter 2, audiences and fans are well versed in paratexts and in the expansion of people 'talking' about television online. This transmedia storytelling is not unusual, as television viewers discuss the programmes they are watching and recount their own stories that run parallel with the broadcast. Marketers and advertisers are keenly aware that media consumers multitask. They may be on discussions boards related to their niche interests or on social network sites with television on in the background. They may be watching television closely and seeking out opinions on more specifically TV-focused discussion sites during or after the broadcast. While Ruth's story is a one-off documentary, it still requires that viewers 'embrace a "collective intelligence" for information, interpretations and discussions', which Jason Mittell has determined as important to the Internet's relationship with television series (2006, 31).

While watching this programme, the authors were keen to see what kinds of comments viewers were making about its content. Would they sympathize with Ruth or be disgusted by her willingness to pose naked for photographs? Would they feel her violation as her private images of erotic and consenting love were not only stolen and enframed as pornography by her boyfriend, but also then mashed up into user-generated porn by anonymous users? How fearful would they be? Or would they blame Ruth for trusting her boyfriend, for not being more suspicious, or for using social networks in the first place? From the UK-based 'The Student Room', the following postings were submitted from young women who would or should identify with Ruth:

> Did anyone just see this story on channel 4? Girl gets 'stalked' by her boyfriend. Sounds pretty awful but just wow at the naivety of the girl involved. Have to watch to believe. (*TSR* Darcie 20.02.12 23:14)
>
> I know this sounds horrible but I can really understand why she was in the lowest class. Although I simply would have phoned the npolice [sic] and that would have been it. (*TSR* Agenda Suicide 20.02.12 23:21)
>
> [...]
>
> As awful an ordeal it must have been for her and this probably sounds really really bad but I was kind of watching in disbelief the whole time. I just think…*surely* there was *someone* around her with some common sense and authority that could have helped her out more. [...] I mean…she was on a computer science course, right? Maybe it was just too sensitive a subject…but still, the harassment and identity theft was pretty serious. That thing with the random guy turning up at her house expecting sex? The phone calls? Awful. (*TSR* Lights 21.02.12 00:02 www.studentroom.co.uk)

Clearly, Karatzogianni's and Kuntsman's notion of 'reverberations' operates here to show how the online–offline divide appears to break down as emotions are communicated and intensified into an 'affective fabric' (2012, 3). Yet what is clear from the quotes above is that while these young women feel *for* Ruth, they do not feel the same *as* Ruth, and they do not really *care for* her (in both senses of this phrase). They use Ruth's case to consolidate their own digital literacy and to demonstrate their collective intelligence that they are aware of the *purchase of intimacy*. They reinforce the ideological position that while the images should not have been misused, neither should Ruth have consented to their production and use at all. On the site 'Hitched' (for the recently married or those about to be married), the documentary is used to share feelings on the remediation of private imagery in the pubic domain and to take a maternal stance that shows off the poster's new status as responsible, family-oriented women:

> I am swinging from wanting to give her a massive cuddle, but also wring her neck at continuing to create images. In saying that, her self esteem must have been in tatters. I had a class today and we were discussing this – freaks me out at how blasé young people are about sending pictures. Had no clue that if they were under 16 it was child pornography. (Hitched Nubbin 20.2.12 22:55 www.hitched.com)

As a media-literate television audience, these women on Hitched are concerned. They reassert the two vulnerable groups that are being targeted by the documentary as the ones needing the most protection: children and young women. Yet what are they to be protected from exactly? From untrustworthy offline relationships or from loved ones they thought they could trust? From the ubiquity of vernacular photography, from the preemptive symbolic and affective value built into images of naked young women, regardless of their context of production and the privacy of their viewing? Perhaps even they need protecting from the images themselves, which are signs and hence commodities that, as we noted in Chapter 1, show forth affect as 'a vector of unqualified intensity seeking future actualization' (Clough 2012, 23). It is Ruth Jeffery's seeming ignorance of this affect/vector in her nudz, which functions as a 'vehicle from one dimension of time to another', that is most derided by other women posting their comments online (Clough 2012, 23). These women have accepted, or are quickly coming to accept, the logic of the media and the online demand for ordinary women's bodies, in the 'technosocial dynamics of the distribution and consumption stages, i.e., [in] the emergence of new audiences for lay photography' (Schwarz 2010b, p. 165).

As we stated in Chapter 1, *affective branding* (Parisi & Goodman 2012) is the control of future memory/emotion. As with the hard work that Ien Ang saw women doing to maintain socially acceptable femininity, it requires that women anticipate the memories and feelings they will have, but are yet to have, about themselves and the feelings that others on and offline will have, but are yet to have, about them. Like online social reputation management (see Solove 2007), it is expected that the individual will retain and maintain control over her identity as an affective brand, and that these identities will fit squarely into predetermined cultural norms. Nevertheless, we are at the beginning of Stanley Cohen's first stage of a moral panic: concern. The irony (50 years after the concerns about television's influence over the vulnerable) is that television steps in to raise awareness of the use and abuse of online media. The televising of Ruth's fraping remediates the exploitation of her sexuality – a danger young women face on a daily basis. Television provides the perfect medium for broadcasting to families the negative impact on Ruth's family and by extension. the potential negative impact to all young women and to civil society as a whole.

In *Folk Devils and Moral Panics* (2002 [1972]), Stanley Cohen marks out the 'moral entrepreneurs' (in this case victims, aggrieved families, and television documentary makers) from the 'folk devils' (digitally literate bullies, ignorant Internet users, and mis/user-generated content makers); the moral entrepreneurs seek escalation of the social and moral 'threat', with the goal of a consensual call to action. From popular music (see Shuker 1994), to film (see Klein 2011), to television (see Holmes & Jermyn 2004), to video games (see Williams & Smith 2007) and now the Internet, moral panics have consistently been produced around deviant behaviour manifested by and through media use by subcultural individuals and collectives. The potential depravation of women and children by and through media content and production is not a new anxiety, and is clearly reiterated in the postings above. Women are persistently remediated as in need of protection and salvation and are made blameworthy for their naivety. As David Oswell argues of the 1970s, when young people, television, and moral panic synergized to mobilize consensus, we again have here the display of 'youth [read in this case the young naked female body and its exploitation] as a public problem, [...] shared and publicly discussed and as a problem concerning the maintenance of order and civility within public spaces [in this case the messy in-between-ness of public/private online spaces]' (Oswell 1998, 36).

The documentary on Ruth Jeffery produces her as ashamed and her body as shameful, the audience as disgusted, and the use of her nudz as attractive/disgusting. Yet, entirely absent from the text is any real understanding of her boyfriend's motivation for the sexual cyberabuse. The only reason offered was jealousy, because Ruth was at university while he was unemployed. Hence, the notion (in line with Schwarz's argument above) that the male Internet user exchanges nudz in order to accrue online social/cultural capital goes unexplored. We have no sense of how Shane Webber used these images to add emotional value to his relationship with Ruth. Nor do we get to explore how the sexual and corporeal capital attached to these images (literally stuck to them in the case of the superimposition of users' genitalia onto the nudz) offered Webber online recognition through his girlfriend's body. The context of a vernacular photo culture online that offers this recognition through trails of comments and 'likes' ensured that Ruth's nudz won the competition for users' attention as soon as they were downloaded, creatively modified, and reuploaded into the amateur porn galleries. This was redoubled with the addition of a television audience. Within this context (and outside of the television text), Webber's girlfriend's body (not Ruth's body) offered the acquisition of social status through *new strong ties* with strangers. While Webber stole the nudz, he was, as the 'image-entrepreneur', offering them to online users as porn, and he was rewarded with the gifts that online culture dispenses to those who share freely: comments, 'likes', compliments, and remediation. Cohen's moral entrepreneurs and folk devils are more intimately connected than before. In fact, moral entrepreneurs can be the folk devils, as in the case of Hunter Moore's IsAnyoneUp.com.

The most hated man on the Internet

The forced closure of the SNS-style website IsAnyoneUp.com (2010–2012) of club and party promoter Hunter Moore, which encouraged users to submit naked photos of former girlfriends/boyfriends without their permission as a form of relationship status update and revenge, stages Cohen's call to action. The story became complete when the anti-bullying site Bullyville purchased the domain and shut the site down in April 2012. Hunter Moore is the opposite of Facebook's Mark Zuckerberg, and yet they espouse exactly the same creative-connections ideology of media online. For our purposes, the discourses performed in and through Moore's site revolve entirely around emotion and around many of the ideas we outlined in Chapters 1 and 2. Hate and revenge fuelled the uploading of images and the linking of these images to the victims' online profiles. 'Global fury' defined the public reaction, according to the *Brisbane Times* in Australia (23 April 2012). Hunter Moore was seen to capitalize upon the labels 'the most hated man on the Internet' and 'Hunter the Horrible', with photo mashups asking, 'Tell me what it's like to not have a soul'. Here, Moore resembles Ruth Jeffery's boyfriend on an industrial scale, an image entrepreneur profiting from thousands of dollars in advertizing revenue from the increased traffic to his site. He provided a space for the offloading of negative feelings (spite, hatred, jealousy, egotistical pride, and self-love) through users naming and shaming ex-partners who had produced private nudz for personal consumption. Moore soon gained a worldwide reputation as the Internet folk devil par excellence, promoting his site in order to promote his 'events' business.

Most notably, the issue of the 'revenge porn' site revealed two deeply contrasting politicized views around who controls women's bodies within a music-roadie-online-fan-party youth culture. These were articulated on the *Anderson Cooper* (CNN) daytime television talk show in which Moore confronted Melissa and Daveeda, whose nude images he had displayed. Moore is prompted by Anderson Cooper to 'feel bad about doing this to these women' (21 November 2011), and in response Moore asserts he is not *doing* anything and that the anonymity of the Internet makes it 'easier' for such sites to exist. In addressing the women he states, 'no one put a gun to your head and made you take these pictures. It's 2011, everything is on the Internet', thus underscoring that sharing is integrated into mobile camera phone pictures and Skype image making by default. As with the case of Ruth Jeffery, these women are positioned to be naïve and trusting of their former boyfriends, who have used their bodies against them within the rational logic of a technosocial lay demand for images of women. Thus, the convention lament in such cases against women: *they should have known better.*

Although the ex-boyfriends might know that the logic of femininity is built upon the avoidance of public shame, Moore himself appears incredulous of the women's naivety. The women's emotional response to the circulation of private images is seen to be at odds with Moore's discourse of the Internet as an open and free culture that undermines the division between public and private. In a queer reading of Moore, we might say that he has claimed the right to *out* their respectable version of femininity as a façade, and their response to his technophilic rationalization is patronised as typically feminine and naively technophobic. According with our earlier reference in chapter 1 to the work of Alison Jaggar: 'Not only has reason been contrasted with emotion, but it has also been associated with the mental, the cultural, the universal, the public and the male, whereas emotion has been associated with the irrational, the physical, the natural, the particular, the private, and, of course, the female' (1989 145).

As with the online comments on Ruth's plight, the television audience seem to either blame the women for taking the photographs in the first place or blame the Internet image entrepreneur for profiting from the already-extant sexualization of women (in this case Ruth's boyfriend). Either way, the logic of the field goes uncritiqued and even is reified as a space that denudes women and strips them of their dignity. For example, it is noteworthy that Moore's site contains numerous images of naked men (a number of them masturbating) that get no airtime as an issue: these bodies are not victims because they are male bodies (sometimes visually encoded as gay). Equally less visible are the users of the site, who actualize the images' future affective value as soft porn for public consumption by enjoying their nudz posted on the site without the women's knowledge. Totally invisible to the debate are the majority of consumers/fans: the audience of the site who assign their 'likes', strings of comments, and ratings, thus contributing to a monetary value in attracting advertizing revenue.

While IsAnyoneUp.com is now closed and the link directs you to Bullyville, there is a Flickr site that archives a good deal of the content. The images there of fragmented nude female bodies, some with messages written on their bodies for their intended viewer, disrupt Ien Ang's fictionalized versions of femininity associated with television and thus fantasy (1996, 92). These are real bodies; in real domestic/leisure situations posing in bedrooms, having fun, getting drunk, partying, and being sexually promiscuous. Their revelation in the public domain disallows the construction of a socially acceptable femininity by those same women in the rest of their public lives. While these uses of images do conform to Ang's 'unallowed' feelings of desire, sexuality, and dominance of the image, these are not confined to the safety of television melodrama consumption but go to the frameworks of Internet soft pornography, which exploit their commodity value outside of the women's control. Not only confined to 'revenge porn' or 'stalker porn' the images also function as one-night-stand-memory/artefacts, as evidence, witnessing and emotion image-objects that signify the sexual conquest the night before (often between band members and roadies associated with Moore's events).

The images and postings work within a specific hierarchy of emotional/ social value. For example, two popular phrases appear to have originated from Hunter Moore's site (either from the man himself or the users). Both are misogynistic and both produce women's bodies as sexual capital with variable exchange values. The hashtag NBHNC frequently occurs on IsAnyoneUp.com and means 'no butthole no care', signifying to users that if a photo (nudz or *noodz*, as they are sometimes termed) does not image the woman showing her 'butthole' then it is not revealing enough and not of affective value to Moore and his fans: they simply do not care because it does not produce the desired affect. Likewise, the frequent use of the term of abuse *gnarg* which appears to be an abbreviation of *gnargoyle* often confounded newbies to the site; this definition was posted on Yahoo! Answers in August 2011:

A Gnargoyle is a gross chick (or dude) who unfortunally [sic] gets their noodz posted. A Gnarg is usually either fat, hairy, has a sloppy vag, or are just plain filthy. Gnargs are anyone with the misocnception [sic] that someone wants to see them naked.

Such nomenclature contributes to an online culture of the denigration of female bodies, body parts, and of any ordinary image that exposes the 'sloppy vag' aspects of a gnarg. The uploaded photo of soiled ladies' underwear after a sexual encounter as proof of conquest is certain to produce an affective response, which then takes time to emotionalize, depending upon the viewer.

On the one hand, Bullyville refers to the concept of 'public good' (which suggests public sentiment), stating that IsAnyoneUp.com did not fulfil this function. We might well agree with this if we uphold the Zuckerbergian 'social good' critiqued in Chapter 5. IsAnyoneUp.com is raping Facebook's own ideological position, despoiling the concept of social networking culture as good, accountable and caring. Moore was often quoted as not caring about the anonymous, low-profile individuals who featured nude. 'People think I'm completely evil and what I'm doing is completely immoral, but at the end of the day I feel like I'm just educating people on technology. As sad as it is, hurting or ruining people's lives as people say, is entertainment for some' (Lee 2012). Shame, laughter, and ridicule were seen to torment the lives of those whose images were on the site (and the attendant abusive comments that sometimes accompanied them) but images could not be removed. Despite being physically attacked several times, Hunter Moore did not 'cease and desist', transmogrifying Facebook's right to a worldwide right to licence users' imagery and making it all his own.

On the other hand, viewers of the site, and especially those who were connected to Moore's clubbing events, derived great textual (and we can only speculate sexual) pleasure from the images and their comments. This is critical, as the issue of digital illiteracy is evoked as both defence and symptom of cyberbullying. Moore's site functioned to show up the real-world, uncontrolled use of media in a mixed-media economy where fandom produced the content entirely, where intimacy can be purchased, and where confessional media cuts across platforms. Many users and so-called victims (female and male) loved the site for the visualization of the provocative, soft-core amateur porn fun that accompanied clubbing events and the bands Moore promoted. It is useful to quote at length a typical user comment [all errors as they appear in the original]:

> Lol I don't get why so many people hate on Hunter Moore and the site, yea it's fucked up but let the guy go down his own destructive path. Do you people realize how many lawsuits he has on him the fact that he can barely pay for his site and he still hands out free shit. It's not like karma hasn't already hit him. Everyone needs to get over themselves it's a stupid funny site, it's a good laugh, everyone needs to lighten up a bit. The human body was meant to be enjoyed naked not covered up. Maybe its because I've already had a video of myself posted up all over Myspace that I have no shame but I don't see why any one else should have any shame either. Most of the people on there are pretty good looking people, beside the gnargs but that's my personal opinion. Beauty is in the eye of the beholder and everyone should just learn to love the naked body already!] (zombiewife: Isanyoneup? http://www.tumblr.com/tagged/gnarg)

Interestingly, Moore too had his limits and bemoaned the under-age pornography sent to him from the UK that he was obliged to endlessly flag and report. While a minority of adult (and always female) 'victims' turned to television to air their distress and create the pressure needed for an old-media call to action, Moore's fans (and in a number of cases other women who desired to be associated with the images) used the site to confront issues of moral control of the Internet. It is important to note that Moore publicized IsAnyoneUp's call for nudz as a way of addressing loneliness and disconnection in the context of Facebook's social goodness. As the site is now redirected to Bullyville, readers can view Moore's obituary to his own endeavour:

> To everyone who got a tattoo, bought a shirt, wrote on your body, self-submitted or came to a party, I truly thank you for the support. Without your support, the site would not have been what it was. To all the girls who submitted those band guy's [sic] and too all the guys who submitted the groupies, you made the Internet fun again. [...] Since we launched Isanyoneup.com a year ago, we received over 500 million page views. Girls got naked of all sizes at the IAU parties; we did it from Canada to Vegas. You made it possible for me to have the best life and made me realize what people will do for a few extra

friend requests & followers on twitter. I'll miss a lot of things but mostly the community. (Moore 2012)

Fans thanked Moore for his entertaining site that had offered them laughs, comfort, friendship, fraternity, desire, passion, knowledge and learning. Rest in peace (RIP) messages to the site, and obituaries on its closure were in abundance. 'Almost cried this morning. I hate how people are talking so much shit. You're a legend and I hope you don't go to the good side. It feels like a [sic] lost a best friend'. In response, Moore posts 'Ill still be here, i am still me and im not changing. I just cant deal with the death, child pornography etc.. being submitted everyday. everyone should understand that' [all errors as quoted]. In response, the founder of Bullyville converts Hunter Moore from Internet folk devil par excellence to moral entrepreneur of a new social media economy:

> I've known Hunter for quite some time now, and the fact of the matter is that he's a very smart guy. While he has been misguided, he is very astute and socially observant. His ability to not only capture the attention of young people, but to spur them into action as well, is truly unique in an era where social media makes it so easy to be a passive consumer of information. (Moore 2012)

The numerous postings to Moore's obituary to IsAnyOneUp.com reinforce the contested discourses we have analysed as circulating around this form of 'bad community', as Debra Ferreday might term it. An entrepreneur who uses the valorized features of creativity, exchange, collaboration, and reciprocity toward creating a community that is not 'good' should not necessarily be considered aberrant. This would only seek to 'normalize the idea of a utopian internet community, from which deviations occur only as a result of insufficient vigilance' (Ferreday 2005). What we have hoped to show in our mixed-media approach to emotion online is that such distinctions between good and bad, online and offline are both unhelpful and outdated. As Ferreday argued early on in her research of the Internet:

> The invocation of a group of right-thinking cyber-citizens – the 'we' who must be 'careful' – reproduces the very liberal rhetoric which [...] tends to perpetuate, or at least obscure, power structures within online communities. Indeed, the notion of 'the online community' [...] seems, ironically, to reproduce the notion of a single unlimited community which, if it is not conterminous with all mankind exactly,

is certainly conterminous with all (responsible) users of the internet.
[...]
   I would suggest, then, that the notion of a community that has
the potential to be good but is constantly under threat from deviant
outsiders, is inadequate. Rather, it is necessary to pay attention to the
ways in which utopian rhetoric might in itself play a role in repro-
ducing inequalities that exist in society more generally, both online
and off. (Ferreday 2005)

This may well mean that Hunter Moore's site is just the emotional anti-
dote to Facebook that the Internet user needs.
   Gorton and Garde-Hansen (2013) have written in depth about
online hate on discussion boards in the context of fan postings about
Madonna's ageing body. In that research, they found the emotions
being performed were not new, just as 'lolcats' have a precedent in late
nineteenth-century photography. Such online hate 'represent(s) an
echo chamber of disgusted voices articulating shame, anger and rage
at the sexualization of the older woman's body' (2013). What may be
new is the widening number of online hate sites and communities of ill
feeling that revolve around individual targets who are ordinary people.
A good example is the televised moral panic around Internet trolls in the
UK's BBC3 channel's broadcast *The Anti-Social Network,* in which Radio
5Live's presenter Richard Bacon hunted online trolls. What is striking
about this documentary, the next in Stanley Cohen's 'concern' phase of
a moral panic process, is that while the programme includes children as
a source of vulnerability to RIP trolls, it is in fact the presenter himself,
an attractive, 36-year-old white family man, who is the victim of two
years of online abuse. In the online BBC magazine *Richard Bacon: My
Battle with the Trolls,* he claims: 'There is something about the alchemy
of a keyboard and a public platform that taps into a side of human
nature that you rarely, if ever, encounter in real-life conversation' (Bacon
2012).
   It is important to end therefore on this middle-class, well educated,
well-presented, married, successful man's incredulity at being 'stalked'
and 'terrorised' by this tool. His clear distinction between 'real-life' and
online life suggests that although the democratization of hate enfolds all
identities, in the real world he considers himself safe. For many women,
young or old, this historically has not been the case.

Conclusion

Don't hate your computer. Change your broadband

In the mid 1980s, the authors (at the time children) were playing PacMan and Asteroids on their first family computers. By 1990, we were sending our first e-mails as college students and worshipping the cut-and-paste function. In the mid-1990s we purchased our own PCs, Macs, and mobile phones. In late 2006, one of the authors opened a Facebook account and used screen shots in lectures to show undergraduates just what this new website could do. By 2009, everyone seemed to be social networking. In those 30 years, the authors have continued to consume electronics (numerous TVs, DVD players, PVRs, PCs, laptops, video game consoles, mobile phones, digital cameras, MP3 players, tablets). This book has unashamedly and clearly expressed our Anglo-American experiences as audiences, users, and consumers of media discourses, forms, and practices through the many media production and delivery technologies we have acquired. Many of the electronics we have used to access media content are now discarded into what has been termed a museum 'of failed and outdated technologies' of media 'that have a built-in tendency toward their own termination' (Gabrys 2011, 15). Yet we have never hated our electronics: their tangibility, shininess, touchability, solidity and *thereness* have guaranteed our desire for them. They may have become smaller (because we need to be with them on the move) but our desire for them as they call out to us in the dark (vibrating, beeping, and glowing) belies the reality that we will soon dump them (in both senses of the term). How can we love these objects if we cannot be loyal to them and they are incapable of staying with us for long? We may be taught never to hate our computer, but this snapshot of a natural history shows the vast amount of electronic rubbish that we shamefully forget.

As Gabrys has eloquently shown in *Digital Rubbish: A Natural History of Electronics*, natural history 'is a provocation for how to think through the material leftovers of electronics' and to refocus on those 'outmoded commodities' that 'through their inert persistence – ultimately unsettle notions of progress' (2011, 7). For us, our love and desire for shiny upgrades produces an affective relationship built upon persistent newness and determined forgetting that makes a politics of hope and the promise of happiness imaginary and continuously deferred. Thus, while 'planned obsolescence' (Hills 2009, 109) is built into our media tools for accessing the Internet, so too is affect, which is distributed as the never-ending pursuit of *something else*. Patricia T. Clough's location of the small possibility that 'there is always a chance for something else, unexpected, new' (2010, 224), could be imagining affect as upgradable in the context of a digital media age. In everyday life, ordinary people's acceptance of the 'openness, emergence, and creativity' of the 'affect turn', which 'is already the object of capitalist capture' (Clough 2010, 224) may only continue to overcode their time, lives, and loves in ways that make them fall in love with themselves and their electronics.

Away from the beautiful new media-delivery systems that allow us to get online, we experience hate, frustration, shame, and dissatisfaction in the omnipresence of our technologized lives. Melissa Gregg in *Work's Intimacy* (2011) has defined this as a schizophrenic condition of affective labour in our knowledge economy. Except these feelings extend well beyond work. If affective labour is 'devoted to developing reserves of emotional resilience to withstand the ontological challenges of the typical working day' (Gregg 2011, 11) what about down time and the emotional resilience required to just being online, as a fan, a blogger, a tweeter, a message poster and more often than not, as simply a reader and watcher. Even the ordinary act of passively seeing online media and culture has become coded and enclosed by emotion-agents seeking to impose unnecessary demands on our attention. There are just too many times when we can hate being online. Technical (hardware/software) obstacles seem to deliberately prevent us getting where we want to be, and total absorption in online worlds means that we may lose touch with other inimtacies, relationships, and even the size of our bodies.[1] The 'cognitive surplus' that Shirky (2010a) claims is stymied by passive television consumption seems to now be controlled by even bigger global media conglomerates, which may or may not have a 'social' mission. For example, let's look at the following ad: 'Don't hate your computer. Change your broadband. Broadband as it should be. Go fibre optic for just £6.75 a month for the first 6 months when you switch to a Virgin phoneline' (Amazon.co.uk). In this online advert on Amazon's website from March 2011, which buffers to the right of reviews of Jaron Lanier's *You Are Not a Gadget: A Manifesto* (2010), Virgin Media solve our emotional problems with technology through better competitor technology. In Lanier's book, we are seeking to understand the viability of the idea that technology has stifled and controlled creativity (the inverse of Shirky's argument). Lanier (2010) observes:

> Ever more extreme claims are routinely promoted in the new digital climate. Bits are presented as if they were alive, while humans are transient fragments. Real people must have left all those anonymous comments on blogs and video clips, but who knows where they are now, or if they are dead? The digital hive is growing at the expense of individuality. (26)

While reviewers determine the usefulness of Lanier's text, which in itself determines the usefulness of amateur online reviewers (who seem to have replaced expert opinions), other reviewers determine the helpfulness of the online reviews. We have no way of knowing who anyone is or their background, and yet we have grown to rely upon these opinions, thoughts, and feelings about products and the world of consumption as leverage in our decision-making.

Here the tension between being ourselves in our daily-lived lives and the risky desire (and perceived need) to extend ourselves beyond our immediate surroundings into our emo-techno-ecology is resented. Lanier laments this tension:

> When developers of digital technologies design a program that requires you to interact with a computer as if it were a person, they ask you to accept in some corner of your brain that you might also be conceived as a progam. When they design an internet service that is edited by a vast anonymous crowd, they are suggesting that a random crowd of humans is an organism with a legitimate point of view. (Lanier 2010, 4)

Serious, reflective, and well-informed debates about the relationship between technology, the environment, and people may well be better located in the customer reviews of Lanier's *Manifesto* than in current academic research. Through reading these, we try to understand how we feel about online culture while *in* online culture, and Internet adverts ask us to consider how we feel about the gadgets we use to access online culture. We may also feel guilty that all this may not be environmentally sustainable: the massive tubes that are the Internet itself may be undermining any efforts to care.

Yet, our entrance into online forums is often prompted by emotion or affect, whether we are fans of a television series or computer game; people searching for information about a disease or condition they fear they might have or a loved one might have; those seeking an opportunity to 'meet' someone, whether romantically or just for friendship; searchers looking for a chance to reconnect with friends and family and/or to share photographs, stories, thoughts; or browsers at a moment where we are not sure what we want but hope to come across something that will make us 'feel better' about life. These entrances into online culture are highly individualized and yet they are, by nature of the events described above, in pursuit of community, togetherness, belonging, reassurance, comfort, and/or emotional support from others. This book has touched upon the individual and social emotions and affects that are mapped out across the Web, which are legible to any reader of the Internet. In so doing, it has uncovered the push and pull between the individual and the social – the desire for belonging and community that coincides with a desire for privacy and intimacy. Whether the Internet is seen as a forum for all or a mechanism for corporate consumerism, it is a place where the individual and the social meet and emotions and affects are exchanged.

Emotions also belong to someone else and not just to the public space of powerful commercialized networks and the emotion agents we have pointed to in this book. The emotional experiences that can be consumed online do not belong only to the individuals who share them. They also belong to those who create the content as well as those who then upload the content: family members, friends, co-workers, opinion leaders, entrepreneurs, news agencies, brand managers, governments, businesses, museums, universities, celebrities, media organizations, entertainment companies, fan activists, religious bodies, think tanks, and terrorists, to name the most obvious individuals and groups who upload, post, and publish emotional content on the World Wide Web. Fear that your emotional and intimate content will appear online without your permission makes for a tool of terror wielded by ordinary people. Yet, this creates a disjuncture between online and offline that is increasingly hard to maintain.

The deep-rooting into place, time, and bodies of emotionalized memory technologies and networked taste-making has been recently noted by Melissa Gregg in her analysis of the 'city singles' dating site

Lovestruck.com (Gregg 2012) and by Leder and Karpovich (2012) in their focus upon 'digital object memories'. The 'Internet of Things' and affective stories around objects that could be given agency through sensors, transmitters, and processors are 'linked via wireless networks'. Thus, 'such objects will be able to record and exchange data about themselves, their locations, and their environments, and respond to Internet protocol in the process' (Leder and Karpovich 2012, 128). Contrary to Lanier's argument, mentioned above, Gregg is keen to show the continuities of taste, leisure, and intimacy built into geomapped online dating that promotes the navigation of known pathways through space, place (and objects): 'Each in their own way makes city space legible, familiar, inhabitable. The taste logic of profile pages establishes the terms of encounter in advance, making the anonymity of the city safe to navigate. With the utmost discretion, social networking sites and their geomapping counterparts domesticate life's unruly potential, online and off' (Gregg 2012, 147). This addresses affect's messy in-between-ness that Gregg and Seigworth noted (2010), which we drew upon in Chapter 1 and have been negotiating in our close readings: by seeking to inhabit, map, and control the liminal space between online and offline worlds, it is emotion agents who claim the territory.

This territory is becoming increasingly premediated as emotionalized and securitized as dangerous, because it seems to be both good and bad – belonging to the Mark Zuckerbergs and the Hunter Moores equally, and it's not clear which one is which. As Nick Mansfield argued before Facebook dominated everyday life:

> Our entertainment, our social values, even the work we do and the governments we elect are all to be understood in terms of satisfaction, pleasure, like and dislike, excitement and boredom, love and hate. A world where we once knew ourselves in terms of values and identities has given way to the uninterrupted intensities of elation and grief, triumph and trauma, loss and achievement; birth, death, survival, crime, consumption, career are all now pretexts for emotion. (Mansfield 2000, 2)

What we have tried to show in our book on emotion online and the premediation and remediation in and of everyday life is that the emotionality of online texts and their (mis)readability needs to become more prominent. In our readings, we have arrived at the notion that pervasive emotions are being extended out of individual psyches and into online spaces or collective experience. We have been less interested in the debates about 'how' emotions come to be (the neuroscientists versus the sociologists), but more interested in the subtleties and nuances of ordinary expressions and readings of online culture as an emotional culture.

In terms of developing media technologies, mobility and intensity is key. Thus, Maxine Sheets-Johnstone's tactile-kinaesthetic body (2011, 505) resonates with the 'pocket technoscapes' and 'affective computing' that can be found in Ingrid Richardson's (2007) focus upon mobile new media. Emotions then become created as mobile and dynamic (both in society and in the academy), as the site of contact between the individual and the social becomes mobilized. The wide-ranging nature of our book has sought to open up questions and keep emotion mobile and move it across media discourses, forms, and practices. The desire in the academy at present to tie emotions, feelings, and affects back down into a disciplinary sphere is indicative of a fear that the affective turn has become too unscientific and that the *mechanics* of emotion and affect would provide just the quantifiable explanations of human behaviour that art, literature, psychoanalysis, and sociology have failed to deliver. 'If you don't think our brains are responsible for our behaviour then what is?' asked Professor Colin Blakemore of Oxford University, 'We need to prepare for explanations of things we hold dear: love, responsibility, friendship, will come from our greater knowledge of how the brain works in this golden age of neuroscience' (Interview with BBC Radio 4, 5 September 2012). All the literature that our book has applied in our close readings only produces more questions, more possibilities, and the need to undertake more readings of how those things we hold dear are being mobilized, securitized, and monetized.[2]

Leaking affects/controlling bodies

Wikipedia notes that 'during the 2008 Mumbai Attacks, eyewitnesses sent an estimated 80 "tweets" every five seconds as the tragedy unfolded. Twitter users on the ground helped in compiling a list of the dead and injured'.[3] A new vocabulary of 'tweets', 'twittering', and 'yammering' entered journalistic discourse as politicians, corporate CEOs, media moguls, and celebrities hastily appropriated 'real-time' reporting. The convergence of Twitter with broadcast media, while clearly having an impact on media production and consumption, meant that an ethical and emotional dimension to social media was now in our midst.

Mumbai 2008 has been described as the day that social media appeared to come of age. Here, Twitter functioned on a biopolitical level as a merging of the social, emotional, and technological, virally marketing itself, networking human bodies, emotions, and lives, making the possibility of 'bioterror', contagious affect, and a global pandemic of sensations all the more real. These are new media 'wars without end' (see Mbembe 2003; Kaplan 2009). In this book, we have not been explicitly focused on highly emotionalized war, terrorism, and crisis. Yet, it has been implicit that in our emo-techno-ecology the emotion agents producing everyday mediations of life are the same as those securitizing our emotions in everyday low-level wars without end. Thus, we have been focused on the leaky affects and uncontrollable bodies (of emotion) of Lanier's 'random crowd of humans' (Lanier 2010, 60).

This 'crowd' may be seen as 'an organism with a legitimate point of view' but it is one that fills Lanier with self-loathing as he is 'drawn into ridiculous pissing matches online' (Lanier 2010, 60). Banks (2010, 238) accords with this, and in researching extremist websites and the growth of hate sites noted by the Simon Wiesenthal Center, he has determined that there is a need to 'reclaim' the Web. This should occur, he recommends, through a multidimensional approach: national and international legal frameworks; ISP-based regulation; education and media literacy; monitoring organizations; terms of service contracts; geo-location tools; firewalls; and individual responses from users to 'promote a culture of intolerance towards online hate' (Banks 2010, 238). Therefore, there is a great deal of cross-cultural, transnational, and cross-departmental work to do, and the sheer enormity of Banks's recommendations suggest there is no good and bad Internet anymore. This is everyday life. In our research for this book, we have seen as much everyday hate, shame, and anger performed by online trolls of a 'mob dynamic' toward 'fragmentary pseudo-people' (Lanier 2010 60) as we do on the streets, in the workplace, or at home. This explains to us, why it seems a 12-minute YouTube video by Anders Behring Brevik hides in plain sight in 2011, because it is, in fact, so ordinary and so unremarkable in its repetition of ubiquitous ideas and images.

Emotion for media studies or the mediation of emotion

For media studies, at stake is the age-old battle between those with power (global corporate media giants; bloated public service broadcasters; horizontally and vertically integrated media conglomerates; state-controlled infrastructure) and those without power (audiences, consumers, citizens, amateur producers, and fans). The assumption made by digital enthusiasts is that we are all now interacting and engaging. Yet, media historians know that the 'right to communicate' was thrashed around by members of UNESCO during the 1970s and 1980s and ultimately was dismantled when the United States and the United Kingdom withdrew in protest over the McBride Report, which recommended dismantling global communications. The United Nations was only ever able to agree upon *a right to an environment in which communication could happen* (Hamelink 2003). But what of a right to communicate emotions, a right to feel and to show those feelings through media, the freedom to express opinions or interact with those whose emotions you share or do not share?

Throughout the writing of this book, we have become increasingly aware of the various dynamics of online media in relation to affect and cognition. Although we may not have had the space to offer precise and distinct landscapes, structures, and logics of emotion, we have sought to sketch the terrain upon which future researchers will plot coordinates of the personal, local, and global accounts of emotion online. Within memory studies, Anna Reading maps the terrain of a 'globital memory field' (2011b, 248), with the 'bit' in the middle of the word representing the smallest unit of information. That is, as with digital memory, we can begin thinking about emotion online in terms of Reading's vectors: its transmediality (it travels), its velocity (at different speeds in terms of time), its extensity (it has limits and reaches), its modality (it has patterns), its valency (its ability to bond), its viscosity (its resistance to flow and change), and its axes (x = its composition and y = its mobilization/securitization) (Reading 2011b).[4] While not directly applicable to our close readings in this book, it would be worth pursuing these and to pose a dynamic of *intensity* in relation to emotion in our digital media era. This could help us to understand emotion also as 'assemblages that have multiple non-linear transmedial trajectories and connectivities that may be uneven and contradictory. These traverse conventional communicative binaries, body/machine, analog/digital, public/private; they include discursive formations and material practices of prosumers, citizen journalists as well as mass media organizations'. (Reading 2011b, 251).

That is, universal feelings, global emotion and emotional noise can become misunderstood as prevailing and prevalent, carving societies and individuals up into those who care because they interact and those who do not because they passively consume. As authors, we belong to the 89 out of 100 people who do not interact, but that does not mean we do not care or pay attention. In our mixed-mediated approach to emotion, we have sought to challenge the discourse that emotion in our increasingly mobile, digital, social, and globalized media era is more felt, more spreadable, and more intense. It would be better to think about emotion in a digital media era as being transmitted and received transmedially as assemblages of contradictory affects with different intensities that are felt in different ways. So, how do we feel about emotion online?

Committing web 2.0 suicide

Interestingly, one of the authors got angry with Facebook and tried to leave (it is hard to leave) during the research for this book. It was the ubiquitous family photography, or better still 'friendship photography', that prompted the drastic action of deleting the most popular social networking site in the world (nearly 1 billion users at the time of writing) from her online profile. After almost seven years of archived friendships, discussions, groups, photographs and links, ordinary life just moved too fast and became too complex for the blunt parameters of Facebook's public and social conformity. Garde-Hansen has written in *Save As...Digital Memories* (2009) about the corporate homogeneity of the data architecture of Facebook and in *Media and Memory* (2011), she has noted that Facebook ceaselessly streams data of ordinariness into a 'repetition of memorable experiences across a diverse network of "friends" from different backgrounds' with 'unremarkable conventionality: new babies, weddings, beloved pets, children on the beach, families skiing, gatherings, nights out, concerts, gardens, home improvement and hobbies' (2011, 136).

This seems to undo the purpose of family photography as Annette Kuhn had theorized it, which 'looks toward a future time when things will be different, anticipating a need to remember what will soon be past' (Kuhn 2002, 49). Facebook does not anticipate difference, rather it seems to cement, fix, and archive relationships as ever present, utopian and happy (as Chapter 4 has analysed), while at the same time shoring up existing alliances through online conversations as presentist. It just does not let you forget and, as Paul Connerton (2008) and Viktor Mayer-Schönberger (2009) have argued, forgetting is very important for individual and community resilience. (One might also venture that dispassion, unfeeling, and lack of care may be equally necessary in order to survive in a hypermediated environment of emotion agents). At least analogue photographs can be lost, taken, put away, and destroyed. Now, so many other people in the network have curatorial control over the online representation of the Self (one's life, loves, and living), something noted by grieving families who find friends of their loved one creating memorial sites over which the family has no control.

The only way out is to commit online suicide, which Terro Karpi (2011) argues would offer a bio-political resistance to the network. Facebook has ways of persuading you not to commit such a dreadful act and, in fact, the vast majority of Facebook users balk at the prospect of leaving, however much they complain that online life is not really worth living. One of the authors has asked hundreds of students in her classes: would you commit Facebook suicide? One will have tried but failed, one would consider it, but the rest are incredulous at the thought, even if they admit that much of their time is now spent untagging themselves from others' photos. Even if you do *go all the way*, as one of the authors of this book did, then Facebook has ways of *making you feel bad*, as Karpi notes:

> Not only the present situation of choosing to confirm the disconnection is mediated but also the future is premediated by showing a set of pictures of friends 'who will miss you' after deactivating the account. Here premediation relies heavily on the affects created by profile pictures and names of the user's *Facebook* friends. (Karpi 2011)

Facebook has numerous groups of many thousands of members that state they 'hate being online'. YouTube is teeming with videos that list the five or ten things people hate about Facebook. Some of these are creative and humorous such as Glove and Boots's '10 Reasons Why We Hate Facebook' (YouTube), which include the imposition of 'likes', getting cartoon gifts, 'friend' suggestions, and default privacy settings. From Twitter's 'fail whales' (service 'going down'), to lengthy terms and conditions, to pop-up adverts, to chain mail, there are many emotional pleas through text, video, and audio that appear to enact hate and loathing toward online culture. The fact is, says Karpi, 'what many of the *Facebook* users fear and loathe' is 'their data being used, distributed and exploited by third parties such as marketing ventures or central intelligence agencies' (2011).

At the time of this writing, the Glove and Boots video has 655,546 views, 5,108 likes, 132 dislikes. Of the 571 comments posted, most simply state how much they love the video while others add to the list their own pet hates about Facebook ('emotional people', 'addiction', 'women who bitch and whine') with one comment stating: 'Twitter is for people you would actually hang out with. Facebook is full of people you're trying to forget' (posted by hulllewis0817, December 2011). The tag description to the Glove and Boots video signals the inescapability of emotion in a digital media age: 'We love facebook. And we hate facebook. This video explains why. Speaking of which...visit us on facebook!'

Notes

Introduction

1. While we have seen an exponential rise in social networking at the end of the first decade of the 21st Century, we should note Geert Lovink's emphasis in *Zero Comments: Blogging and Critical Internet Culture* that 'if you get a group of 100 people online then one will create content, 10 will interact with it, and the other 89 will just view it' (2008, xxvii).

2. 'The only way my life makes sense is if, regardless of culture, race, religion, tribe, there is this commonality, these essential truths and passions and hopes and moral precepts that are universal. And that we can reach beyond our differences.' (President Barack Obama in interview with biographer David Maraniss, 10 November 2011.)

3. Among other scholars, Anna Reading has used the term 'memory agents' to describe the 'struggle of cultural production, circulation, and consumption' over 'the assemblage, mobilization, and securitization of memory capital' (2011b, 242). While this idea is clearly focused upon memory and not on emotion, we find the term useful for describing the powerful ways in which emotion might also be assembled, mobilized, and securitized (particularly in terms of media).

4. Our rethinking connects with Joanna Zylinska and Sarah Kember's (2012) *Life after New Media: Mediation as Vital Process*, which argues in favour of 'mediation' rather than media as the focus of theories of biological and social lives.

5. At the time of our writing, the Indian-born UK nurse at King Edward VII hospital, London, committed suicide three days after a hoax call from Australian radio presenters. She mistook them for the Queen enquiring about the Duchess of Cambridge's health. She was a victim of national differences within and between spreadable media content, which meant that the impact of the traditionally and socially mediated audio of her mistake inevitably humiliated her, an ordinary member of the public, nationally and globally.

6. On 11 November 2012, the director general of the BBC, George Entwistle, resigned when it emerged its flagship news programme *Newsnight* wrongly implied that a senior politician had abused children in the 1980s. Widely shared tweets and online postings fuelled the impression this was 'accurate' news.

7. A particularly striking example of this (again concerning children – but this time a child yet to be born) was the handful of images of Feng Jianmei, who lost her 7-month-old foetus to alleged forced abortion in June 2012 in Shaanxi province, China. The 'unheimlich' photos of mother and dead baby lying next to each other on the hospital bed were uploaded to the microblogging site Weibo, created public fury in China and abroad, and could not be controlled by the Great Firewall.

8. The theme of passion at the heart of the emotional economy within media, culture and society was throughly interrogated at the *Media and Passion International Conference*, Lund, Sweden 21st March 2013.
9. We are very grateful to Professor Henry Jenkins for this insight provided to us in conversation at the Popular Cultures Symposium, London, 19 May 2012. Professor Jenkins's research team had been following Invisible Children as an example of fan activism and spreadable media as part of the Civic Paths project. For further information see Jenkins's blog posting 12 March 2012 at www.henryjenkins.org.
10. In 'The Anatomy of the Facebook Social Graph' (2011) Ugander et al. do not find a strong gender homophily but do find a strong effect of age on friendship preferences as well as an effect of nationality. Their research is important because one of the authors is Facebook's own sociologist, Cameron Marlow, who has been analysing in depth what is the largest social network ever.
11. King et al. (2008) undertook research of the bystander effect in *Second Life* (the virtual social networking world in which users take on avatars) to see if 'in-world' witnessing of antisocial behaviour leads to collective action. They tested this by shadowing an avatar called Thomas, who engaged in sexual acts and attacks upon other avatars. Regardless of the level of aggression displayed and the feelings of discomfort represented by the users, users displayed a reluctance to get involved, report the behaviour, or directly stop Thomas and instead agreed that the unseen presence of Linden Labs (makers of Second Life) would enforce the rules and evict Thomas. The bystander effect in the real world is well established.
12. In her work on 'Global Care Chains and Emotional Surplus Value,' Arlie Russell Hochschild argues that 'global care chains,' which she defines as 'a series of personal links between people across the globe based on the paid or unpaid work of caring,' are 'usually made up of women and men, or, in rare cases, made up of just men' (2000, 131).
13. During the Edinburgh Festival 2012, Charlotte De Bruyne and Nathalie Marie Verbeke from *Ontroerend Goed* (a Belgian youth theatre) presented a piece with laptops and data projector of themselves crying to films and news reports. They photographed themselves (using the built-in camera) crying to the online content, projecting the images back to the audience on the screen behind them.
14. For example, what was most striking about the 12-minute YouTube video created and posted by the Norwegian mass murderer Anders Behring Brevik before he killed 77 civilians in 2011 in Norway was the nonspecific reiteration of 1000 years of artistic, historical, and political representations of racism, from the Crusades to the Nazi Holocaust. Brevik's online audiovisual and textual expression of how he felt about multiculturalism seemed safe because it was and could be endlessly copied and de-historicized to any audience and through any means.
15. In his TED talk 'How Social Media Can Make History' Clay Shirky (2009a) passionately argues in favour of new media as social rather than technological as 'the largest increase in expressive capability in human history' and proves this through (only) four (not widely known) stories that he argues 'create an environment for convening and supporting groups' posted June

2009. http://www.ted.com/talks/clay_shirky_how_cellphones_twitter_
facebook_can_make_history.html

16. Google Chrome adverts such as 'Dear Sophie' indicate a need for this
powerful Internet company to be seen as family friendly and a builder/sharer
of human emotion in everyday contexts.

17. *Lost* was produced almost entirely on US soil. Locations in Oahu, Hawaii,
substituted for California, New York, Miami, South Korea, Iraq, Nigeria, UK,
Paris, Thailand, Berlin, Australia and the other locations around the world
that featured in the series.

1   Theorizing Emotion and Affect

1. See also Gorton, (2007) 'Theorising Emotion and Affect: Feminist
Engagements', *Feminist Theory*, 8: 3: 333–348.

2. The mass-produced simplicity of an Apple iPod Classic can be engraved. 'Just
add a personal message such as a name, a favourite saying or song title, and
"I love you" or "Happy Birthday," just about anything. It's easy, it's free and
delivery will be just as fast' (www.apple.com).

3. In June 2012, Nicola Brookes (abused on Facebook by so-called Internet
trolls) won high court backing to force Facebook to reveal the identities of
her cyberbullies. The case rested upon the inciting of hatred (particularly
against women) and the emotional impact this had upon the victim.

4. Note also that the concept of the public is thoroughly contested/disputed
in terms of public versus private attention. See Couldry, Livingstone, and
Markham (2007).

5. For example, the self-reflexive anonymity of The Secret Footballer (his newspaper column and book) alongside the online fan determination to 'out'
him on sites such as www.whoisthesecretfootballer.co.uk perform a 'self'
(in this case the concept of a Premier League player) publicly as emotionally competent within an industry that produces footballers as emotionally
incompetent.

2   Screening Emotion

1. The latter is informed by the perception that 'smart' young viewers under
35 years of age are discussing the TV shows they are watching using social
networking sites, fan sites, and mobile phones as a form of 'virtual togetherness' (see Fiona Graham's (2011) BBC News item 'Beyond the Couch').
Moreover, it is worth noting the rise of the Lean In Community based around
the launch of Facebook COO Sheryl Sandberg's *Lean In: Women, Work and the
Will to Lead* (2013).

2. Since 2008, many major cities have seen a pillow-fight day, promoted via the
Internet. It is interesting to note that www.pillowfightday.com defines the
main goal of International Pillow Fight Day 'to make these unique happenings in public space a significant part of popular culture, partially replacing
passive, non-social consumption experiences like watching television, and

consciously celebrating public spaces' as part of the urban playground movement.

3. Highly attuned to their target market, CBS released *The Big Bang Theory Flash Mob!* on 15 Nov 2012, which saw cast and crew of the hit TV show *The Big Bang Theory* interrupt production of the last scene to engage in a flashmob, danced to Carly Rae Jepsen's 'Call Me Maybe', to the delighted surprise of Chuck Lorre, the senior producers, and the studio audience.

4. Mimi White notes that 'On television, confessional and therapeutic strategies figure centrally in a range of reality genres' (2002, 314). See also Rebecca Coleman's (2013) *Tranforming Images: Screens, Affect, Futures*, London: Routledge.

5. Thanks to Heather McClendon for this example.

6. Thanks to Professor Andrew Hoskins of Glasgow University for this insight.

3 Global Emotion

1. By September 2012, Facebook shares had fallen 52 per cent and on 14 November 2012 the largest shareholder (Zuckerberg) was free to sell 1.32 billion shares.

2. Other more recent organisations such as AVAAZ or Ushahidi have similar philosophies integrated into their use of online journalism and social networking. Thank you to our Kenyan postgraduate student, Hillary Okech, who drew our attention to the editing out of 'hate comments' from Ushahidi during and after the Kenyan election crisis 2007–2008.

3. BBC News [online] 'Where are you on the global fat scale? (12 July 2012), is a good example of a metageographic tool for global responsibility, regardless of difference. That is, if a 37-year-old woman weighing 8 stone 12 pounds from the United Kingdom inputs her data, she is instantly presented with: Obesity Index: 20 BMI, National: below average (93 per cent of females are above this bmi), Global: below average (78 per cent of females are above this bmi), and 'You're most like someone from *Ethiopia*'. Personal contribution to global civic responsibility is calculated as: 'If everyone in the world had the same BMI as you, it would remove 48,754,368 tonnes from the total weight of the world's population'.

4. Numerous publications have emerged/are emerging with titles that define media in terms of connected, connectivity, and creativity (see, for example, Baym 2010; Gauntlett 2011; van Dijck [2013]).

5. Sarita Yardi and danah boyd (2010) make the same point about the use of Twitter during two local events in the USA – a shooting in Kansas and a building collapse in Georgia – that proved the benefits of being technologically connected to others who were physically nearby.

4 Social Media, Happiness, and Virtual Communities

1. There are also a number of remediated McDonald's logos found through a Google Image search that show quite the opposite emotion/affect: 'I was lovin' it', 'I'm hatin' it' and 'I'm vomitin' it', for example.

2. It is worth noting here that as online viewers we are able to partake in the nuptials of thousands of married couples that post their wedding videos online. Some of these include the couple flashmobbing the guests with a surprise dance routine that may or may not include forewarned guests as participants (e.g., see 'Wedding First Dance' on ebaumsworld.com with over 700,000 views or 'Wedding Thriller' on YouTube with over 16 million views).

3. It is worth highlighting Elizabeth Siegel's groundbreaking research of nineteenth-century American *cartes de visite* and cabinet card albums, which were exchanged and displayed by families as a record and social register. Her findings show a continuum of self-presentation, now found in Facebook imagery (see *Galleries of Friendship and Fame: A History of 19th Century Photograph Albums* 2010).

4. See also data on 'Facebook friends' in 'Tastes, ties and time: a new social network dataset using Facebook.com,' by Kevin Lewis et al. in *Social Networks*, 2008.

5. See CBS News, 'Facebook ramps up efforts to prevent suicide', 14 December 2011.

5 Emo-Techno-Ecology: Fear and Anger about Climate Change

1. Critical and cultural theory (in the context of posthumanism and transhumanism) have begun to deeply interrogate animality, technics, humanity, and the future of life in a digital age; see Zylinska and Kember (2012) and Zylinska (2012, 2009).

2. See for example the Royal Geographical Society's Annual International Conference 2011, which covered a session of papers on the theme 'Meteorological Imaginations: Towards Geographies of Affective Practices of Weather, Atmospherics and Landscapes'.

3. In fact, one of the authors is part of a team of researchers on an Economic and Social Research Council (ESRC) funded project, *Sustainable Flood Memories* (2011–2013), the results of which will explore the personal, local, and regional representations of extreme weather in terms of lay knowledge, folk memories, media archives, and memory performances.

4. The 'Emotional Geographies Conference', 6–8 April 2010, Adelaide, Australia. This was the third international conference on this topic, preceded by conferences held in UK (2008) and Canada (2009).

5. In 2012 the University of Liverpool's Dr Neil Gavin delivered a paper, 'The Media and Climate Change', alongside Richard Black (BBC environment correspondent) on 'Reporting Climate Change' and Dr Lorraine Whitmarsh's (Cardiff University) on 'Climate Attitudes & Attitude Change.'

6. See Andrew Hoskins's edited series Media, War and Security (Routledge), which has titles covering war, violence, 9/11, race, and religion, all in their relationships to and with media.

7. It is worth noting that IMDb began as an archive of movie information that was noncorporate; searches were often triggered by a simple query, such as the one that was positioned as the banner on the early interface: 'What was that film they were both in?'

8. An excellent example of product reviews being hijacked for political purposes can be found on Amazon.com for BIC Cristal For Her Ball Pen, 1.0mm, Black, 16 pens $8.65. At first glance this is a pack of pens with a healthy 583 reviews. Look closely and the reviews reveal a relentless satirical political attack on BIC for producing a range of pens in pretty pastel colours. The architecture of Amazon's interface is redefined with the top-selected comment: 'As if men hadn't been stripped of everything good already, BIC steps in and piles on by encouraging women to learn to write, just like their male counterparts.'—JohnnyTubesteak. Ninety-three reviewers made a similar statement (http://www.amazon.com/BIC-Cristal-1-0mm-Black-MSLP16-Blk/dp/B004F9QBE6).

9. See danah boyd's presentation 'The Power of Fear in Networked Publics', SXSW, Austin, Texas, 10 March 2012 (Boyd 2012b). We use the phrase 'attention economy' less in terms of cognitive issues of information overload and more in terms of emotional issues of paying attention and caring for.

10. Note the case in the UK in 2010 of Colm Cross the man who went to jail for leaving obscene messages on Internet tribute sites. The UK police were supplied with the evidence to convict him from an anonymous troll hunter.

6 The Hate and Shame of Women's Bodies Online

1. A troll is online slang for someone who is deceptive, derogatory or tangential in his or her postings to an online community, discussion board, blog or twitter feed. Trolling has been a very common feature of online communities for decades but has grown in prominence due to the increased media exposure of and moral panics about the desecration of RIP sites and celebrity twitter accounts by trolls

2. One only has to track the online reports and their comments about the well-publicised 'Haidl Gang Rape' case in Orange County in 2002 and the recent public appearances of Jane Doe (the victim) as a 'survivor' whose rape was recorded on video, to get a sense of just how emotionally charged online discussions can be regarding women and their bodies. The case revolved around that pivotal question 'Did she use her body or was her body used?' and at what point in the transaction of intimacy a sexual exchange took place. The fact that she became unconscious left in doubt when that moment was to the perpetrators, even though it seemed clear to viewers of the video.

3. 'It is worth noting the now-frequent announcement: 'Please help us safeguard our children by not sharing any of their images on social networking sites', as teachers implore parents who are busily videoing and taking photos of their children at sports days.

4. The loss of control of one's body or one's senses has become the main point of argument regarding high-profile sexual assault cases, where the victim is not in a position to consent, even though she may have consented previously (i.e., she is asleep or intoxicated). A similar argument is used to justify the use of nudz, in that consent to the photograph's being taken is therefore considered to be consent to its being uploaded to the Internet.

7 Conclusion

1. In fact, alongside a whole range of media forms that produce human inactivity, the computer is being blamed for making us obese and slothful (the latter affect has been derided by previous generations).
2. That the journal *Feminist Media Studies* should devote a whole issue to the relationship between affect, intimacy and mobile technologies while we were writing this book, is a timely counter-narrative to the emotion-agents within scientific discourses who seek to explain those things we hold dear (see Hjorth and Lim, 2012).
3. Twitter, http://en.wikipedia.org/wiki/Twitter accessed 11 March 2009.
4. The authors would like to thank Anna Reading for her insightful discussions and feedback at the *Digital Memories Seminar*, London, 10 July 2012. Although Reading's six dynamics (2011b, 248–251) pertain to temporality as a defining aspect of commemoration, remembering and witnessing, they are very useful contextually for understanding the 'multimodal, transversal' dynamics of media in a digital age.

Bibliography

Abbott, Stacey (2010) *The Cult TV Book*, London: I.B. Tauris.

Abu-Lughod, Lila (2002) 'Egyptian Melodrama – technology of the modern subject?' in Faye Ginsburg, Lila Abu-Lughod, and Brian Larkin (eds) *Media Worlds: Anthropology on New Terrain*, Berkeley: University of California Press, pp. 115–133.

—— (1986) *Veiled Sentiments: Honor and Poetry in a Bedouin Society*, Berkeley: University of California Press.

Adorno, Theodor and Max Horkheimer (1979) *Dialectic of Enlightenment*, London: Verso.

Ahmed, Sara (2010) *The Promise of Happiness*, Durham, NC: Duke University Press.

—— (2004) *The Cultural Politics of Emotion*, Edinburgh: Edinburgh University Press.

Allen, Matthew J. and Steven D. Brown (2011) 'Embodiment and living memorials: the affective labour of remembering the 2005 London bombings', *Memory Studies*, 4: 312–327.

Andrejevic, Mark (2004) *Reality TV: The Work of being Watched*, Lanham, MD: Rowman and Littlefield.

Ang, Ien (1996) *Living Room Wars: Rethinking Media Audiences*, London: Routledge.

—— (1985) *Watching Dallas: Soap Opera and the Melodramatic Imagination*, London: Methuen.

Angel, Maria and Anna Gibbs (2006) 'Media, affect and the face: biomediation and the political scene', *Southern Review*, 38(2): 24–39.

—— (1994) *Descartes' Error: Emotion, Reason and the Human Brain*, New York: Putnam.

Appadurai, Arjun (1996) *Modernity at Large: Cultural Dimensions of Globalization*, Minneapolis, MN: University of Minnesota.

Aristotle (1976) *The Ethics of Aristotle: The Nicomachean Ethics*, translated by J.A.K. Thomson, London: Penguin. Revised edition, 1976 (original translation published 1953).

Atton, Chris (2004) *An Alternative Internet: Radical Media, Politics and Creativity*, Edinburgh: Edinburgh University Press.

Aveyard, Karina (2011) 'The place of cinema and film in contemporary rural Australia', *Participations: Journal of Audience and Reception Studies*, 8: 294–307.

Bacon, Richard (2012) 'Richard Bacon: my battle with the trolls', *BBC News Magazine*, 19 March 2012. Available at: http://www.bbc.co.uk/news/magazine-17399027 (Accessed 20 April 2012).

Baker, Andrea J. (2005) *Double Click: Romance and Commitment Among Couples Online*, New York: Hampton Press Communication Series: New Media.

Banks, James (2010) 'Regulating hate speech online', *International Review of Law, Computers and Technology*, 24(3): 233–239.

Balibar, Etienne and Immanuel Wallerstein (1991) *Race, Nation, Class: Ambiguous Identities*, London: Verso.

Barker, Chris (1999) *Television, Globalization and Cultural Identities*, Buckingham: Open University Press.

Barney, Darin (2004) *The Network Society*, Cambridge: Polity.

Baudrillard, Jean (1995 [1991]) *The Gulf War Did Not Take Place*, translated by Paul Patton, Sydney: Power Publications.

Baym, Nancy (2010) *Personal Connections in the Digital Age*, Cambridge: Polity.

—— (2000) *Tune In, Log On: Soaps, Fandom and Online Community*, Thousand Oaks, CA: Sage.

Beaverstock, Jonathan, R. G. Smith, and P. J Taylor (2005) 'World-city network: a new metageography?' in N. R. Fyfe and J. T. Kenny (eds) *The Urban Geography Reader*, London: Routledge, pp. 63–73.

Beck, Ulrich (2009) *World at Risk*, Cambridge: Polity.

—— (2006) *Cosmopolitan Vision*, Cambridge: Polity.

Beeton, Sue (2005) *Film-Induced Tourism*, Clevedon: Channel View Publications.

Behringer, Wolfgang (2010) *A Cultural History of Climate*, Cambridge: Polity.

Bell, David and Barbara M. Kennedy (eds) (2000) *The Cybercultures Reader*, London: Routledge.

Bendelow, Gillian and Simon J. Williams (eds) (1998) *Emotions in Social Life: Critical Themes and Contemporary Issues*, London: Routledge.

Ben-Ze'ev, Aaron (2004) *Love Online: Emotions on the Internet*, Cambridge: Cambridge University Press.

Berlant, Lauren (2011) *Cruel Optimism*, Durham, NC: Duke University Press.

—— (2004) (ed.) *Compassion: The Culture and Politics of an Emotion*, New York: Routledge.

—— (2000) (ed.) *Intimacy*, Chicago, IL: The University of Chicago Press.

—— (1997) *The Queen of America Goes to Washington City: Essays on Sex and Citizenship*, Durham, NC: Duke University Press.

Bernstein, Gabrielle (2010) *Add More ~ing to Your Life: A Hip Guide to Happiness*, New York: Three Rivers Press.

Blackman, Lisa (2011) 'Affect, performance and queer subjectivities', *Cultural Studies*, 25(2): 183–199.

—— (2010) 'Embodying affect: voice-hearing, telepathy, suggestion and modeling the non-conscious', *Body and Society: Special Issue on Affect*, 16(1): 163–192.

—— (2007) 'Feeling FINE: social psychology,suggestions and the problem of social influence', *International Journal of Critical Psychology: Special Issue on Affect and Feeling*, 21: 23–49.

—— (2001) *Mass Hysteria: Critical Psychology and Media Studies*, Basingstoke: Palgrave Macmillan.

Blackman, Lisa, and John Cromby (2007) 'Editorial: affect and feeling', *Critical Psychology*, 21: 5–22.

Blackman, Lisa, and Janet Harbord (2010) 'Technologies of mediation and the affective': a case study of the mediated environment of mediacityUK', in Deborah Hauptmann and Warren Neidich (eds) *Cognitive Architecture: From Biopolitics to Noopolitics, Architecture and Mind in the Age of Communication and Information*, Rotterdam: 010 Publishers, pp. 302–323.

Boehner, Kirsten, Rogério DePaula, Paul Dourish, and Phoebe Sengers (2007) 'How emotion is made and measured', *International Journal of Human-Computer Studies*, 65: 275–291.

Booth, Paul (2010) *Digital Fandom: New Media Studies*, New York: Peter Lang.

Bortoluzzi, Maria (2009) *'An Inconvenient Truth*: multimodal emotions in identity construction', in Jane Vincent and Leopoldina Fortunati (eds) *Electronic Emotion: The Mediation of Emotion via Information and Communication Technologies*, Bern: Peter Lang, pp. 137–154.

Bos, N., Olson, J. S., Olson, G. M., Wright, Z., and Gergle, D. (2002) 'Rich media helps trust development', *CHI 2002 Conference Proceedings*, New York: ACM Press.

boyd, danah (2012a) 'Nancy Baym, Kate Crawford, Mary L. Gray to join Microsoft Research', *danah boyd | apophenia: Making connections where none previously existed*. Available at www.zephoria.org (12 June 2012)

—— (2012b) 'The Power of Fear in Networked Publics', *SXSW*, Austin, Texas, 10 March 2012.

—— (2010) 'Social network sites as networked publics: affordances, dynamics, and implications', in Zizi Papacharissi (ed.) *A Networked Self: Identity, Community, and Culture on Social Network Sites*, London: Routledge, pp. 39–58.

—— (2008) 'None of this is Real', in Joe Karaganis (ed.) *Structures of Participation in Digital Culture*, New York: Social Science Research Council, pp. 132–157.

—— (2005) 'Sociable technology and democracy', in Jon Lebkowsky and Mitch Ratcliffe (eds) *Extreme Democracy*, Lulu, pp. 198–209. Available at http://www. danah.org/papers/ExtremeDemocracy.pdf (5 April 2012).

Brabazon, Tara (2005) *From Revolution to Revelation: Generation X, Popular Memory and Cultural Studies*, Hants: Ashgate.

Brace, Catherine and Hilary Geoghegan (2011) 'Human geographies of climate change: Landscape, temporality, and lay knowledges', *Progress in Human Geography*, 35(3): 284–302.

Braidotti, Rosi (1994) *Nomadic Subjects: Embodiment and Sexual Difference in Contemporary Feminist Theory*, New York: Columbia University Press.

Brennan, Teresa (2004) *The Transmission of Affect*, Ithaca, NY: Cornell University Press.

Brooker, Will (2002) *Using the Force: Creativity, Community and Star Wars Fans*, London: Continuum.

Broughton, Lee (2011) 'Crossing borders virtual and real: a transnational Internet-based community of Spaghetti Western fans finally meet each other face to face on the wild plains of Almeria, Spain', *Language and Intercultural Communication*, 11(4): 304–318.

Bury, Rhiannon (2008) 'Praise you like I should: Cyberfans and *Six Feet Under*', in Leverette, Ott, and Buckley-Ott (eds) *It's Not TV: Watching HBO in the Post-Television Era*, New York: Routledge, pp. 190–208.

Butler, Judith (1997) *The Psychic Life of Power: Theories in Subjection*, Stanford, CA: University of California Press.

CBS News (2011) 'Facebook ramps up effort to prevent suicide', 14 December 2011.

Callard, Felicity (2006) 'Understanding agoraphobia: women, men, and the historical geography of urban anxiety', in Carol Berkin, Judith Pinch, and Carole Appel (eds) *Exploring Women's Studies: Looking Forward, Looking Back*, London: Prentice-Hall, pp. 201–217.

Callard, Felicity and Constantina Papoulias (2010a) 'Affect and embodiment', in Susannah Radstone and B. Schwartz (eds) *Memory: Histories, Theories, Debates*, New York: Fordham University Press, pp. 246–262.

—— (2010b) 'Biology's gift: interrogating the turn to affect', *Body and Society: Special Issue on Affect*, 16(1): 29–56.

Calloway-Thomas, Carolyn (2010) *Empathy in the Global World: An Intercultural Perspective*, London: Sage.

Campbell, Scott W. and Yong Jin Park (2008) 'Social implications of mobile telephony: the rise of personal communication society', *Sociology Compass*, 2(2): 371–387.

Cantor, Joanne (2009) 'Fright reactions to mass media', in Jennings Bryant and Mary Beth Oliver (eds) *Media Effects: Advances in Theory and Practice*, 3rd Edition, New York: Routledge, pp. 287–303.

Carpentier, Nico and Salvatore Scifo (2010) 'Introduction: community media's long March', *Telematics and Informatics*, 27: 115–118.

Carroll, Noël (1999) 'Film, Emotion, and Genre', in Carl Plantinga and Greg M. Smith (eds) *Passionate Views: Film, Cognition, and Emotion*, Baltimore: The John Hopkins University Press, pp. 21–47.

Caspi, Avner and Paul Gorksy (2006) 'Online deception: prevalence, motivation and emotion', *Cyberpsychology and Behavior*, 9(1): 54–59.

Castells, Manuel (1996) *The Rise of the Network Society*, 1st Edition, Oxford: Blackwell.

Chen, Hsinchun (2012) *Dark Web: Exploring and Data Mining the Dark Side of the Web, Integrated Series in Information Systems 30*, New York: Springer.

Ciochetto, Lynne (2011) *Globalisation and Advertising in Emerging Economies*, London: Taylor and Francis.

Climate Change Communication Advisory Group (CCCAG) (2010) *Communicating Climate Change to Mass Public Audiences*. Available at http://pirc.info/downloads/communicating_climate_mass_audiences.pdf (12 January 2012).

Cloud, Dana L. (1998) *Control and Consolation in American Culture and Politics: Rhetoric of Therapy*, Thousand Oaks, CA: Sage.

Clough, Patricia T. (2012) 'War by any other means: what difference do(es) the graphic(s) make?' in Athina Karatzogianni and Adi Kuntsman (eds) *Digital Cultures and the Politics of Emotion: Feelings, Affect and Technological Change*, Basingstoke: Palgrave Macmillan, pp. 21–32.

—— (2010) 'The affective turn: political economy, biomedia and bodies', in Gregg, M. and Seigworth, G.J. (eds) *The Affect Theory Reader*, Durham, NC: Duke University Press, pp. 206–224.

—— (2009) *The Becoming of Bodies: Girls, Images, Experience*, Manchester: Manchester University Press.

—— (ed.) (2007) Patricia Ticiento Clough, *The Affective Turn: Theorizing the Social*, with Jean Haley, Durham, NC: Duke University Press.

—— (2000) *Autoaffection: Unconscious Thought in the Age of Teletechnology*, Minneapolis, MN: University of Minnesota Press.

—— (1998) *The End(s) of Ethnography*, New York: Peter Lang.

Clough, Patricia T. and Craig Willse (eds) (2012) *Beyond Biopolitics: Essays on the Governance of Life and Death*, Durham, NC: Duke University Press.

Cochrane, Kira (2012) 'Creepshots and revenge porn: how paparazzi culture affects women', *The Guardian*, 22 September 2012. Available at http://www.guardian.co.uk/culture/2012/sep/22/creepshots-revenge-porn-paparazzi-women (23 September 2012).

Cohen, Stanley (2002 [1972]) *Folk Devils and Moral Panics*, 3rd Edition, London: Routledge.

Coleman, Rebecca (2012) *Transforming Images: Screens, Affect, Futures*, London: Routledge.

—— (2009) *The Becoming of Bodies: Girls, Images, Experience*, Manchester: Manchester University Press.

—— (2008) 'The becoming of bodies: Girls, media effects and body image', *Feminist Media Studies*, 8(2): 163–179.

Connerton, Paul (2008) 'Seven types of forgetting', *Memory Studies*, 1(1): 59–71.

Cottle, Simon and Libby Lester (2009) 'Visualizing climate change: television news and ecological citizenship', *International Journal of Communication*, 3: 920–936.

Cottle, Simon (2006) *Mediatized Conflict: Developments in Media and Conflict Studies*, Maidenhead: Open University Press.

Couldry, Nick, Sonia Livingstone and Tim Markham (2007) *Media Consumption and Public Engagement: Beyond the Presumption of Attention*. Basingstoke: Palgrave Macmillan.

Couldry, Nick (2003) *Media Rituals: A Critical Approach*, London: Routledge.

Crawford, Kate (2009a) 'These foolish things: on intimacy and insignificance in mobile media', in Goggin, G. and Hjorth, L (eds) *Mobile technologies: From telecommunications to media*, New York: Routledge, pp. 252–266.

—— (2009b) 'Following you: disciplines of listening in social media', *Continuum: Journal of Media and Cultural Studies*, 23(4): 525–535.

Crothers, Lane (2010) *Globalization and American Popular Culture*, Plymouth: Rowman and Littlefield Publishers, Inc.

Csigo, Peter (2010) 'Permanent turbulence and reparatory work: a dramaturgical approach to late modern television', in N. Couldry, A. Hepp and K. Krotz (eds) *Media Events in a Global Age*, London: Routledge, pp. 141–155.

Cumiskey, Kathleen (2010) '"Simply leaving my house would be even scarier": how mobile phones affect women's perception of safety and experience of public places', *Media Asia: An Asian Communication Quarterly*, 37(4): 205–214.

Curran, James (2002) *Media and Power*, London: Routledge.

Curran, James and Jean Seaton (2009) *Power without Responsibility: The Press, Broadcasting and New Media in Britain*, 7th Edition, London: Routledge.

Curtin, Michael (2007) *Playing the World's Biggest Audience: The Globalization of Chinese Film and TV*, Berkeley, CA: University of California Press.

Cvetkovich, Ann (2003) *An Archive of Feelings: Trauma, Sexuality, and Lesbian Public Cultures*, Durham, NC: Duke University Press.

CyberEmotions (2009–2013) 'Objectives' (website) www.cyberemotions.eu/objectives

Damasio, Antonio (2000) *The Feeling of What Happens: Body, Emotion and the Making of Consciousness*, London: Vintage.

Danet, Brenda and Susan C. Herring (2007) *The Multilingual Internet: Language, Culture and Communication Online*, Oxford: Oxford University Press.

Daniels, J. (2008) 'Race, civil rights, and hate speech in the digital era', in A. Everett (ed.) *Learning Race and Ethnicity: Youth and Digital Media*, Cambridge, MA: MIT Press, pp. 129–154.

Dasgupta, Romit (2011) 'Emotional spaces and places of Salaryman anxiety in *Tokyo Sonata*', *Japanese Studies*, 31(3): 373–386.

Davidson, J., Bondi, L. and Smith, M. (eds) (2005) *Emotional Geographies*, Ashgate: Aldershot.

Davis, Erik (1999) *TechGnosis: Myth, Magic and Mysticism in the Age of Information*, London: Serpents Tail.

Dayan, Daniel and Elihu Katz (1992) *Media Events: the Live Broadcasting of History*, Harvard: Harvard University Press.

Dean, Jodi (2005) 'Communicative capitalism: circulation and the foreclosure of politics', *Cultural Politics*, 1(1). Available at: http://jdeanicite.typepad.com/i_cite/2005/01/communicative_c.html (16 April 2012).

Deleuze, Gilles (1988) *Spinoza: Practical Philosophy*, trans. Robert Hurley, San Francisco: City Lights Books.

Delwiche, Aaron and Jennifer Jacobs Henderson (eds) (2012) *The Participatory Cultures Handbook*, London: Routledge.

Demos, E. Virginia (ed.) (1995) *Exploring Affect: The Selected Writings of Silvan S. Tompkins*, New York: Cambridge University Press.

Dicks, Bella (2011) *Digital Qualitative Research Methods*, 4 Volumes, London: Sage.

Donath, Judith S. (1999) 'Identity and deception in the virtual community', in M. A. Smith and P. Kollock (eds) *Communities in Cyberspace*, London: Routledge, pp. 29–59.

Dourish, Paul and Genevieve Bell (2011) *Divining a Digital Future: Mess and Mythology in Ubiquitous Computing*, Cambridge, MA: MIT Press.

Döveling, Katrin, Christian von Scheve, and Elly A. Konijn (eds) (2010) *The Routledge Handbook of Emotions and Mass Media*, London: Routledge.

Döveling, Katrin, Christian von Scheve, and Elly A. Konijn (2010) 'Emotions and mass media: an interdisciplinary approach', in Döveling, Katrin, Christian von Scheve, and Elly A. Konijn (eds) The Routledge *Handbook of Emotions and Mass Media*, London: Routledge, pp. 1–12.

Easton, Mark (2006) 'Britain's happiness in decline', http://news.bbc.co.uk/1/hi/programmes/happiness_formula/4771908.stm, accessed 20 July 2012.

Ellison, Nicole, Charles Steinfield and Cliff Lampe (2007) 'The benefits of facebook "Friends:" social capital and college students' use of online social network sites', *Journal of Computer –Mediated Communications*, 12: 1143–1168.

Ellison, Nicole, Rebecca Heino, and Jennifer Gibbs (2006) 'Managing impressions online: self-presentation processes in the online dating environment', *Journal of Computer- Mediated Communication*, 11(2). Available at http://jcmc.indiana.edu/vol11/issue2/ellison.html (12 May 2012).

Eng, David L. and David Kazanjian (eds) (2003) *Loss: The Politics of Mourning*, Berkeley, CA: University of California Press.

Evans, Dylan and Pierre Cruse (eds) (2004) *Emotion, Evolution and Rationality*, Oxford: Oxford University Press.

Evans, Elizabeth (2011a) 'The evolving media ecosystem: an interview with Victoria Jaye, BBC', in *Ephemeral Media: Transitory Screen Culture from Television to YouTube*, Paul Grainge (ed.) Houndmills: Palgrave, pp. 105–121.

Evans Elizabeth (2011b) *Transmedia Television: Audiences, New Media and Daily Life*, London: Routledge.

Evans, Mary and Carolyn Williams (eds) (2012) *Gender: The Key Concepts*, London: Routledge.

Featherstone, Mike (ed.) (1990) *Global Culture: Nationalism, Globalization and Modernity*, London: Sage.

Featherstone, Mike and Scott Lash (1995) 'Globalization, modernity and the spatialization of social theory: an introduction', in M. Featherstone and S. Lash (eds) *Global Modernities*, London: Sage, pp. 1–24.

Fenton, Natalie (2009) 'My media studies: getting political in a global, digital age', *Television and New Media*, 10(1): 55–57.

—— (2008) 'Mediating hope', *International Journal of Cultural Studies*, 11, 230–248.

Ferreday, Debra and Rebecca Coleman (2010) 'Introduction: hope and feminist theory', *Journal for Cultural Research*, 14(4): 313–321.

Ferreday, Debra (2010) 'Reading disorders: online suicide and the death of hope', *Journal for Cultural Research*, 14(4): 409–426.

—— (2009) *Online Belongings: Fantasy, Virtuality, Community*, Oxford: Peter Lang.

—— (2005) 'Bad communities: internet communities and hate speech', *M/C Online*, 8(1). Available at http://journal.media-culture.org.au/0502/07- ferreday.php (4 April 2012).

—— (2003) 'Unspeakable bodies: erasure, embodiment and the pro-ana community', *International Journal of Cultural Studies*, 6(3): 277–295.

Fiske, John (1989a) *Reading the Popular*, Boston: Unwin Hyman.

—— (1989b) *Understanding Popular Culture*, Boston: Unwin Hyman.

Flint, Colin (ed.) (2004) *Spaces of Hate: Geographies of Discrimination and Intolerance in the USA*, New York: Routledge.

Fortunati, Leopoldina (2008) 'Reflections on mediated gossip', in *Mobile Communication and the Ethics of Social Networking*, Conference Pre-proceedings http://www.socialscience.t-mobile.hu/2008/Preproceedings.pdf, pp. 71–78.

Franklin, Sarah, Celia Lury and Jackie Stacey (2000) *Global Nature, Global Culture*, London: Sage.

Franks, David D. and E. Doyle McCarthy (eds) (1989) The *Sociology of Emotions: Original Essays and Research Papers*, Greenwich, CT: Jai Press.

Freud, Sigmund (2001 [1958]) *The Standard Edition of the Complete Psychological Works: An Infantile Neurosis and Other Works*, Volume XVII (1917–1919), London: The Hogarth Press.

Friedman, Kasja Ekholm and Jonathan Friedman (2008) *Modernities, Class and the Contradictions of Globalization: The Anthropology of Global Systems*, Lanham, MD: AltaMira Press.

Frith, Simon (1988) *Music for Pleasure: Essays in the Sociology of Pop*, London: Routledge

Fuller, Matthew and Andrew Goffey (2012) *Evil Media*, Cambridge, MA: MIT Press

Furedi, Frank (2007) *Invitation to Terror: Expanding the Empire of the Unknown*, London: Continuum.

—— (2006) *Culture of Fear*, 2nd Edition, London: Continuum.

Gabrys, Jennifer (2011) *Digital Rubbish: A Natural History of Electronics*, Ann Arbor: University of Michigan Press.

Garde-Hansen, Joanne (forthcoming) 'Friendship photography: memory, mobility and social networking', in Mette Sandbye and Jonas Larsen (eds) *Digital Snaps: The New Face of Photography*, London: I.B. Tauris.

—— (2011) *Media and Memory*, Edinburgh: Edinburgh University Press.

—— (2009) 'My memories?: personal digital archive fever and Facebook', in J. Garde-Hansen, A. Hoskins and A. Reading (eds) *Save As...Digital Memories*, Basingstoke: Palgrave Macmillan, pp. 135–150.

Garde-Hansen, Joanne, Andrew Hoskins, and Anna Reading (2009) *Save As…Digital Memories*, Basingstoke: Palgrave Macmillan.

Gauntlett, David (2011) *Making is Connecting: The Social Meaning of Creativity from DIY and Knitting to YouTube and Web 2.0*, Cambridge: Polity.

Gauntlett, David and Annette Hill (1999) *TV Living: Television Culture and Everyday Life*, London: Routledge.

Geraghty, Christine (1991) Women and Soap Opera: A Study of Prime Time Soaps, Cambridge: Polity.

Gibbs, Anna (2011) 'Affect theory and audience', in Virginia Nightingale (ed.) *The Handbook of Media Audiences*, Oxford: John Wiley and Sons, pp. 251–266.

—— (2010) 'After affect: sympathy, synchrony, and mimetic communication', in Gregg, M. and Seigworth, G.J. (eds), *The Affect Theory Reader*, Durham, NC: Duke University Press, pp. 186–205.

—— (2008) 'Panic! Affect contagion, mimesis and suggestion in the social field', *Cultural Studies Review*, 14(2): 130–145.

—— (2005) 'In Thrall: affect contagion and the bio-energetics of media', *M/C Journal of Media and Culture*, 8(6). Available at http://journal.media- culture. org.au/0512/10-gibbs.php (10 June 2012).

—— (2002) 'Disaffected', *Continuum: Journal of Media and Cultural Studies*, 16(3): 335–341.

—— (2001) 'Contagious feelings: Pauline Hanson and the epidemiology of affect', *Australian Humanities Review*. Available at www.australianhumanitiesreview.org (11 July 2011).

Gibbs, Jennifer L., Nicole B. Ellison, and Chi-Hui Lai (2010) 'First comes love, then comes Google: An investigation of uncertainty reduction strategies and self- disclosure in online dating', *Communication Research*, 38(1): 70–100.

Giddens, Anthony (2011) *The Politics of Climate Change*, Cambridge: Polity.

—— (1991) *Modernity and Self-Identity: Self and Society in the Late Modern Age*, Cambridge: Polity Press.

—— (1990) *The Consequences of Modernity*, Stanford, CA: Stanford University Press.

Giddings, Seth and Martin Lister (eds) (2011) *The New Media and Technocultures Reader*, London: Routledge.

Gilbert, Daniel (2005) *Stumbling on Happiness*, London: Random House.

Gilbert, Elizabeth (2006) *Eat, Pray, Love: One Woman's Search for Everything Across Italy, India and Indonesia*, London: Penguin.

Gitlin, Todd (2002) *Media Unlimited: How the Torrent of Images and Sounds Overwhelms Our Lives*, New York: Henry Holt & Co.

Gladwell, Malcolm (2010) 'Small change: why the revolution will not be tweeted', *New Yorker* (4 October). Available at: www.newyorker.com/ reporting/2010/10/04/101004fa_fact_gladwell (16 April 2012).

Glassner, Barry (2009 [1999]) *Culture of Fear: Why Americans are Afraid of the Wrong Things*, New York: Basic Books.

Glotz, Peter, Stephan Bertschi, and Chris Locke (eds) (2005) *Thumb Culture: The Meaning of Mobile Phones for Society*, New Brunswick, NJ: Transaction Publishers.

Goggin, G. and Hjorth, L (eds) (2008) *Mobile Technologies: From Telecommunications to Media*, New York: Routledge.

Goffman, Erving (1961) *Encounters: Two Studies in the Sociology of Interaction*, Indianapolis, IN: Bobbs-Merrill.

Gopnik, Adam (2011) 'How the internet gets inside us', *The New Yorker*, 14 February, pp. 1–5. Available at http://www.newyorker.com/ (4 April 2012).

Gorton, Kristyn and Joanne Garde-Hansen (2013) 'From old media whore to new media troll: The Online Negotiation of Madonna's Ageing Body', *Feminist Media Studies*, 13(3)

Gorton, Kristyn (2009) *Media Audiences: Television, Meaning, and Emotion*, Edinburgh: Edinburgh University Press.

—— (2007) 'Theorizing Emotion and Affect: Feminist Engagements', *Feminist Theory*, 8(3): 333–348.

Gould, Deborah (2010) 'On affect and protest', in Ann Cvetkovich, Ann Reynolds, and Janet Staiger (eds) *Political Emotions*, London: Routledge, pp. 18–44.

Graham, Fiona (2011) 'Beyond the couch: TV goes, social, goes everywhere', *BBC News* 16 September 2011. Available at: http://www.bbc.co.uk/news/business-14921491 (17 December 2012).

Gray, Ann (1992) *Video Playtime: The Gendering of a Leisure Technology*, London: Comedia and Routledge.

Gray, Jonathan (2010) *Show Sold Separately: Promos, Spoilers, and Other Media Paratexts*, New York: New York University Press.

Gray, Mary (2009) *Out in the Country: Youth, Media, and Queer Visibility in Rural America*, New York: New York University Press

Gregg, Melissa and Gregory J. Seigworth (eds) (2010) *The Affect Theory Reader*, Durham, NC: Duke University Press.

Gregg, Melissa (2012) 'White collar intimacy', in Athina Karatzogianni and Adi Kuntsman (eds) *Digital Cultures and the Politics of Emotion: Feelings, Affect and Technological Change*, Basingstoke: Palgrave Macmillan, pp. 147–164.

—— (2011) *Work's Intimacy*, Cambridge: Polity Press

—— (2010) 'On friday night drinks: workplace affects in the age of the cubicle', in Melissa Gregg and Gregory J. Seigworth (eds) *The Affect Theory Reader*, Durham, NC: Duke University Press, pp. 250–268.

—— (2006) *Cultural Studies' Affective Voices*, Basingstoke: Palgrave Macmillan.

Gregory, D. and Pred, A. (2007) *Violent Geographies: Fear, Terror and Political Violence*, London: Routledge.

Grodal, Torben (1997) *Moving Pictures: A New Theory of Film Genres, Feelings, and Cognition*, Oxford: Clarendon Press.

Gross, Daniel M. (2006) *The Secret History of Emotion: From Aristotle's Rhetoric to Modern Brain Science*, Chicago: University of Chicago Press.

Grossberg, Lawrence (2010) 'Affect's future: rediscovering the virtual in the actual' (An Interview with Gregory J. Seigworth and Melissa Gregg), in Melissa Gregg and Gregory J. Seigworth (eds) *The Affect Theory Reader*, Durham, NC: Duke University Press, pp. 309–338.

—— (1992) 'Is there a fan in the house?: the affective sensibility of fandom', in Lisa A. Lewis (ed.) *The Adoring Audience: Fan Culture and Popular Media*, London: Routledge, pp. 50–68.

—— (1988) 'Postmodernity and affect: all dressed up with no place to go', *Communications*, 10, 271–293.

Grusin, Richard (2010) *Premediation: Affect and Mediality after 9/11*, Basingstoke: Palgrave: Macmillan.

Halbwachs, Maurice (1992[1950]) *The Collective Memory*, translated by Lewis. A. Coser, Chicago, IL: University of Chicago Press.

Hall, P. Cougar, Joshua H. West, and Emily McIntyre (2012) 'Female self-sexualization in MySpace.com personal profile photographs', *Sexuality and Culture*, 16(1): 1–16.

Hamelink, Cees J. (2003) 'The right to communicate in theory and practice: a test for the world summit on the information society', Montreal, 13 November 2003 and Vancouver, 17 November 2003. Available at: http://www.com.umontreal.ca/spry/old/spry-ch-lec.html (12 June 2012).

Haraway, Donna (1991) 'A cyborg manifesto: science, technology, and socialist-feminism in the late twentieth century', *Simians, Cyborgs, and Women: The Reinvention of Nature*, New York: Routledge, pp. 149–181.

Harding, Jennifer and E. Deidre Pribram (eds) (2009) *Emotions: A Cultural Studies Reader*, London: Routledge.

Harding, Jennifer and E. Deidre Pribram (2002) 'The power of feeling: locating emotions in culture', *European Journal of Cultural Studies*, 5(4): 407–426.

Hardt, Michael (2007) 'Foreword: what affects are good for', in Patricia Ticineto Clough (ed.) *The Affective Turn: Theorising the Social*, Durham, NC: Duke University Press, pp. ix–xiii.

Hardt, Michael and Antonio Negri (2000) *Empire*, Cambridge: MA: Harvard University Press.

Harley, Trevor A. (2003) 'Nice weather for the time of year: the british obsession with the weather', in Sarah Strauss and Benjamin Orlove (eds) *Weather, Climate, Culture*, Oxford: Berg, pp. 103–120.

Harold, Christine (2009) 'On target: aura, affect, and the rhetoric of design democracy', *Public Culture*. 21: 599–618.

Hartley, John (2009) *The Uses of Digital Literacy*, St Lucia: University of Queensland Press.

—— (1999) *Uses of Television*, London: Routledge.

—— (1992a) *The Politics of Pictures: The Creation of the Public in the Age of Popular Media*, London: Routledge.

—— (1992b) *Teleology: Studies in Television*, London: Routledge.

Haythornthwaite, Caroline (2005) 'Social networks and Internet connectivity effects', *Information, Communication & Society*, 8(2): 125–147.

Hearn, A. (2006) '"John, a 20-year-old Boston native with a great sense of humor": on the spectacularization of the "self" and the incorporation of identity in the age of reality television', in P. D. Marshall (ed.) *The Celebrity Culture Reader*, London: Routledge, pp. 618–633.

Heim, Michael (1993) *The Metaphysics of Virtual Reality*, New York: Oxford University Press.

Hellekson, Karen and Kristina Busse (eds) (2006) *Fan Fiction and Fan Communities in the Age of the Internet*, Jefferson, NC: McFarland & Company Inc Publishers.

Hemer, Susan (2010) 'Grief as social experience: death and bereavement in Lihir, Papua New Guinea', *The Australian Journal of Anthropology*, 21: 281–297.

Hemmings, Clare (2005) 'Invoking affect: cultural theory and the ontological turn', *Cultural Studies*, 19(5): 548–567.

Hesmondhalgh, David (2007) *The Cultural Industries*, 2nd Edition, London: Sage.

Herring, Susan, Kirk Job-Sluder, Rebecca Scheckler, and Sasha Barab (2002) 'Searching for safety online: managing "Trolling" in a feminist forum', *The Information Society*, 18: 371–384.

Highmore, Ben (2010a) 'Bitter after taste: affect, food and social aesthetics', in Melissa Gregg and Gregory J. Seigworth (eds) *The Affect Theory Reader*, Durham, NC: Duke University Press, pp. 118–137.

Highmore, B. (2010b) *Ordinary Lives: Studies in the Everyday*, London: Routledge.

Hills, Matt (2010) *Triumph of a Time Lord: Regenerating Doctor Who in the Twenty-First Century*, London: I.B. Tauris.

—— (2002) *Fan Cultures*, London: Routledge.

Hindman, Matthew (2009) *The Myth of Digital Democracy*, Princeton: Princeton University Press.

Hjarvard, Stig (2008) 'The mediatization of religion: a theory of the media as agents of religious change', *Northern Lights: Film & Media Studies Yearbook*, 6(1): 9–26.

Hjorth, Larissa and Sun Sun Lim (2012) 'Mobile intimacy in an age of affective mobile media', *Feminist Media Studies*, 12: 4, 477–484

Hjorth, Larissa (2011a) 'Still mobile: cross-generational SNS usage in Shanghai', in R. Wilken and G. Goggin (eds) *Mobile Technologies and Place*, London: Routledge.

—— (2011b) 'Mobile spectres of intimacy: the gendered role of mobile technologies in love – past, present and future', in R. Ling and S. Campbell (eds) *The Mobile Communication Research Series: Volume II, Mobile Communication: Bringing Us Together or Tearing Us Apart?* Edison, NJ: Transaction books.

—— (2010) 'The price of being mobile: youth, gender and mobile media', in S. Donald, T. Anderson, and D. Spry (eds) *Youth, Society and Mobile Media in Asia*, London: Routledge, pp 73–87.

—— (2009) 'Photo shopping: a snapshot on camera phone practices in an age of web 2.0', *Knowledge, Technology and Policy*, 22(3): 157–159.

—— (2008a) 'Gifts of presence: a case study of a South Korean virtual community, Cyworld's mini-hompy', in Goggin and McLelland (eds) *Internationalising Internet Studies: Beyond Anglophone Paradigms*, London: Routledge.

—— (2008b) 'Framing imaging communities: gendered ICTs and SNS (social networking systems) in the Asia-Pacific', *T-Mobile Hungarian Academy of Sciences Conference, Budapest, Pre-Proceedings*. Available at http://www.socialscience.t-mobile.hu/2008/Preproceedings.pdf (1 May 2012).

—— (2007) 'Snapshots of almost contact', *Continuum: Journal of Media and Cultural Studies*, 21(2): 227–238.

Hochschild, Arlie Russell (2003 [1983]) *The Managed Heart: Commercialization of Human Feeling*, Berkeley, CA: University of California Press.

—— (2000) 'Global care chains and emotional surplus value', in W. Hutton and A. Giddens (eds) *On The Edge: Living with Global Capitalism*, London: Jonathan Cape, pp. 130–146.

—— (1990) *The Second Shift*, London: Penguin.

Hogan, Patrick Colm (2009) *The Mind and its Stories: Narrative Universals and Human Emotion*, Cambridge: Cambridge University Press.

Holmes, Su and Deborah Jermyn (eds) (2004) *Understanding Reality Television*, London: Routledge.

hooks, bell (1989) *Talking Back: Thinking Feminist, Thinking Black*, London: Sheba Feminist Publishers.

Horton, John and Peter Kraftl (2012) 'Clearing out a cupboard: memory, materiality and transitions', in O. Jones and J. Garde-Hansen (eds) *Geography and Memory*, Basingstoke: Palgrave Macmillan, pp. 25–44.

Hoskins, Andrew (2011) '7/7 and connective memory: interactional trajectories of remembering in post-scarcity culture', *Memory Studies*, 4(3): 269–280.
—— (2004) *Televising War: From Vietnam to Iraq*, London: Continuum.
Hoskins, Andrew and Ben O'Loughlin (2010) *War and Media: The Emergence of a Diffused War*, Cambridge: Polity Press.
Huang, Yen-Pei, Tiong Goh, and Chern Li Liew (2007) 'Hunting suicide notes in web 2.0 – preliminary findings', *Ninth IEEE International Symposium on Multimedia Workshops* (ISMW).
Hulme, Mike, Suraje Dessai, Irene Lorenzoni, and Donald Nelson (2009) 'Unstable climates: exploring the statistical and social constructions of "normal" climate', *Geoforum*, 40: 197–206.
Hutchings, Stephen and Galina Miazhevich (2010) 'Photography, new media and the peculiarities of post-sovietness as translocal affect: the case of the social networking website Odnoklassniki.ru', *Affective Fabrics of Digital Cultures: Feelings, Technologies, Politics Conference*, 3–4 June 2010, The University of Manchester.
Huyssen, Andreas (2003) *Present Pasts: Urban Palimpsests and the Politics of Memory*, Stanford, CA: Stanford University Press.
Illouz, Eva (2012) *Why Love Hurts: A Sociological Explanation*, Cambridge: Polity Press.
—— (2007) *Cold Intimacies: The Making of Emotional Capitalism*, Cambridge: Polity.
Isin, Engin Fahri (2004) 'The Neurotic citizen', *Citizenship Studies*, 8(3): 217–235.
Izard, Carroll E., Jerome Kagan, and Robert B. Zajonc (eds) (1984) *Emotions, Cognition and Behavior*, Cambridge: Cambridge University Press.
Jaggar, Alison M. (1989) 'Love and knowledge: emotion in feminist epistemology', in A. Jaggar and S. Bordo (eds) *Gender/Body/Knowledge: Feminist Reconstructions of Being and Knowing*. New Brunswick, NJ: Rutgers University Press, pp. 145–171.
James, William (1950 [1890]) 'The emotions', in *Principles of Psychology*, Vol. 2, New York: Dover Publications.
Jameson, Frederic (1991) *Postmodernsim or The Cultural Logic of Late Capitalism*, Durham, NC: Duke University Press.
Jenkins, Henry, Sam Ford, and Joshua Green (2013) *Spreadable Media: Creating Value and Meaning in a Networked Culture*, New York: New York University Press.
Jenkins, Henry (2007) *The Wow Climax: Tracing the Emotional Impact of Popular Culture*, New York: New York University Press.
—— (2006a) *Convergence Culture: Where Old and New Media Collide*, New York: New York University Press.
—— (2006b) *Fans, Bloggers and Gamers: Exploring Participatory Culture*, New York: New York University Press.
—— (1992) *Textual Poachers: Television Fans and Participatory Culture*, London: Routledge.
Jenkins Jr, Holman W. (2010) 'Google and the search for the future', *The Wall Street Journal*, 14 August 2010. Available at www.online.wsj.com (16 February 2012).
Jones, Jonny (2011) 'Social media and social movements', *International Socialism: A Quarterly Journal of Socialist Theory*, Issue 130. Available at http://www.isj.org.uk/?id=722 (16 April 2012).
Jones, Owain and Joanne Garde-Hansen (eds) (2012) *Geography and Memory*, Basingstoke: Palgrave Macmillan.

Kagan, Jerome (2007) *What is Emotion? History, Measures, and Meanings*, New Haven, CT: Yale University Press.

Kamvar, Sep and Jonathan Harris (2009) *We Feel Fine: An Almanac of Human Emotions*, London: Scribner.

Kaplan, C. (2009) 'Twitter terrorists, cell phone Jihadists and citizen bloggers: the "global matrix of war" and the biopolitics of technoculture in Mumbai', *Theory, Culture and Society*, 26(7–8): 1–14.

Kappas, Arvid and Nicole C. Krämer (eds) (2011) *Face-to-face Communication Over the Internet: Emotions in a Web of Culture*, Cambridge: Cambridge University Press.

Karatzogianni, Athina and Adi Kuntsman (eds) (2012) *Digital Cultures and the Politics of Emotion: Feelings, Affect and Technological Change*, Basingstoke: Palgrave Macmillan.

Karatzogianni, Athina (ed.) (2009) *Cyber-Conflict and Global Politics*, London: Taylor and Francis.

Karpi, Tero (2011) 'Digital suicide and the biopolitics of leaving facebook', *Transformations: Slow Media* 20. Article 2. Available at: http://www.transformationsjournal.org/journal/issue_20/article_02.shtml (12 July 2012).

Kavka, Misha (2008) *Reality Television, Affect and Intimacy: Reality Matters*, Basingstoke: Palgrave.

Kear, Adrian and Deborah Lynn Steinberg (eds) (1999) *Mourning Diana: Nation, Culture and the Performance of Grief*, London: Routledge.

Kellner, Douglas (2002) 'Theorizing Globalization' *Sociological Theory*, 20(3): 285–305.

Kidd, Dorothy (2011 [2003]) 'INDYMEDIA.ORG: a new communications commons', in Seth Giddings and Martin Lister (eds) *The New Media and Technocultures Reader*, London: Routledge, pp. 407–420.

King, Tanya J., Ian Warren, and Darren Palmer (2008) 'Would Kitty Genovese have been murdered in Second Life? Researching the "bystander effect" using online technologies', in *TASA 2008: Re-imagining Sociology: The Annual Conference of The Australian Sociological Association*, Australia: University of Melbourne, pp. 1–23.

Kitch, Carolyn and J. Hume (2008) *Journalism in a Culture of Grief*, New York: Routledge.

Klein, Amanda Ann (2011) *American Film Cycles: Reframing Genres, Screening Social Problems and Defining Subcultures*, Austin, TX: University of Texas Press.

Knudsen, Britta Timm and Carsten Stage (2011) 'Contagious bodies. an investigation of affective and discursive strategies in contemporary online activism', *Emotion, Space and Society*, 30: 1–8.

Kompare, Derek (2010) 'More "Moments of Television": Online cult television authorship', in Michael Kackman, Marnie Binfield, Matthew Thomas Payne, Allison Perlman, Bryan Sebok (eds) *Flow TV:Television in the Age of Media Convergence*, New York: Routledge, pp. 95–113.

Kuhn, Annette (2002) *Family Secrets: Acts of Memory and Imagination*, 2nd Edition, London: Verso.

Kuntsman, Adi (2012) 'Introduction: affective fabrics of digital cultures', in Athina Karatzogianni and Adi Kuntsman (eds) *Digital Cultures and the Politics of Emotion: Feelings, Affect and Technological Change*, Basingstoke: Palgrave Macmillan, pp. 1–19.

—— (2010) 'Online memories, digital conflicts and the cybertouch of war', *Digital Icons: Studies in Russian, Eurasian and Central European New Media*, 4: 1–12. Available at http://www.digitalicons.org/issue04/adi-kuntsman/ (27 July 2011).

—— (2009) *Figurations of Violence and Belonging: Queerness, Migranthood and Nationalism in Cyberspace and Beyond*, Oxford: Peter Lang.

Landsberg, Alison (2004) *Prosthetic Memory: The Transformation of American Remembrance in the Age of Mass Culture*, New York: Columbia University Press.

Lanier, Jaron (2010) *You are Not a Gadget: A Manifesto* London: Allen Lane.

Lasén, Amparo (2011) '"Mobiles are not that personal": The unexpected consequences of the accountability, accessibility and transparency afforded by mobile telephony', in R. Ling and S. Campbell (eds) *Mobile Communication: Bringing Us Together or Tearing Us Apart*, Piscataway, NJ: Transaction Publishers, pp. 83–105.

—— (2010a) 'Mobile media and affectivity: some thoughts about the notion of affective bandwidth', in J.R. Höflich, G. F. Kircher, C. Linke, and I. Schlote (eds) *Mobile Media and the Change of Everyday Life*, Frankfurt am Main: Peter Lang, pp. 131–154.

—— (2010b) 'Mobile culture and subjectivities: an example of the shared agency between people and technology', in L. Fortunati, J. Vincent, J. Gebhardt, A. Petrovcic and O. Vershinskaya (eds) *Interacting with Broadband Society*, Frankfurt am Main: Peter Lang, pp. 109–124.

Lasén, Amparo and E. Gómez-Cruz (2009) 'Digital photography and picture sharing: redefining the public/private divide', *Knowledge, Technology and Policy*, 22: 205–215.

Lash, Scott and John Urry (1987) *The End of Organized Capital*, Oxford: Blackwell.

Lash, Scott and Celia Lury (2007) *Global Culture Industry: The Mediation of Things*, Cambridge: Polity.

Leadbeater, Charles (2010) *We Think: Mass Innovation not Mass Production*, London: Profile Books.

Leder, Kerstin Mackley and Angelina Karpovich (2012) 'Touching tales: emotion in digital object memories', in Athina Karatzogianni and Adi Kuntsman (eds) *Digital Cultures and the Politics of Emotion: Feelings, Affect and Technological Change*, Basingstoke: Palgrave Macmillan, pp. 127–146.

Lee, Dave (2012) 'IsAnyoneUp's hunter moore: "the net's most hated man"', *BBC News Technology*, 20 April 2012. Available at: http://www.bbc.co.uk/news/technology-17784232 (13 June 2012)

Lee, Dong-Hoo (2005) 'Women's creation of camera phone culture', *Fibreculture* 6 Mobility. Available at http://six.fibreculturejournal.org/ (25 April 2012).

Lewis, Kevin, Jason Kaufman, Marco Gonzalez, Andreas Wimmer, and Nicholas Christakis (2008) 'Tastes, ties and time: A new social network dataset using Facebook.com', *Social Networks*, 30(4): 330–342.

Lewis, Lisa A. (ed.) (1992) *The Adoring Audience: Fan Culture and Popular Media*, London: Routledge.

Lewis, Martin W. and Kären E. Wigen (1997) *The Myth of Continents: A Critique of Metageography*, Berkeley, CA: University of California Press.

Li, Chin-Chuan (2003) *Chinese Media: Global Contexts*, London: Routledge.

Licklider, J. C. R. and Robert Taylor (1968) 'The Computer as Communication Device', *Science and Technology*, pp. 21–41. Available at http://www.comunicazione.uniroma1.it/materiali/20.20.03_licklider-taylor.pdf (4 April 2012).

Lindtner, S., Mainwaring, S., Dourish, P., and Y. Wang (2009) 'Situating productive play: online gaming practices and Guanxi in China', *Proceedings of the IFIP Conference Human-Computer Interaction, INTERACT 2009*, Stockholm, Sweden.

Ling, Richard Seyler and Scott Campbell (2011) *Mobile Communication: Bringing us Together or Tearing Us Apart*, Piscataway, NJ: Transaction Publishers.

Lister, Martin, Jon Dovey, Seth Giddings, Iain Grant, and Kieran Kelly (2009 [2003]) *New Media: A Critical Introduction*, 2nd Edition, London: Routledge.

Livingstone (2009) 'On the mediation of everything: ICA presidential address 2008', *Journal of Communication*, 59(1): 1–18.

Lloyd, Genevieve (1996) *Routledge Philosophy Guidebook to Spinoza and the Ethics*, London: Routledge.

Löffelholz, Martin (2008) 'Heterogeneous – multidimensional – competing: theoretical approaches to journalism – an overview', in Löffelholz, M. and Weaver, D. (eds) *Global Journalism Research, Theories, Methods, Findings, Future*, Oxford: Blackwell, pp. 15–27.

Lovink, Geert and Sabine Niederer (eds) (2008) *Video Vortex Reader: Responses to YouTube*, INC Reader No 4, Institute of Network Cultures. Available at http://networkcultures.org/wpmu/portal/publications/inc- readers/videovortex/ (7 July 2012).

Lovink, Geert (2011) *Networks Without a Cause: A Critique of Social Media*, Cambridge: Polity Press.

—— (2008) *Zero Comments: Blogging and Critical Internet Culture*, New York: Routledge.

Lutz, Catherine (1986) 'Emotion, thought and estrangement: emotion as a cultural category', *Cultural Anthropology*, 1(3) 287–309.

Maffesoli, Michel (1996) *The Time of the Tribes: The Decline of Individualism in Mass Society*, London: Sage.

Maltby, Sarah, and Richard Keeble (eds) (2007) *Communicating War: Memory, Media and Military*, Suffolk: Arima Publishing.

Manovich, Lev (2008) 'The practice of everyday (media) life', in Geert Lovink and Sabine Niederer (eds) (2008) *Video Vortex Reader: Responses to YouTube*, INC Reader No 4, Institute of Network Cultures, pp. 33–44. Available at http://networkcultures.org/wpmu/portal/publications/inc- readers/videovortex/ (7 July 2012).

Mansfield, Nick (2000) *Subjectivity: Theories of the Self from Freud to Haraway*, New York: New York University Press.

Manstead, Antony S.R., Martin Lea, and Jeannine Goh (2011) 'Facing the future: emotion communication and the presence of others in the age of video-mediated communication', in Kappas, Arvid and Nicole C. Krämer (eds),*Face-to-Face Communication Over the Internet: Emotions in a Web of Culture*, Cambridge: Cambridge University Press, pp. 144–175.

Marks, Nic (2010) 'The Happy Planet Index', *TED Talks* http://www.ted.com/talks/nic_marks_the_happy_planet_index.html. (Accessed 11 November 2012).

Marlow, Cameron et al. (2009) 'Maintained relationships on Facebook', *Overstated. net*, posted 9 March 2009 (12 June 2011).

Marwick, Alice E. and danah boyd (2011a) 'I tweet honestly, I tweet passionately: Twitter users, context collapse, and the imagined audience', *New Media and Society*, 13(1): 114–133.

—— (2011b) 'To see and be seen: celebrity practice on Twitter', *Convergence: The International Journal of Research into New Media Technologies*, 17(2): 139–158.

—— (2011) 'National enterprise emergency: steps toward an ecology of powers', in Patricia T. Clough and Craig Willse (eds) *Beyond Biopolitics: Essays on the Governance of Life and Death*, Durham, NC: Duke University Press, pp. 19–45.

—— (2008) 'The thinking-feeling of what happens', *Inflexions: A Journal for Research Creation* 1.1 'How is Research-Creation?' Available at: http://inflexions.org/n1_ massumihtml.html (12 May 2012).

—— (2002) *Parables for the Virtual*, Durham, NC: Duke University Press.

—— (ed.) (1993) *The Politics of Everyday Fear*, Minneapolis, MN: University of Minnesota Press.

Matei, Sorin (2003) 'The internet as magnifying glass: marital status and on-line social ties', *The Public*, 10(1): 101–112.

Matravers, Derek (1998) *Art and Emotion*, Oxford: Oxford University Press.

Mayer-Schönberger, Viktor (2009) *Delete: The Virtue of Forgetting in the Digital Age*, Princeton: Princeton University Press.

Mbembe, Achille (2003) 'Necropolitics', *Public Culture*, 15(1): 11–40.

McCarthy, Anna (2001) *Ambient Television: Visual Culture and Public Space*, Durham, NC: Duke University Press.

McChesney, Robert and John Nichols (2002) *Our Media, Not Theirs: The Democratic Struggle Against Corporate Media*, New York: Seven Stories Press.

McCormack, Derek P. (2007) 'Molecular affects in human geographies' *Environment and Planning A*, 39(2): 359–377.

McIntosh, Heather (2012) *KONY2012: Analyzing the Viral Documentary Video*. Available at http://www.pbs.org/pov/blog/2012/03/kony-2012-analyzing-the-viral-documentary-video. Accessed 20 June 2012.

McLuhan, M. and Powers, B. R. (1989) *The Global Village: Transformations in World Life and Media in the 21st Century*. New York: Oxford University Press.

McLuhan, Marshall (1994 [1964]) *Understanding Media: The Extensions of Man*, Cambridge, MA: MIT Press.

—— (1967) *The Medium Is the Massage* (with Quentin Fiore), London: Penguin.

—— (1951) *The Mechanical Bride: Folklore of Industrial Man*, New York: Vanguard Press.

McNair, Brian (2006) *Cultural Chaos: Journalism, News and Power in a Globalised World*, London: Routledge.

McRobbie, Angela (2008) 'Young women and consumer culture', *Cultural Studies*, 22(5): 531–550.

—— (2009) *The Aftermath of Feminism: Gender, Culture and Social Change*, London: Sage.

Meikle, Graham, and Sherman Young (2012) *Media Convergence: Networked Digital Media in Everyday Life*, Basingstoke: Palgrave.

Merrin, William (2009) 'Media studies 2.0: upgrading and open-sourcing the discipline', *Interactions: Studies in Communication and Culture*, 1(1): 17–34.

Milton, Kay (2005) 'Meanings, feelings and human ecology', in K. Milton and M. Svaek (eds) *Mixed Emotions: Anthropological Studies of Feeling*, Oxford: Berg, pp. 25–42.

Mittell, Jason (2010) *Television and American Culture*, Oxford: Oxford University Press.
—— (2006) 'Narrative complexity in contemporary American television', *The Velvet Light Trap*, 58, 29–40.
Moore, Hunter (2012) *From Hunter Moore* BullyVille.com 19 April 2012. Available at: http://liveweb.archive.org/http://www.bullyville.com/?page=articles&id=358# comments (20 April 2012).
Morley, David (1992) *Television, Audiences and Cultural Studies*, London: Routledge.
Munt, Sally (2008) *Queer Attachments: The Cultural Politics of Shame*, London: Ashgate.
Nakamura, Lisa and Peter Chow-White (eds.) (2011) *Race after the Internet*, London: Routledge.
Nayak, A. and A. Jeffrey (2011) *Geographical Thought: An Introduction to Ideas in Human Geography*, Harlow: Pearson Prentice Hall.
Neiger, Motti, O. Meyers, and E. Zandberg (eds) (2011) *On Media Memory: Collective Memory in a New Media Age*, Basingstoke: Palgrave Macmillan.
Neu, Jerome (2000) *A Tear Is an Intellectual Thing: The Meanings of Emotion*, Oxford: Oxford University Press.
Ngai, Sianne (2005) *Ugly Feelings*, Cambridge, MA: Harvard University Press.
Nicholson, Linda (1999) *The Play of Reason: From the Modern to the Postmodern*, Buckingham: Open University Press.
Nightingale, Virginia (1999) 'Are media cyborgs?' in Angel Gordon-Lopez and Ian Parker (eds) *Cyberpsychology*, London: Macmillan, pp. 226–235.
—— (1989) 'What's ethnographic about ethnographic audience research?' *Australian Journal of Communication*, 16: 50–63.
Nip, Joyce Y. M. (2009) 'Citizen journalism in China: the case of the Wenchuan earthquake', in Stuart Allan and Einar Thorsen (eds) *Citizen Journalism: Global Perspectives*, New York: Peter Lang, pp. 95–106.
Oswell, David (1998) 'A question of belonging: television, youth and the domestic', in Tracey Skelton and Gill Valentine (eds) *Cool Places: Geographies of Youth Cultures*, London: Routledge, pp. 35–49.
Outhwaite, William (ed.) (1996) *The Habermas Reader*, Cambridge: Polity Press.
Pain, Rachel (2009) 'Globalized fear? Towards an emotional geopolitics', *Progress in Human Geography*, 33(4): 466–486.
Pain, R. and Smith, S. J. (eds) (2008) *Fear: critical geopolitics and everyday life*, Ashgate: Aldershot.
Parikka, Jussi and Tony D. Sampson (eds) (2009) *The Spam Book: On Viruses, Porn, and Other Anomalies from the Dark Side of Digital Culture*, Cresskill: Hampton Press.
Parisi, Luciana, and Steve Goodman (2012) 'Mnemonic control', in Patricia T. Clough and Craig Willse (eds) *Beyond Biopolitics: Essays on the Governance of Life and Death*, Durham, NC: Duke University Press, pp. 163–176.
Parisi, Luciana (2004) *Abstract Sex: Philosophy, Bio-Technology and the Mutations of Desire*, London: Continuum.
Perry, Barbara and Patrik Olsson (2009) 'Cyberhate: the globalization of hate', *Information and Communications Technology Law*, 18(2): 185–199.
Peters, Chris (2011) 'Emotion aside or emotional side? Crafting an "experience of involvement" in the news', *Journalism*, 12(3): 297–316.
Pile, S. J. (2009) 'Emotions and affect in recent human geography', *Transactions of the Institute of British Geographers*, 35: 5–20.

Pink, Sarah (2009) *Doing Sensory Ethnography*, London: Sage.

Plant, Sadie (2002) 'On the mobile: the effects of mobile telephones on social and individual life', *Report for Motorola*, 19–87.

Plantinga, Carl (2009) *Moving Viewers: American Film and the Spectator's Experience*, Berkeley, CA: University of California Press.

Plantinga, Carl and Greg M. Smith (eds) (1999) *Passionate Views: Film, Cognition, and Emotion*, Baltimore, MD: The John Hopkins University Press.

Pribram, E. Deidre (2011) *Emotions, Genre, Justice in Film and Television: Detecting Feeling*, London: Routledge

Probyn, Elspeth (2005) *Blush: Faces of Shame*, Minneapolis, MN: University of Minnesota Press.

Radstone, Susannah and Katherine Hodgkin (2005) *Memory Cultures: Memory, Subjectivity and Recognition*, New Brunswick, New Jersey: Transaction Publishers.

Radway, Janice (1988) 'Reception Study: Ethnography and the Problems of Dispersed Audiences and Nomadic Subjects', *Cultural Studies*, 2(3): 359–376.

Raun, Tobias (2012) 'DIY therapy: exploring affective self-representations in trans video on YouTube', in Athina Karatzogianni and Adi Kuntsman (eds) *Digital Cultures and the Politics of Emotion: Feelings, Affect and Technological Change*, Basingstoke: Palgrave Macmillan, pp. 165–180.

Ravindran, Gopalan (2009) 'Moral panics and mobile phones: the cultural politics of new media modernity in India', in Erwin Alampay (ed.) *Living the Information Society in Asia*, Singapore: ISEAS Publishing, pp. 93–108.

Reading, Anna (2011a) 'The London bombings: mobile witnessing, mortal bodies and globital time', *Memory Studies*, 4(3): 298–311.

—— (2011b) 'Six dynamics of the globital memory field', in Motti Neiger, Oren Meyers and Eyal Zandberg (eds) *On Media Memory: Collective Memory in a New Media Age*, Basingstoke: Palgrave Macmillan, pp. 241–252.

—— (2009) 'The globytal: towards an understanding of globalised memories in the digital age', in A. Maj and D. Riha (eds) *Digital Memories: Exploring Critical Issues*. Available at: www.inter-disciplinary.net. (4 April 2012).

Reese, Stephen D. (2008) 'Theorizing a globalized journalism', in M. Löffelholz and D. Weaver (eds) *Global Journalism Research: Theories, Methods, Findings, Future*, Oxford: Blackwell, pp. 240–252.

Rheingold, Howard (2012) *Net Smart: How to Thrive Online*, Cambridge, MA: MIT Press.

—— (2003) *Smart Mobs: The Next Social Revolution: Transforming Cultures and Communities*, Cambridge, MA: Perseus Publishing.

—— (1993) *The Virtual Community: Homesteading on the Electronic Frontier*, London: Harper Collins.

—— (1992) *Virtual Reality*, London: Simon and Schuster.

Ribes, Alberto (2010) 'Theorising Global Media Events: Cognition, Emotions and Performances', *New Global Studies*, 4(3): 1–20.

Richards, Barry (2007) *Emotional Governance: Politics, Media and Terror*, Basingstoke: Palgrave Macmillan.

Richardson, Ingrid (2007) 'Pocket technoscapes: the bodily incorporation of mobile media', in *Continuum: Journal of Media & Cultural Studies*, 21(2): 205–216.

—— (2005) 'Mobile Technosoma: some phenomenological reflections on itinerant media devices', *Fibreculture* 6 http://journal.fibreculture.org/issue6/issue6_richardson_print.html

Ricoeur, Paul (2004) *Memory, History and Forgetting*, Chicago: University of Chicago Press.

Riley, Denise (2005) *Impersonal Passion: Language as Affect*, Durham, NC: Duke University Press.

Rocamora, Agnes (2011) 'Personal fashion blogs: screens and mirrors in digital self-portraits', *Fashion Theory: The Journal of Dress, Body and Culture*, 38: 407–424.

Roeser, Sabine (ed.) (2010) *Emotions and Risky Technologies*, New York: Springer.

Roversi, Antonio (2008) *Hate on the Net: Extremist Sites, Neo-Fascism On-line, Electronic Jihad*, Farnham: Ashgate.

Rubin, Gretchen (2011 [2009]) *The Happiness Project: Or, Why I Spent a Year Trying to Sing in the Morning, Clean My Closets, Fight Right, Read Aristotle, and Generally Have More Fun*, New York: Harper Collins.

Salkin, Allen (2009) 'Seeing yourself in their light', *New York Times*, http://www.nytimes.com/2009/09/20/fashion/20Guru.html?_r=1&ref=allensalkin, first accessed 20 September 2009.

Sandberg, Sheryl (2013) *Lean In: Women, Work, and the Will to Lead*, Virgin Digital.

Sandvoss, Cornel (2005) *Fans: The Mirror of Consumption*, Cambridge: Polity.

Schwarz, Ori (2010a) 'Going to bed with a camera: on the visualisation of sexuality and the production of knowledge', *International Journal of Cultural Studies*, 13(6): 637–656.

—— (2010b) 'On friendship, boobs and the logic of the catalogue: online self-portraits as a means for the exchange of capital', *Convergence*, 16(2): 163–183.

—— (2010c) 'Negotiating romance in front of the lens', *Visual Communication*, 9(2): 151–169.

—— (2009) 'Good young nostalgia: camera phones and technologies of self among Israeli youths', *Journal of Consumer Culture*, 9(3): 348–376.

Sedgwick, Eve Kosofsky and Adam Frank (2003) *Touching Feeling: Affect, Pedagogy, Performativity*, Durham, NC: Duke University Press.

Sedgwick, Eve Kosofsky (1995) *Shame and Its Sisters: A Silvan Tomkins Reader*, Durham, NC: Duke University Press.

Seigworth, Gregory J. and Melissa Gregg (2010a) 'An inventory of shimmers', in Melissa Gregg and Gregory J. Seigworth (eds) *The Affect Theory Reader*, Durham, NC: Duke University Press, pp. 1–28.

—— (eds) (2010b) *The Affect Theory Reader*, Durham, NC: Duke University Press.

Shaviro, Steve (2010) *Post Cinematic Affect*, Hants: Zero Books.

Sheets-Johnstone, Maxine (2011) *The Primacy of Movement: Expanded Second Edition*, Amsterdam: John Benjamins Publishing Co.

Shinkle, Eugénie (2012) 'Videogames and the digital sublime', in Athina Karatzogianni and Adi Kuntsman (eds) *Digital Cultures and the Politics of Emotion: Feelings, Affect and Technological Change*, Basingstoke: Palgrave Macmillan, pp. 97–108.

—— (2008) 'Video games, emotion and the six senses', *Media, Culture and Society*, 30(6): 907–915.

Shirky, Clay (2010a) *Cognitive Surplus: Creativity and Generosity in a Connected Age*, London: Allen Lane.

—— (2010b) 'The Collapse of Complex Business Models', *Clay Shirky* blog posted 1 April 2010. Available at www.shirky.com (15 March 2011).

—— (2009a) 'How social media can make history', *TED Talks* posted June 2009. Available at http://www.ted.com/talks/clay_shirky_how_cellphones_twitter_facebook_can_ make_history.html (30 June 2011).

—— (2009b) 'Clay shirky big idea: social media enhances the emotional dimension of news', *Ideas Project* [online video] *YouTube* uploaded 22 May 2009. Available at http://www.youtube.com/watch?v=q5itra-Jkmw (15 March 2011).

—— (2008) *Here Comes Everybody: The Power of Organizing without Organizations*, London: Allen Lane.

Shouse, Eric (2005) 'Feeling, emotion, affect', *M/C: A Journal of Media and Culture* 8:6. Available at http://journal.media-culture.org.au/0512/03-shouse.php (12 May 2012).

Shuker, Roy (1994) *Understanding Popular Music*, London: Routledge.

Siegel, Elizabeth (2010) *Galleries of Friendship and Fame: A History of Nineteenth-Century American Photograph Albums*, New Haven, CT: Yale University Press.

Sirkin, Harold L., James W. Hemerling, and Arindam K. Bhattacharya (2008) *Globality: Competing with Everyone from Everywhere for Everything*, New York: Business Plus.

Sirisena, Mihirini (2012) 'Virtually yours: reflecting on the place of mobile phones in romantic relationships', in Athina Karatzogianni and Adi Kuntsman (eds) *Digital Cultures and the Politics of Emotion: Feelings, Affect and Technological Change*, Basingstoke: Palgrave Macmillan, pp. 181–196.

Skeggs, Beverley and Helen Wood (2012) *Reacting to Reality Television: Performance, Audience and Value*, Oxford: Blackwell.

Skeggs, Beverley (2001) 'The Toilet Paper: Femininity, Class and Mis-recognition', *Women's Studies International Forum*, 24(3): 295–307.

Smiles, Samuel (2002) *Self-Help*, Oxford: Oxford University Press.

Smith, Adam (1976) *Theory of Moral Sentiments*, Oxford: Oxford University Press.

Smith, Greg M. (2003) *Film Structure and the Emotion System*, Cambridge: Cambridge University Press.

—— (1999) 'Local emotion, global moods: the emotion system and film structure', in Carl Plantinga and Greg M. Smith (eds) *Passionate Views: Film, Cognition, and Emotion*, Baltimore: The Johns Hopkins University Press, pp. 103–126.

Smith, Jeff (1999) 'Movie music as moving music: emotion, cognition, and the film score', in Carl Plantinga and Greg M. Smith (eds) *Passionate Views: Film, Cognition, and Emotion*, Baltimore: The John Hopkins University Press, pp. 146–167.

Solnit, Rebecca (2009) *A Paradise Built on Hell: The Extraordinary Communities that Arise in Disaster*, New York: Viking.

Solomon, Robert C. (ed.) ([1984] 2003) *What Is an Emotion? Classic and Contemporary Readings*, 2nd Edition, Oxford: Oxford University Press.

Solove, D.J. (2007) *The Future of Reputation: Gossip, Rumor, and Privacy on the Internet*, New Haven, CT: Yale University Press.

Sontag, Susan (2004) *Regarding the Pain of Others*, London: Penguin.

Spinoza, Baruch (1993 [1677]) *Ethics and Treatise on the Correction of the Intellect*, trans. by Andrew Boyle, London: Everyman's Library.

Sproull, Lee and Sara Kiesler (1991) *Connections: New Ways of Working in the Networked Organization*, Cambridge, MA: MIT Press.

Staiger, Janet, Ann Cvetkovich, and Ann Reynolds (eds) (2010) *Political Emotions: New Agendas in Communication*, London: Routledge.

Stepanova, Ekaterina (2011) *The Role of Information Communication Technologies in the Arab Spring: Implications Beyond the Region*, PONARS Eurasia Policy Memo No 159 http://ponarseurasia.org/blog/policy-memos/2011–2/ (1 February 2012).

Stevenson, Nick (2002) *Understanding Media Cultures: Social Theory and Mass Communication*, London: Sage

Stewart, Kathleen (2007) *Ordinary Affects*, Durham, NC: Duke University Press.

—— (2005) 'Cultural poesis: the generativity of emergent things', in N. Denzin and Y. Lincoln (eds) *Handbook of Qualitative Research*, 3rd Edition, Thousand Oaks: Sage, pp. 1027–1042.

Stiegler, Bernard (2012a) 'Interview', *World Wide Web 2012 Conference*, Lyon, France 16–20 April 2012. Available at: http://www2012.wwwconference.org/hidden/interview-of-bernard-stiegler/ (8 February 2012).

—— (2012b) 'Care: within the limits of capitalism, economizing means taking care' Tom Cohen (ed.) in *Telemorphosis: Theory in the Era of Climate Change*, University of Michigan Library: Open Humanities Press. Available at http://quod.lib.umich.edu/o/ohp/10539563.0001.001 (25 February 2013).

—— (2008) 'Biopower, psychopower and the logic of the scapegoat', *Ars Industrialis*. Available at: http://www.arsindustrialis.org/node/2924 (12 July 2012).

Sturken, Marita (2007) *Tourists of History: Memory, Kitsch, and Consumerism from Oklahoma City to Ground Zero*, Durham, NC: Duke University Press.

Sugiyama, Satomi (2009) 'Decorated mobile phones and emotional attachment for Japanese youths', in Jane Vincent and Leopoldina Fortunati (eds.), *Electronic Emotion: The Mediation of Emotion via Information and Communication Technologies*, Bern: Peter Lang, pp. 85–106.

Surakka, Veikko and Toni Vanhala (2011) 'Emotions in human-computer interaction', in Arvid Kappas and Nicole C. Krämer (eds) *Face-to-face Communication over the Internet: Emotions in a Web of Culture, Language and Technology*, Cambridge: Cambridge University Press, pp. 213–236.

Surowiecki, James (2005) *The Wisdom of Crowds*, New York: Random House.

Szerszynski, Bronislaw, John Urry, and Greg Myers, G. (2000a) 'Mediating global citizenship', in J. Smith (ed.) *The Daily Globe: Environmental Change, the Public and the Media*, London: Earthscan, pp. 97–154.

—— (2000b) *Global Citizenship and the Environment*, Full Report of Research Activities and Results, ESRC. Available at www.esrc.ac.uk/my ... /37dc265f-f20a-4dbf-81af- d09d8bb66051 (12 July 2012).

Tan, S. (ed.) (2011) *Emotion and the Structure if Narrative Film: Film as an Emotion Machine*, London: Taylor and Francis.

Terranova, Tiziana (2011 [2004]) 'Free labour', in Seth Giddings and Martin Lister (eds) *The New Media and Technocultures Reader*, London: Routledge, pp. 350–368.

Thayer, E. C. (1880) *Wired Love: A Romance of Dots and Dashes*, New York: W.J. Johnson.

Thelwall, Mike, Buckley, K., and Paltoglou, G. (2011) 'Sentiment in Twitter Events', *Journal of the American Society for Information Science and Technology*, 62(2): 406–418.

Thelwall, Mike, P. Sud, and F. Vis (2012) 'Commenting on YouTube videos: From Guatemalan Rock to El Big Bang', *Journal of American Society for Information Science and Technology*, 63(3): 616–629.

Thelwall, Mike, Wilkinson, D., and Uppal, S. (2010) 'Data mining emotion in social network communication: Gender differences in MySpace', *Journal of the American Society for Information Science and Technology*, 6(1): 190–199.

Thrift, Nigel (2008) *Non-Representational Theory: Space, Politics, Affect*, London: Routledge.

—— (2007) 'Immaculate warfare? The spatial politics of extreme violence', in Gregory, D. and Pred, A. (eds) *Violent Geographies: Fear, Terror and Political Violence*, London: Routledge, pp. 273–294.

—— (2004a) 'Summoning life', in P. Cloke, M. Goodwin, and P. Crang (eds) *Envisioning Human Geography*, London: Arnold, pp. 81–103.

—— (2004b) 'Intensities of Feeling: towards a spatial politics of affect', *Geografiska Annaler*, 86(B): 57–78.

—— (1999) 'Steps to an ecology of place', in D. Massey, P. Sarre, and J. Allen (eds) *Human Geography Today*, Cambridge: Polity, pp. 295–352.

—— (1992) 'Muddling through: World orders and globalization', *The Professional Geographer*, 44(1): 3–7.

Thompson, John H. (1990) *Ideology and Modern Culture: Critical Social Theory in the Era of Mass Communication*, Cambridge: Polity Press.

Thumim, Nancy (2012) *Self-Representation and Digital Culture*, Basingstoke: Palgrave.

Tichi, Cecelia (1991) *Electronic Hearth: Creating an American Television Culture*, Oxford: Oxford University Press.

Tolia-Kelly, D. P. (2006) 'Affect – an ethnocentric encounter? Exploring the 'universalist' imperative of emotional/affective geographies', *Area*, 38(2): 213–217.

Tomkins, Silvan (1995) *Exploring Affect: The Selected Writings of Silvan S. Tomkins* (ed.) Virginia E. Demos, Cambridge: Cambridge University Press

Turkle, Sherry (2011) *Alone Together: Why We Expect More from Technology and Less from Each Other*, New York: Basic Books.

—— (1997) *Life on the Screen: Identity in the Age of the Internet*, London: Simon and Schuster.

Turner, Graeme (2010) *Ordinary People and the Media: The Demotic Turn*, London: Sage.

—— (2003) *British Cultural Studies: An Introduction*, 3rd Edition, London: Routledge.

—— (1999) *Film as Social Practice*, 3rd Edition, London: Routledge.

Turner, Jonathan H. and Jan E. Stets (eds) (2005) *The Sociology of Emotions*, Cambridge: Cambridge University Press.

Ugander, Johan, Brian Karrer, Lars Backstrom, and Cameron Marow (2011) *The Anatomy of the Facebook Social Graph*, Cornell University Library. Available at http://arxiv.org/abs/1111.4503 (12 July 2012).

Uribe, Rodrigo and Barrie Gunter (2007) 'Are "sensational" news stories more likely to Trigger viewers' emotions than non-sensational news stories?: a content analysis of British TV news', *European Journal of Communication*, 22: 207–228.

van Compernolle, Rémi A. (2011) 'Use and variation of French diacritics on an Internet dating site', *Journal of French Language Studies*, 2(2): 131–148.

van Dijck, José (2013) *The Culture of Connectivity: A Critical History of Social Media*, Oxford: Oxford University Press.

—— (2012) 'Facebook as a tool for producing sociality and connectivity', *Television and New Media*, 13(2): 160–176.

— (2009) 'Users like you? Theorizing agency in user-generated content', *Media, Culture and Society*, 31(1): 41–58.

Vernallis, Carol (2004) *Experiencing Music Video: Aesthetics and Cultural Context*, New York: Columbia University Press.

Vincent, Jane (2005) 'Emotional attachment and mobile phones', in Peter Glotz, Stephan Bertschi, and Chris Locke (eds) *Thumb Culture: The Meaning of Mobile Phones for Society*, New Brunswick, NJ: Transaction Publishers, pp. 117–122.

Vincent, Jane, and Leopoldina Fortunati (eds) (2009) *Electronic Emotion: The Mediation of Emotion via Information and Communication Technologies*, Bern: Peter Lang.

Wallis, Neil (2012) Interview with *The Media Show*, BBC Radio 4, broadcast 11 July 2012.

Walter, Tony, Rachid Hourizi, Wendy Moncur, and Stacey Pitsillides (2011–12) 'Does the internet change how we die and mourn? overview and analysis', *OMEGA: Journal of Death and Dying*, 64(4): 275–302.

Walther, Joseph. B., Brandon Van Der Heide, San-Yeon Kim, David Westerman, and Stephanie Tom Tong (2008) 'The role of friends' appearance and behavior on evaluations of individuals on facebook: are we known by the company we keep?' *Human Communication Research*, 34: 28–49.

Weimann, Gabriel (2006) *Terrorism on the Internet: The New Arena, the New Challenges*, New York: United States Institute of Peace.

White, Michele (2012) *Buy It Now: Lessons from eBay*, Durham, NC: Duke University Press.

White, Mimi (2002) 'Television, therapy, and the social subject; or, the TV therapy machine', in James Friedman (ed.) *Reality Squared: Televisual Discourses on the Real*, New Brunswick, New Jersey: Rutgers University Press, pp. 313–332.

Whitty, Monica T., Andrea J. Baker, and James A. Inman (eds) (2007) *Online Matchmaking*, Basingstoke: Palgrave Macmillan.

Whitty, M. T. and Carr, A.N. (2006) *Cyberspace Romance: The Psychology of Online Relationships*, Basingstoke: Palgrave Macmillan.

Williams, J. Patrick and Jonas Heide Smith (eds) (2007) *The Players' Realm: Studies on the Culture of Video Games and Gaming*, Jefferson NC: McFarland and Co, Inc.

Williams, Raymond (1974) *Television: Technology and Cultural Form*, New York: Schocken Books.

— (1961) *The Long Revolution*, London: Chatto & Windus.

Williams, Simon (2001) *Emotion and Social Theory*, London: Sage.

Wilson, Edward O. (2012) *The Social Conquest of Earth*, New York: W.W. Norton.

Wissinger, Elizabeth (2007) 'Always on display: affective production in the modeling industry', in *The Affective Turn: Theorizing the Social* (ed.) Patricia Ticineto Clough, Durham: Duke Univesrity Press: pp. 231–260.

Wolf, Alicia (2000) 'Emotional expression online: gender differences in emoticon use', *CyberPsychology and Behavior*, 3(5): 827–833.

Wolf, Naomi (2012) *Vagina: A New Biography*, London: Harper Collins.

Wood, Helen (2009) *Talking with Television: Women, Talk Shows and Modern Self-Reflexivity*, Chicago Il: University of Illinois Press

Woodward, Kathleen (1996) 'Global cooling and academic warming: long-term shifts in emotional weather', *American Literary History*, 8(4): 759–779.

Yardi, Sarita and danah boyd (2010) 'Tweeting from the Town Square: Measuring geographic local networks', *Proceedings of the Fourth International AAAI Conference on Weblogs and Social Media*, pp. 192–201.

Zelizer, Viviana A. (2005) *The Purchase of Intimacy*, Princeton, NJ: Princeton University Press.

Zizek, Slavoj (2012) 'Occupy wall street: What is to be done next?' *The Guardian*, 24 April. Available at: http://www.guardian.co.uk/commentisfree/cifamerica/2012/apr/24/occupy- wall-street-what-is-to-be-done-next (7 July 2012).

Zylinska, Joanna (2012) 'Bioethics otherwise, or, how to live with machines, humans, and other animals', in Tom Cohen (ed.) *Telemorphosis: Theory in the Era of Climate Change*, University of Michigan Library: Open Humanities Press. Available at http://quod.lib.umich.edu/o/ohp/10539563.0001.001 (12 July 2012).

—— (2009) *Bioethics in the Age of New Media*, Cambridge, MA: MIT Press.

Zylinska, Joanna and Sarah Kember (2012) *Life after New Media: Mediation as Vital Process*, Cambridge, MA: MIT Press.

Films

2012, 2009, dir. Roland Emmerich, Columbia Pictures.

An Inconvenient Truth, 2006, dir. Davis Guggenheim, Participant Productions.

Armageddon, 1998, dir. Michael Bay, Touchstone Pictures.

Deep Impact, 1998, dir. Mimi Leder, Paramount Pictures.

Earthquake, 1974, dir. Mark Robson, Universal Pictures.

Eat Pray Love, 2010, dir. Ryan Murphy, Columbia Pictures.

Forrest Gump, 1994, dir. Robert Zemeckis, Paramount Pictures.

Princess Mononoke, 1997, dir. Hayao Miyazaki, Miramax Films.

Sex and the City and *Sex and the City 2*, 2008, 2010, dir. Michael Patrick King, HBO films and New Line Cinema.

Sunshine, 2007, dir. Danny Boyle, DNA Films/UK Film Council.

The Day After Tomorrow, 2004, dir. Roland Emmerich, 20th Century Fox.

The Day the Earth Caught Fire, 1961, dir. Val Guest, British Lion Films.

The Elephant Man, 1980, dir. David Lynch, EMI Films.

Television

10 O'Clock Live, Channel 4 (2010–)

24, Fox (2001–2010)

Anderson Cooper, CNN (2003–)

Candid Camera, original run, abc (1948–1949)

Coronation Street, ITV1 (1960–)

Dallas, original run, CBS (1978–1991)

Doctor Who, BBC1, original series (1963–1989); new series (2005–)

EastEnders, BBC1 (1985–)

Forbrydelsen, DR1 (2007) [in English: *The Killing*]

Good Morning ITV1

Heroes, NBC (2006–1010)

How do you Solve a Problem Like Maria?, BBC1 (2006)

Loose Women, ITV1 (1999–)

Lost, abc (2004–2010)
Mad Men, AMC (2007–)
Mobbed, Fox (2010–)
Modern Family, abc (2009–)
My Social Network Stalker, C4 (20 February 2012)
Sex and the City, HBO (1998–2004)
Sherlock, BBC1 (2010–)
The Anti-Social Network, BBC3 (19 March 2012)
The Ellen DeGeneres Show, NBC (2003–)
The Only Way Is Essex, Channel 4 (2010)
The Simpsons, Fox (1989–)
Wife Swap, RDF, Channel 4 (2003–2009)

Internet Media

Climate Change Communication Advisory Group (http://www.pirc.info/projects/cccag/)
Climate Crisis (www.climatecrisis.org)
E20 (www.bbc.co.uk/programmes/p00k0b4b)
Earth Hour (www.earthhour.org)
Facebook (www.facebook.com)
Heroeswiki (heroeswiki.com)
Happy Planet Index (www.happyplanetindex.org)
Hitched (www.hitched.com)
IMDb (www.imdb.com)
IsAnyoneUp.com
I Will Survive Auschwitz (http://www.youtube.com/watch?v=cFzNBzKTS4I)
Kony 2012 (www.kony2012.com)
Lovestruck (www.lovestruck.com)
Mobbed (www.fox.com/mobbed)
MSNBC (www.msnbc.msn.com)
News of the World (www.newsoftheworld.com)
Rate My Vagazzle (www.ratemyvagazzle.com)
Save the Planet for 60 Minutes (www.earthhour.org)
Second Life (secondlife.com)
Spaghetti Western Web Board (http://disc.yourwebapps.com/Indices/160642.html)
Supermodels Take It Off for Climate Change (350.org)
The Happiness Project (http://www.happiness-project.com)
The Student Room (www.studentroom.co.uk)
Thriller, Cebu Prison (http://www.youtube.com/watch?v=hMnk7lh9M3o)
Twitter (http://twitter.com)
We Feel Fine (www.wefeelfine.org)
World of Warcraft (battle.net/wow/)

Index

Note: Page numbers in *italics* denote tables or figures

global emotion, 84–5, 94, 95–9
globality, 19–20, 82–5, 87, 88–90
Globality: Competing (Sirkin, *et al.*), 19
globalization, 25, 131
  consumerism, 89
  cultural sharing, 77
  of culture, 82–3
  fear, 99
  media campaigns, 152
  online communities, 89–90
Global Nature, Global Culture (Franklin,
  Lury & Stacey), 77
global psyche, 75, 156
global scrutiny, 86, 88
globital concept, 25, 95, 184
Glotz, Peter, 42, 157
Glove and Boots video, 186–7
gnarg, 173, 174
Goffey, Andrew, 79, 94
Goffman, Erving, 51
Goh, Jeannine, 80, 110
Goodman, Steve, 41, 67
Good Morning (ITV), 60
Google, 16, 18, 63, 190n16
Gopnik, Adam, 75, 92, 99
Gore, Al, 140, 141
Gorton, Kristyn, 58–9, 62, 176
gossip, mediated, 155
Gould, Deborah, 111–12
Gray, Mary, 97–8
Gregg, Melissa, 21, 34–5, 129,
  178, 180–1
Grodal, Torben, 55
Gross, Daniel M., 29
Grossberg, Lawrence, 30, 37, 64
Grusin, Richard, 66, 67, 78–9
Guardian, 156
Guggenheim, David, 139–40

Habermas, Jurgen, 62, 147
hacking, 154
Haidl Gang Rape, 193n2
Halbwachs, Maurice, 32
Hall, P. Cougar, 155
happiness, 103–4, 112–14
  fandom, 26
  flashmobs, 109
  as project, 123, 125
  responsibility for self, 125

  social networking, 114, 125, 161
  from unhappiness, 119
  viewing pleasure, 71
  wealth, 104
The Happiness Project (Rubin), 122–4
The Happy Planet Index, 104, 111, 133
haptics, 43, 157
Haraway, Donna, 92–3, 94
Harding, Jennifer, 29, 30, 48
Hardt, Michael, 94
Harris, Jonathan, 87, 88
Hartley, John, 134
hate, 156, 170, 176
Hate on the Net (Roversi), 156
hate sites, 183
Haythornthwaite, Caroline, 116
Heim, Michael, 94
Hellekson, Karen, 65
Hemerling, James W., 19
Hemmings, Clare, 36
Heroeswiki.com, 69–70
Hesmondhalgh, David, 18
hierarchy online, 15–16
Highmore, Ben, 33–4, 134
Hills, Matt, 8, 63–4
Hindman, Matthew, 15
'Hitched', 168
Hjorth, Larissa, 157, 159, 161
Hochschild, Arlie Russell, 31, 38,
  44–5, 189n12
Hogan, Patrick Colm, 129
Hoggart, Richard, 37
homophily, 7, 151, 189n10
Hoskins, Andrew, 48, 95
hostile worlds view, 156, 165
  see also intimacy, hostile
Huang, Yen-Pei, 80
Huffington Post, 133
Hulme, Mike, 128
human-computer interaction, 73, 97
human geography, 129–30
Hume, David, 29, 37
humiliation, 188n5
Hurricane Katrina, 126
Huyssen, Andreas, 76, 78
hyper-attention, 2, 3, 137

ICTs, 40, 42, 100
identity, 71, 147, 157, 163

media ecology, 6, 18, 107
  see also mixed-media ecology
mediality, 67, 68
  see also transmediation
Media Rituals (Couldry), 90
media studies
  affective turn, 20, 23, 37, 53–4,
    56, 76
  challenged, 79
  emotion, 15, 37, 53–4, 56, 82, 183–5
  new, 68–9
  participatory, 6
media technologies, 42, 177, 182
mediation
  dynamics of, 3
  of emotion, 24–5, 53–4, 183–5
  mediatization, 16, 18
  as term, 188n4
mediatization, 16, 18, 82, 134,
    136, 138
The Medium is the Message
    (McLuhan), 94
Meikle, Graham, 66, 112
memory, 32, 82, 184
  see also remembering
Memory, History and Forgetting
    (Ricoeur), 32
memory agents, 188n3
Me on the Web, 118
Merrin, William, 68, 79
metadata, 94, 96, 98
metageographical constructs, 83, 84,
    86, 191n3 (Ch 3)
Meyers, Oren, 48
Microsoft Research, 98–9
Milton, Kay, 128
Mind, 29
The Mind and Its Stories (Hogan), 129
misogyny, 26, 153, 172, 173
Mittell, Jason, 68, 167
mixed-media activity online, 65,
    173–4, 175–6, 184–5
mixed-media ecology, 136, 165
mnemonic ecology, 67
Mobbed (Fox), 108
mob dynamic, 108, 183
  see also flashmobs
Mobile Communication (Ling &
    Campbell), 97

mobile phone photographs, 95, 157,
    161, 162, 171
mobile phones
  decorations on, 81
  emotion, 12, 158
  fear/protection, 96
  keeping in touch, 42–3
  public sphere, 96–7
  studies of, 23
  visualization of life, 157
  YouTube, 52–3
mobility, 96, 159
mobisodes, 67
Modern Family, 109
Moore, Hunter, 170–2, 173–5, 176, 181
moral panic, 162, 169, 176, 193n1
Morley, David, 22
Morozov, Evgeny, 111
mourning, public, 48
Mourning Diana (Kear & Steinberg), 32
Moving Pictures (Grodal), 55
Moving Viewers (Plantinga), 56, 70
multiplayer games, 127
multiuser domain sites, 72
Mumbai attacks, 182–3
Murdoch, Rupert, 17
Music for Pleasure (Frith), 70–1
Myers, Greg G., 131
MySpace, 145, 155
The Myth of Continents (Lewis &
    Wigen), 83–4
The Myth of Digital Democracy
    (Hindman), 15

National Union of Students, 143
Negri, Antonio, 94
Neiger, Motti, 48
Net Smart (Rheingold), 87
Networks without a Cause (Lovink), 4
Neu, Jerome, 31
neuroscience approaches, 25, 30, 56,
    76, 182
New Economics Foundation, 105
newness, 2, 178
news coverage, 32, 52–3, 73, 126–7,
    188n6
Newsnight, 188n6
The News of the World, 16–17
New Yorker, 92, 99

Richardson, Ingrid, 96, 97, 182
Ricoeur, Paul, 32
ridicule, 64, 173
    see also gnarg
right to communicate, 184
Riley, Denise, 48, 119
The Rise of the Network Society
    (Castells), 83
*The Routledge Handbook of Emotions
    and Mass Media* (Döveling, von
    Scheve, & Konijn), 54
Roversi, Antonio, 156
Rubin, Gretchen, 122–4
Russell, Jason, 1, 2, 5, 6–8, 9

Salkin, Allen, 120–1
Sampson, Tony D., 157
Sandvoss, Cornel, 8
Save As…Digital Memories (Garde-
    Hansen, Hoskins, & Reading), 48,
    185
Save the Planet for Sixty Minutes
    (WWF), 143
    see also Earth Hour
Schmidt, Eric, 16
Schwarz, Ori, 158, 159, 160, 162
science/emotion, 140
The Science of Deduction website, 65
Scifo, Salvatore, 90, 92
screen studies
    audience, 51
    disgust, 39–40
    drives, 56
    emotion/affect, 25, 51, 53, 64
    face-to-face communication, 73–4
    television/computer, 52
    touch, 43
Second Life, 71–2, 73, 151
The Second Shift (Hochschild), 31
The Secret History of Emotion (Gross), 29
securitization, 14, 80, 159
security, 7, 99, 115, 136
Sedgwick, Eve Kosofsky, 35–6
Seigworth, Gregory J., 21, 34–5, 129,
    181
self
    construction of, 118–20, 125
    representation of, 117–18, 162
    sexualization, 155

self-help, 104, 120–2, 124–5
self-portraiture online, 158, 160
Self-Representation and Digital Culture
    (Thumim), 117, 118
sensibility, 36–7
sentiment, 47–51, 100, 118–20, 150
sentimentalism, 48, 110
Sex and the City, 120, 121
sexuality, 30, 46, 59, 88, 154, 156,
    169, 172
shame
    avoidance, 171
    emotional geographies, 132–3,
        143–52
    empathy, 166
    environment, 130
    female body, 156
    intimacy, 160
    online, 134
    parenting, 59
    ridicule, 173
    sexuality, 154
    on television, 59–60
shared spaces of dwelling, 104, 105,
    112, 155
sharing, 103
    alienation, 110
    Facebook, 79, 112
    friendship photography, 154
    images of female body, 154–5, 158
    male users, 160
    mobile phone photographs, 171
    nudz, 155, 156–7
    online media, 57, 74, 110
    Wikipedia, 88
Shaviro, Steve, 21
Sheets-Johnstone, Maxine, 96, 182
Sherlock (BBC), 65
Shirky, Clay, 16, 81–2, 88–9, 178,
    189–90n15
Shouse, Eric, 44, 134
Siegel, Elizabeth, 192n3 (Ch 4)
Simondon, Gilbert, 43
Simon Wiesenthal Center, 183
single medium concept, 24
Sirkin, Harold L., 19
Skeggs, Beverley, 58, 153
    Reacting to Reality Television, 63
slacktivism, 4, 111, 144

GPSR Compliance
The European Union's (EU) General Product Safety Regulation (GPSR) is a set
of rules that requires consumer products to be safe and our obligations to
ensure this.

If you have any concerns about our products, you can contact us on

ProductSafety@springernature.com

In case Publisher is established outside the EU, the EU authorized
representative is:

Springer Nature Customer Service Center GmbH
Europaplatz 3
69115 Heidelberg, Germany